Interpreting
the Truth

Changing the Paradigm
of Biblical Studies

L. WILLIAM COUNTRYMAN

Interpreting
the Truth

Changing the Paradigm
of Biblical Studies

TRINITY PRESS INTERNATIONAL
A Continuum imprint
HARRISBURG • LONDON • NEW YORK

Trinity Press International, P.O. Box 1321, Harrisburg, PA 17105
Trinity Press International is a member of the Continuum International Publishing Group.

Cover art: Botticelli, Alessandro (1444–1510). Saint Augustine. 1480. Fresco. Copyright Scala/Art Resource, NY. Chiesa di Ognissanti, Florence, Italy.

Design: Corey Kent

Library of Congress Cataloging-in-Publication Data

Countryman, Louis William, 1941-
  Interpreting the truth : changing the paradigm of Biblical studies /
L. William Countryman.
      p. cm.
Includes bibliographical references and index.
  ISBN 1-56338-410-8 (pbk.)
  1. Bible—Hermeneutics. I. Title.
  BS476.C67 2003
  227'.0601—dc21
                                2003008785

Printed in the United States of America

03 04 05 06 07 08   10 9 8 7 6 5 4 3 2 1

*This work is dedicated
to my colleagues,
the faculty and students of the
Committee for Interdisciplinary Studies
at the
Graduate Theological Union,
Berkeley, California,
who can be counted on to disagree with it
in provocative and stimulating ways.*

—◻—

Religious symbol is open to various forms of misinterpretation. It is generally recognized that the interpreter can err through literalism. He can also err by too prosaic an approach. A third form of faulty exegesis is that of the rationalist who insists on seeking what he calls a clear idea in imaginative discourse.

Amos N. Wilder

Removing inconsistencies by slicing up documents is a fascinating task . . . , but it rarely produces convincing results, especially in dealing with an author [Paul] whose correspondents regarded him as inconsistent.

Robert M. Grant

Contents

Acknowledgments

Since the ideas presented here have been in formation throughout my education and work as a scholar of scriptural studies, I cannot possibly thank all who have contributed to them—or even identify them at this point in my life. The epigraphs of this work, however, acknowledge a particular debt to exemplars and advocates of an earlier, less fragmented practice of New Testament studies, embodied in such scholars as Robert M. Grant, who was my doctoral advisor, and Amos N. Wilder, whom I knew only from his writings.

For time to write this work, I am indebted to The Church Divinity School of the Pacific for sabbatical leave, during which much of it took shape, and to the Episcopal Church's Board for Theological Education and its Conant Fund for support in the form of a challenge grant. Hal Rast was unfailingly encouraging over the years it has taken for this book to mature.

Two people read the manuscript for me. Henry Carrigan, my editor, was very helpful both with his encouragement and with suggestions about organization of a rather complex argument. Sean Burke helped me see where I was not making clear connections for the reader and gave me the sense of being in conversation with the newest generation of biblical scholars. I do not assume that either of them would agree altogether with the final form of the work.

The sources of the epigraphs are as follows: Amos N. Wilder, "Scholars, Theologians, and Ancient Rhetoric," *Journal of Biblical Literature* 75 (1956): 1–11; Robert M. Grant, *A Historical Introduction to the New Testament* (New York: Harper & Row, 1963), 180.

All biblical translations are my own except where otherwise noted.

Abbreviations

AB   The Anchor Bible

ABD   *The Anchor Bible Dictionary*

AV   Authorized (King James) Version

BDAG   *Greek-English Lexicon of the New Testament and Other Early Christian Literature,* 3d ed.

HBC   *Harper's Bible Commentary*

ICC   International Critical Commentary

JBL   *Journal of Biblical Literature*

LSJ   Liddell & Scott, *A Greek-English Lexicon,* rev. ed. by Henry Stuart Jones and Roderick McKenzie

LXX   Septuagint

NEB   New English Bible

NRSV   New Revised Standard Version

NT   New Testament

RSV   Revised Standard Version

SP   Sacra Pagina

Introduction
The Aim of the Present Volume

The work of the biblical interpreter has perhaps never been more confusing and complex than it is now. The replacement of "modern" historical-critical study as the dominant paradigm by the much more diffuse and varied practices of "postmodern" scholarship is one factor. No one can expect to master the whole array of possibilities; indeed, they seem to become increasingly unintelligible to one another and even incommensurate with one another, so that there is no way to bring them into fruitful conversation. Yet the most basic problem we face is not the potential confusion created by the postmodern era. Indeed, on the whole, I think the resulting diversity makes a contribution to the richness of our studies. The most basic problem is the tendency already well underway by the middle of the twentieth century toward a fragmenting of the field into distinct and narrowly defined "methodologies," each pursued in increasing isolation from the others.

My purpose in the present work is to recover a more unified field of discourse, not to limit the possible conclusions of our work, but to restore our ability to talk with one another about them. Indeed, I am concerned not only for our ability to talk with one another, but for the possibility of conversation with larger communities in the world around us and even for the internal conversation which can and should occupy each of us personally. The fragmentation of methodologies tends to produce a fragmentation of the text, a fragmentation of scholarly discourse, a disconnect between academics and nonacademics concerned for Scripture, and an internal division within the interpreter's self, resulting in a mind that too often does not confer with the rest of the human being.

I am not quite foolish enough to imagine that one book can offer a cure for all these ills. But it seems important to me to put into writing an approach to interpretation that I first learned more by osmosis than from being deliberately taught it, and for which I have long sought adequate and explicit language. This approach is interdisciplinary, seeing the text as a human artifact with dimensions that are literary, social, cultural, historical, personal, theological, spiritual, and more. It also maintains a consciousness of the social role of interpreters—the reality that we interpret to and for larger communities that have a basic investment in Scripture, regarding it not primarily as an object of study, but as a medium through which they expect to encounter God and to learn something true both about themselves and about the reality of the world around them.

As I have argued elsewhere, for Christians the Bible exists not merely to ratify what we think we already know—by definition, never very much—about God, the world, and ourselves. If that is all the Scriptures do, then they are worthless. One thing all human beings rarely need is further reinforcement of our existing prejudices or prejudgments. Christians need Scripture rather for the ways in which it allows new discovery within the context of our faith. I do not suggest that the discovery need be entirely new, the radical overthrow of all that we earlier thought and believed. But it will be significantly new, providing fresh perspective even on what was already known. Only then will it offer an opportunity for what some NT writers call, in Greek, *metanoia,* "conversion, renewal of mind, repentance."[1]

What I am seeking, then, is a way of bringing discrete methods (literary, social scientific, historical, etc.) into conversation within biblical studies and, at the same time, a way of bringing biblical studies itself into a richer, more productive conversation with communities interested in the Bible—particularly communities of Christian faith, but also the more general public that, in Western culture, also has strong reason to care about what its religious classics have to say in conversation with the culture's values and working presuppositions.

The problems addressed here are not unique to biblical studies. In a broad sense, they appear across the board in the academic world. Scholars in the natural sciences experiment with ways of bringing different disciplines to bear on common questions. Scholars in the humanities wonder how to overcome the increasing fragmentation of method. There is a perennial plea for better, clearer communication with the larger world. Only with difficulty, over the last half century, have natural scientists begun to recognize that they have some responsibility to reflect on ethics and the public use of their discoveries. Schools of law, medicine, and business have begun to recognize that it is not enough to prepare specialists who have no concern for the larger contexts in which they work, whether social, psychological, or ethical. Academics at large have begun looking to revive the tradition of the "public intellectual," the person who brings contemporary scholarship into conversation with the needs and realities of public discourse.

But even if this is not a uniquely religious issue, it is particularly acute when the subject matter is made up of writings esteemed as canonical, classified as the scriptures or classics of a particular group. People, over time, have esteemed such writings because they found them to have a revelatory quality, to offer wisdom, direction, indeed *truth* for life in this world. It is strange if scholars claim to understand them without having discovered in them some of their depth—even if that simply means having discovered what in them moved others to canonize them. When I was a doctoral student in the 1970s, we did not think it unusual that a prominent biblical scholar told a seminary student it was not the scholar's business to say what the NT texts mean for today. The scholar studied what they meant in antiquity; it was up to the theologians and the clergy to think about what they mean here and now. While the two subjects are indeed somewhat distinct, they cannot be so neatly separated.

I doubt that what I am proposing can be laid out clearly in a purely theoretical discussion. Indeed, part of my purpose is to bring the *practice* of interpretation back into consideration as a significant factor in this discussion. In part 1 of this book, I present a general picture of how I understand interpretive practice and then give an illustration, in relation to the Letter of Jude, of the most basic way in which the interpreter's work can contribute to a richer and more surprising conversation. Part 2 argues that only a more synthetic process of reading can give us the foundation for the broader conversation I seek; again, there is an illustration based on Jude. Part 3 looks at the broad category of NT letters and offers guidelines for interpreting them in a more synthetic mode. After a brief return to the Letter of Jude, I offer readings of two other quite different NT books: James and Romans. I endeavor to show that careful academic study with a synthetic as well as analytic movement sets the stage for a richer conversation between the complexities of the text and those of the communities of readers. The Epilogue returns to the work of the interpreter, suggesting how the practice of interpretation calls for a certain "ethos" or "character" in those who pursue it, because integration of the sort I am proposing will take place only if it can in fact find a residence in our own souls.

One thing that gives me some hope in such an ambitious undertaking is the recognition that this is indeed the practice—even if somewhat disregarded of late—of my own Christian tradition, Anglicanism. Anglican theology has not proceeded, on the whole, by spinning out large theories, but by seeking to understand the issues, questions, and problems of the moment in the larger context of our ancient, scriptural, and catholic faith. It may well be that, in biblical studies, too, it can be helpful to place principles and practice into intimate conversation with one another, as I endeavor to do here.

Many barriers stand in the way of such a procedure, the greatest single barrier being the complexity of the whole project. Again and again, we are tempted to interpret a single crux, a single word, a single passage, a single theme, in isolation from the larger complexity that gave it meaning in its age of origin. Some such narrowing of the field of vision is inevitable, at least on a provisional basis, if biblical studies is to exist at all. But it often leads us to miss the fact that the true significance of a text is contained in the whole as it interacts with the full complexity of human life and faith, then and now. Above all, this book, then, is a call to acknowledge such complexity and bring it to the fore in our thinking and writing. Our task is not to simplify but to confront one complexity with another—ancient with modern, modern with ancient—and encourage conversation between them.

Notes

1. L. William Countryman, *Biblical Authority or Biblical Tyranny? Scripture and the Christian Pilgrimage* (Valley Forge, Pa.: Trinity Press International, 1994).

Part 1

Interpreting the Interpreter

1. The Interpreter and the Practice of Interpretation

Beginning Where We Are

The Contemporary Situation

In itself, the contemporary chaos in biblical studies is not bad. It is frustrating, to be sure: interpreters have difficulty talking with one another and with the people for whom they interpret. We lack the common assumptions, signs, and symbols that would facilitate such conversation. On the other hand, no single language, no single theology or theory, no single cultural mind-set has ever been adequate to the task of interpreting reality as a whole or even a single important text. Because of limitations inherent to human existence, there is always some need for change—a need to break open existing prejudgments and discover where they are wanting and how we might move toward a deepening understanding of God, our world, our communities, and ourselves. Though chaos is a distressing state, it is also an opportunity for just such discovery.

Our present chaos manifests itself in a number of ways. Perhaps the most important—because deeply grounded in human experience and therefore fertile with future possibilities—is the multiplication of contexts for interpretation. Some of this diversity has developed within the academy itself, arising from the fact that biblical studies are pursued in both secular contexts and schools that have a religious affiliation. In either kind of location, scholars may find themselves working with a good deal of freedom—or they may be constricted by the prevailing ideology of the place, secular or religious. But this sort of academic diversity makes a relatively small contribution to the overall multiplicity of our time, which has more to do with the movement of peoples, the interaction of diverse cultures, and the entry of previously marginalized voices into the conversations of the West.

New voices are interpreting the Christian Scriptures in an extraordinary multiplicity of social and perspectival contexts that were rarely heard from before. These include social groupings within the West whose voices were previously little represented in the biblical studies establishment—women, people of color, members of sexual minorities, and people whose social class or educational level put them outside the mainstream discourse of interpretation (e.g., *campesinos*). They also include groups outside Western culture who have taken up the Scriptures of Christianity as significant for their relationship with God and their world. To the reading of these texts, such groups bring types of experience and a cultural take on the world often quite different from the male and officially heterosexual scholars of European extraction who have long dominated biblical studies; hence, it would be surprising if such newly heard groups did not read the texts rather differently.[1]

Yet another source of multiplicity in the current scholarly situation is the modern and postmodern multiplication of analytical and ideological perspectives.[2] The shifting fashions in academic methodologies found in other university departments affect biblical studies as well. Unfortunately, this is not a neutral development. The tendency toward narrower and narrower specialization, whether in terms of subject matter or in terms of modes of analysis, can create fragmentation and a narrowing of discourse. Those who approach Scripture with literary methods often find themselves hard-pressed to carry on a mutually intelligible conversation with those who use methods from the social sciences. Indeed, the variety of literary methods can prove mutually unintelligible among themselves. Similarly, on the social-scientific side, there are suspicions between those, for example, who practice "social study" of Scripture as a high-theory sociological approach and those who practice "social history," using modern social sciences as suggestive rather than prescriptive.

Alongside this multiplicity of methodologies lies a multiplicity of ideologies and theories. The dogmatic Christian approach of the post-Reformation era is still alive and well in many places, where it prescribes rather precisely what the Bible must be found to say on issues of major importance. But a Marxist or Freudian or Jungian approach will often function in much the same way for scholars who assume, at some level or other, that these theoretical stances give one access to the fundamental realities of the world, and that the Bible therefore must, if it is to make sense at all, make sense in terms of them. Still other ideological stances arise out of the emergence of hitherto silenced voices and enter the conversation, as, for example, feminist/womanist approaches or postcolonial interpretation or queer hermeneutics. And there is also the mixed bag of "theory" that goes by the name of "postmodernism" proper, which may or may not include any of the above. While much of the postmodern impetus originates in a desire to undermine the hegemonic metanarratives (such as patriarchalism) we have inherited from the past, it now frequently functions within academic circles as just such a metanarrative in its own right, summarily forbidding discussion of such imponderables as "truth" and prohibiting efforts to argue that some interpretations are better grounded than others.[3]

It is not my purpose in this work to offer a sustained critique of the varied possibilities currently available. I do not reject any of them *a priori*. My point rather is that diversity becomes a problem when methodologies assume relatively closed forms in an effort to protect themselves from criticism. One may as easily experience this on the left—in, say, Marxist or feminist circles—as on the right—for example, in the context of conservative Presbyterian or Baptist dogmatism. There is an important difference between methodologies that are employed in order to gain new and potentially unexpected insight into a text and those that are employed rather to conform the text to preexisting theory, whether doctrinal, political, psychological, or whatever. This latter usage serves only to confirm the theory, not to illuminate the text; indeed, it actually diverts attention from the text's individual peculiarities and, therefore, its complexity. The same methodology, of course, may be put to either use; and much depends upon the horizon of the interpreter, whether it embraces only one's academic colleagues and partisans or a larger public.[4]

Of all these elements of diversity that I have pointed out, those that come from specific experiential roots deserve to be taken more seriously than those that embody purely intellectual perspectives. Postcolonial interpretation, partly because of its very resistance to strict formulation, has more to offer than the more highly structured and rigid varieties of theory. Mary Ann Tolbert's "poetics of location" is particularly suggestive in this regard because of her alertness to the particular and contingent, basic components of human complexity.[5] The problem with more purely ideological approaches to interpretation is that they know too much in advance. They tend to know the answers before they have asked the questions and to frame only such questions as can be answered in the predetermined way. The kind of interpretive practice I am advocating here is precisely the opposite. It expects both questions and answers to emerge, develop, and change in the living process of interpretation through a conversation involving many partners and significant human complexity on all sides.[6]

Not "Hermeneutics" but "Practice of Interpretation"

What I am exploring in this writing is not what is now usually meant by the word "hermeneutics," though it certainly fits the etymological meaning of the term. Over the last few decades, biblical scholars have evinced great interest in philosophical hermeneutics, and that discipline has been immensely helpful by reminding us that there is no simple, unproblematic return to the text itself, much less through the text to the author. The meaning of a text is not self-evident; even the most unself-conscious reading is already an act of interpretation, whether one knows it or not. Philosophical hermeneutics, above all, seeks to make explicit the interpreter's own complex relation to the text. In doing so, it has helped us absorb the emergence of a vastly enlarged and more diverse community of discourse in the world of biblical interpretation. We are no longer quite so surprised to discover that what had seemed self-evident to oneself or one's tradition of faith or one's scholarship may seem quite improbable to those reading the text from a different perspective, with different sets of presuppositions.[7]

What philosophical hermeneutics has not done for us, however, is to clarify the living, social practice of interpretation. Philosophical hermeneutics speaks more to the individual and intellectual aspects of interpretation than to its social and spiritual realities. It omits from consideration, on the one hand, much of the hard work that qualifies a person as a biblical scholar in the first place, above all, the mastery of languages and the specialized knowledge of other cultures, ancient times, and, for most of us, distant places. No theoretical knowledge can substitute for these. Hermeneutics also tends to overlook the question of how the interpreter relates to others—to those people and communities to whom and for whom we interpret the Scriptures. As a result, it comes to focus on an idealized process within the scholar's own brain, a process by which the scholar, assumed to be already competent in the broad knowledge necessary to read the texts for oneself, assigns to and/or elicits from the text a meaning. While this is a critical part of the process of interpretation, it is far from being the whole. It stops short of the process that carries the individual's reading out into a larger conversation of interpretation with whatever community for which we interpret. This is not to fault the philosophers in question, but to fault ourselves for resting content with the limitations of their perspective. The rest of the process needs to be taken at least as seriously.

In addition, philosophical hermeneutics, though it acknowledges the constructive element in interpretation, does not pull us effectively toward it. Indeed, often we forget that there is a constructive side to biblical interpretation, that there is something beyond reading the text and interpreting it in my own head or in the only slightly broader circle of the like-minded. Yet as soon as we remember that the interpreter interprets *for* someone, it is inconceivable that the interpretation of ancient works in modern contexts should be without an element of the constructive. If nothing else, the very act of translation means substituting a contemporary language and cultural context for an ancient one. To choose an example from a nonbiblical sphere, one may translate the Greek δημοκρατία into English as "democracy," but there is no point in pretending that the two mean the same thing. What the Greeks called δημοκρατία would, in today's world, surely be seen as patriarchal oligarchy, not democracy. There is no way to convert even a single ancient Greek word into a modern English one without losing much of its cultural and historical context and connotations— and also adding new and different ones. There is no way to translate without some degree of creative alteration. The interpreter, then, is not simply a functionary, a bureaucrat, a technician, but a creator, continually creating the culture of the present and future in the act of interpreting that of the past. We may and do ignore this aspect of our work, but that does not mean that we escape it—only that we create absentmindedly, unintentionally, and often in clumsy ways.[8]

Modern biblical scholarship, to be sure, came by its avoidance of the constructive element honestly. In the eighteenth and early nineteenth centuries, perhaps nothing could have been more important for biblical scholars than to declare their independence of the existing expectations of their faith traditions. Where the Western denominations had long imposed on scholars the duty of defending the local theology—Lutheran or Presbyterian or Roman Catholic or what have you—scholars began to insist that the study of the Scriptures must be as free from a priori demands as any other academic specialization. There was still a continuing thread of "biblical theology," and many scholars, including people as theologically diverse as Harnack and Schweitzer, Barth and Bultmann, were in fact quite interested in the constructive implications of their work. But, as a whole, modern biblical criticism has come to be focused primarily on analytical tasks. The text is disassembled into its presumed components, to be identified and studied separately through critical methods ranging from historical enquiry into authorship and date; to source, form, redaction, and rhetorical criticism; and on to more recent initiatives such as sociological criticism or reader-response criticism. What marked all these modalities of biblical studies was a strong tendency to take the text apart without the sense of a corresponding need to put it back together or relate it to contemporary realities.

This analytical tendency has been reinforced by the analytical reductionism characteristic of both modernism and postmodernism. The scientific model that has dominated modern thinking is particularly that of physics, with its goal of reducing complex realities to the interplay of a small number of forces or "laws."[9] When such a model is applied in areas where it is less congenial, it can result in a sort of notional reductionism in which one kind of reality is treated as an epiphenomenon or even a disguise of some other kind. Biology, for example, may be reduced to elements of physics or chemistry, and for some purposes this proves quite useful. And yet, chemistry cannot fully predict or encompass the complexities revealed in, say, field observations of baboon societies. Only because of the modernist academic prestige of the so-called hard sciences will some suppose that knowing the chemistry of fight-or-flight situations fully explains the phenomenon and makes the actual observation of behavior irrelevant or superfluous.[10]

Such reductionism has been particularly popular with regard to the complexities of religion, which both modern and postmodern thinkers frequently interpret simply as a by-product of, or mask for, psychological, sociological, economic, or other more quantifiable forces. Biblical scholarship's desire to appear scientific (to justify its place in the academy) has encouraged us to accept this reductionism more or less without question. As an example, we may note the interesting fact that relatively few recent studies of the "historical Jesus" seem to treat Jesus' religion or spirituality as a central issue.[11] It is somehow easier for the contemporary scholar to think of Jesus as a political leader or a philosopher than to conceive of him as what he was assumed for nearly two thousand years to be, a teacher of faith whose spiritual movement eventually became a world religion. But is the political Jesus really any more plausible, historically? Or is he simply more acceptable academically?

Reductionism has implied an objectifying stance. The object of study is assumed to lie inert before the observer, to be poked and prodded, dissected and experimented upon—without any dangerous connection of personal involvement with it. Being an object, it does not have a voice or threaten to take an active role in the examination. It will not question the questioner. We cannot be surprised, then, if the end product of much modern biblical scholarship is a dead and disassembled text of purely historical interest. The academic predilection for increasingly abstruse and narrow superstructures of methodology and vocabulary has intensified this objectifying and analytical dismemberment of the text by embalming its results in language that has no everyday meaning. If we could remember that the great issues of human existence are discussed every day by ordinary people in ordinary human language, and if we thought of the materials with which we work as belonging to that discussion—then we would, in our writing, avoid erecting such barriers against the outsider, the layperson, the plebeian. They are, after all, barriers even against our own everyday selves.

In terms of method, the modern and postmodern bias for analytical approaches has sometimes led biblical studies to defeat its own purpose by focusing too narrowly. Form criticism of the Gospels, as an example, has a value in that it concretizes the basic recognition that the materials incorporated in the written gospels had a prehistory of a generation or more as oral texts. Unfortunately, some scholars pursue form criticism mechanically, as if every individual word in a text could be identified either as part of the oral tradition or as a literary insertion. Some even propose to identify layers within the oral tradition. Such an approach becomes possible only if scholars ignore the probability that these texts were shaped in an oral tradition of composition in performance, not one of memorized texts. There never was a completely predictable form that could be modified word by word; there was simply a tradition whose performer used (to borrow the phrase of an ancient student of the subject) "to adapt his instructions to the needs" of the occasion.[12] As a result, the practice of form criticism, pursued in an unreflectively analytical way, winds up creating word-perfect versions of traditions that were never, in reality, verbally fixed until they eventually were written—and then treats these versions as if they represented some privileged access, independent of the written documents, to the messy realities of oral performance.

On the broader stage of contemporary society, modern biblical scholarship has driven a wedge between biblical interpreters and other readers of the Bible, especially communities of faith. The discourse of academic interpreters has come to be of marginal interest to most of these groups. The historic, "mainline" denominations have perfected the art of tipping their hats to biblical scholarship while ignoring it in practice. Seminarians learn

about biblical scholarship; but in many cases, once they are in positions of
parish leadership, it has little effect on their preaching, which leans more
to a sentimental than a critical use of the text. More ideologically uniform
faith groups, on the other hand, are inclined to create cadres of tame interpreters who are forbidden, on pain of dismissal, to say anything the community does not want to hear. In both cases, biblical scholarship is
basically ignored. Without excusing either sort of faith community, one
may ask whether scholars are themselves partly at fault for this state of
affairs.

In addition to churches, there is also a more secular public that is
intrigued by what it learns of current scholarship (e.g., the Jesus Seminar).
They may find it refreshing to have the Bible taken away from the control
of churches; there is an old tradition of this in the United States, going
back at least to Thomas Jefferson. They may also hope to hear from it
something of value for their own lives. In any case, it is increasingly clear
that religion is not "going away," as modernists once imagined, and the
noncommitted public may think it worthwhile to know something of the
Bible for that reason alone. As things currently stand, this wider audience
must sometimes wonder about the apparent disconnect between what
scholars tell them about the Bible and the actual ways in which communities of faith put the Bible to use. I do not suggest that scholars should give
up having distinct perspectives on the Bible—only that the almost complete failure of conversation between scholarship and communities of faith
needs to be reversed.

However one looks at it, the biblical interpreter today, standing at the
conclusion of the modern era and the beginning of something else that has
not yet become clear, is in an oddly isolated spot. Intensifying this situation is the fact that many of us belong to university departments, where we
have no concretely articulated responsibility to any broader community,
whether a religious tradition or the general public. We are in danger of
thinking of ourselves almost exclusively in terms of the community of our
colleagues, whose interest in the texts, at least so far as our work is concerned, is intellectual and not spiritual or religious. We are apt to find ourselves talking only to one another. We then wonder if our discipline has
become sterile and irrelevant. Our efforts to ransack neighboring disciplines for new methodologies, fruitful or not, are often inspired as much
by claustrophobia as by curiosity.[13]

I do not mean to criticize philosophical hermeneutics, the science of
physics, the churches, the media (which seem quite befuddled by the contemporary religious scene), postmodernism, or even my own colleagues.

We are, after all, heirs to a long process of historical development. I mean rather to criticize a certain state of disconnectedness that has grown up as the result of good intentions launched into motion two or more centuries ago. Biblical studies did need to assert its independence of post-Reformation religious establishments in the West. More recently, philosophical hermeneutics has helped us to become more sophisticated about what is going on in our own heads as we attempt to read and interpret ancient texts. Now we must rediscover a larger process, a *practice* of interpretation that can take better account of the social nature of interpretation and replace the reductionism of the recent past with an ability to take spiritual dimensions in the interpretation of sacred scriptures seriously.

Reclaiming Our Connections

The true challenge for interpreters today is not so much to find new methods of analysis as to discover what broader kind of integration our work and our lives are capable of. We need a synthesis that is genuinely rooted in what we do. It is not enough that it be defined by the various communities to which we are related, academic or religious, because none of them can know our whole discipline, the actual work of the interpreter, from the inside. The dictates of academic fashion now easily change several times over the average scholar's working life. Some of the changes will be useful and some will not; and in any case, the wise interpreter will keep the texts at the center of focus rather than the methodologies. Religious communities do not always really want to know what their scriptures say, particularly if it might conflict with existing assumptions. The larger, apparently secular Western world, though fitfully interested, has adopted a dilettante's perspective toward religion. Often, it is not even aware of where or how deeply it is influenced by its own culturally constitutive documents. Interpreters are the people who stand at the juncture of these demands and influences; we are the people who know what it is like to live out the practice of interpretation.

We are tempted by modernist and postmodernist reductionisms partly because we know only too well exactly how complex our position really is.[14] We juggle the often competing demands of the text itself; the craft by which we come to read and understand it; the academic guilds of accrediting agencies, schools, and scholarly associations; the churches with which we are associated; and so forth. We know that the text itself is complex and does not give simple answers to its own questions, much less to modern ones. We know that we may have to be very careful, at times, in

our interpretive work in order not to scuttle the interpretive conversation
before it gets well underway. On the other hand, if we simply retreat into
the dry and impenetrable thickets of scholarship, we have abandoned an
essential element in our job, and then where does our own spirit go for
nourishment? It is not easy to overcome these problems, but it is vital. In
attempting to respond to them, I want to begin by offering a basic model of
interpretation as a social practice.

The Practice of Interpretation

A Triangular Conversation

The practice of interpreting a text is intrinsically triangular, the three
points of the figure being constituted by the text, the interpreter, and the
community with which the interpreter communicates. This is merely to
describe the process of interpretation in the simplest possible terms. There
is no such process without some equivalent of a text, on the one hand (a
verbal one in the case of the Bible, though the visual, gestural, and musical
arts generate similar issues), and on the other, those who are interested but
feel unable to understand the text fully. The interpreter stands alongside
these two, turning one sort of meaning into another—one more accessible,
it is hoped, to those in need of interpretation. Whether the interpreter is
turning Spanish into French or explaining Gilgamesh to someone with no
prior knowledge of ancient Mesopotamian civilization, there is always a
kind of translation going on.

The proportions of the triangle thus determined can vary greatly. Some
texts seem less opaque to their readers or hearers than others and therefore less in need of interpretation; in this case, the role of the interpreter
becomes minimal because the readers feel that they already have access to
the text. In other cases, the text (even the same text) may come to seem
quite difficult and remote, and those who wish to read it may feel that they
must put great trust in an interpreter to explain its meaning. Readers and
interpreter may easily disagree at times as to the exact configuration of the
triangle and, therefore, the importance of the interpreter's role.

The conversation among the three points of the triangle is the substance
of interpretation. It is a conversation that can never be brought to completion because none of the three points is stationary or unchanging. Communities of readers and interpreters change, in response to external
pressures and to their own internal dynamism. Individual readers or interpreters can grow in existing perspectives or discover new ones. The text

itself, while relatively (seldom absolutely) fixed as a form of spoken words or written characters, will at least appear to change as interpreters and communities bring new knowledge or new perspectives to its interpretation. Like a musical score, a written text is constantly being brought to life anew by its performance, its interpretation; and no two performances, even by the same performer, are ever quite identical.

Each point of the interpretive triangle deserves consideration here in its own right. At the same time, no one of the three can exist in isolation from the others, for it would either wither away on its own or else survive by generating the other two. Texts, for example, may fall out of the interpretive triangle either by being lost or by being ignored; but if they return to attention, they will generate interpreters and communities, as seen, for example, in the modern rediscovery of Gnostic documents at Nag Hammadi. From being isolated documents, long cut off from any community that might take them seriously, they have once again become part of an interpretive triangle with learned interpreters and a community, however diffuse, that has a high interest in their meaning.

Communities, in their turn, can and do generate texts, as the NT and the Talmud demonstrate. Both Christianity and Judaism already had canonical texts, inherited from ancient Israel; but both generated additional ones that are in many ways more decisive for them because they express more explicitly the central focus of each. Once such new texts come into being, the necessity for new interpretation quickly becomes apparent as the life of the community moves on in time and changes in response to its own internal logic or to outside stimuli. Already within the NT, one can see this at work: the writers of the Synoptic Gospels reinterpret one another's work, for example, or the (probably second-century) author of 2 Peter expresses concern about the way the "uneducated and unstable" are appropriating Paul's letters, in which there are many things that are "hard to understand" (3:16).

Interpreters, one supposes, are the least creative of the three points of the triangle. After all, we claim to be doing nothing more than improving the access between text and reader. But we, too, "create" texts through our choice and ordering of them. After Luther, the NT was not quite the same text that it was before. Quite apart from his physical relegation of certain books to an appendix in his German translation, he refocused his followers' reading of the whole with reference to Paul's teaching on justification. This interpretive transformation of the text intertwined with the transformation of communities, too. Whether Luther meant to found a distinct Christian tradition or not, his role as interpreter had that effect.

Interpretation, then, is a dynamic process that cannot lose its dynamism without ceasing to exist. A work of interpretation may sometimes become a text in its own right (e.g., patristic commentaries that have become classics in Christian theology). But this does not foreclose the ongoing process of interpretation. Even in the so-called Dark Ages, when reverence for the classical early Christian writers was at a peak, new interpretive writing continued apace from the hands of scholars like the Venerable Bede. After all, even the classic interpretations needed interpreting by then.

Interpretation and the Larger World: The Issue of Reality

I shall return to further discussion of each point of the interpretive triangle; but first it is important to make a further observation about the triangle as a whole. Interpretation is not a purely intellectual process, but a social one. Nor does it float unanchored by space and time. Rather, it is situated in a larger environment that I shall call, while recognizing the difficulty of the term, "reality." When text, interpreter, and community are carrying on their conversation, they do it in awareness that there is a larger world around them—a world of life and death, a world of body and soul as well as mind or spirit, a world that demands and receives, one way or another, our fundamental attention. This is a world that we can approach only in interpretive ways. I am not suggesting that we have some simple, direct access to reality that bypasses the cultural preconceptions with which we approach it. Yet reality is bigger and more powerful than we. It can foster us or cut us off short. It stands over all our thinking and living as a question mark, even when it does not force itself on us in the form of specific, demanding, unresolved, individual questions.

The cultural element in our interpretation of reality has not always seemed obvious to interpreters. Because writing frees speech, in certain ways, from the constraints of time, the written word can cross boundaries of culture, coming to appear timeless because of this decontextualization. Thus Philo of Alexandria could read the Books of Moses as eternally clear and valid, unrestricted by age or culture.[15] In his case, this meant reading them as if they had been written in the cultural context of his own time, virtually the day before he read them—in the sense that they contained an account of reality that he could readily recognize, which meant an account of something not unlike the Middle Platonist philosophy that Philo took as the standard description of reality. The same is true of much ancient textual interpretation, whether Gentile or Jewish or Christian. Texts that had become difficult by reason of their antiquity were seen as allegories disguising more familiar messages—or else as oracles, divine messages rendered intentionally difficult in order to force the recipient to become existentially involved in the search for their meaning.

In the history of interpretation, the same drive to cut texts loose from time and place crops up repeatedly and in a variety of forms. In the West, for example, the heirs of John Calvin supposed that an attentive and unbiased reader could derive from the miscellaneous and often contradictory contents of the Christian Bible a concrete, detailed, and timeless constitution for the Christian religion and for church life. It is a fantasy still dear to many Christian communities, despite its complete failure to create unanimity of doctrine or polity even among those who hold to it. But other schools of thought are equally capable of launching out into such abstract, universalist projects. Jungian thinkers, for example, have a long habit of treating sacred texts as a veneer masking what they feel are timeless mental constructs.[16] And advocates of some postmodern critical modes seem to proceed in a kind of solipsistic vein, as if neither the era in which the text was written nor the text itself had any significance outside the mind of the critic.[17]

I am convinced that the opposite is the true case. We continue to preserve, perform, and interpret texts from the past precisely because they are *not* contemporary with us.[18] Whether we recognize this in theory or only in practice, a text from another historical and cultural horizon raises questions for us and offers us perspectives that are scarcely available within our own. Every culture—indeed, every distinct historical era within a given culture—is a particular exploration of human possibilities. It has made its choices, however unconsciously, about which possibilities to explore and which to leave aside. Such choices are inevitable, but they are not permanent nor self-explanatory. They create certain opportunities and foreclose others.

Accordingly, every culture will mask, isolate, or circumscribe within itself human possibilities that it does not satisfy or honor or even acknowledge. And we preserve and perform "classical" or "canonical" ancient texts not only because they embody values and concerns we have made central, but also because they embody other possibilities that the culture we have inherited has chosen, in our place and time, not to realize. The past and its texts do not, of course, exhaust all human possibilities; nor do we need them to. We do not need them to give us a perfect paradigm of human life. We only need them to relativize the certainties of the present, break their apparent stranglehold on human possibility, offer a few alternative directions, and so set our collective imagination free to continue into the future.

No text is free of its own time and place. That is a principal reason why we find texts worth attending to and also needful of interpretation. It does not mean that the text's time and place and culture of origin is entirely determinative of its meaning. But it does mean that the very foreignness, the alien character, of a classical text is part of its meaning and part of what makes it desirable to us. If it also makes the text partly unintelligible and even objectionable to us, that is merely part of the bargain. We are not unlike the ancient Greeks, who were both enchanted and estranged by the foreignness of those they called βάρβαροι, "barbarians." They could never quite decide whether the βάρβαροι possessed all wisdom or no wisdom, whether their discourse was supreme sense or utter nonsense. So it is with canonical texts, even our own. The Greeks of late antiquity both revered Homer and found the Homeric epics strange and objectionable and in need of allegorization.

What I have written thus far, of course, implies that the whole purpose of reading and interpreting such texts is intimately tied up with a human desire to know the broader, more fundamental reality in which we live and to find meaning for human life in that context. This desire, of course, can come to life only in specific cultures and persons and is always shaped and limited by that fact. Yet the possibility of larger meaning is what fires our interest in reading and understanding the texts. As Wilfred Cantwell Smith has observed, people of faith have always read their canonical texts not simply to find out about the texts themselves, but to find out about their world and the meaning of human life in it.[19]

Some readers will perhaps take exception to this way of formulating the matter. They would prefer to speak in terms not of "finding out about," but of "constructing" reality. Such constructivist terminology has had a useful function in recent discourse, reminding us how much our view of the world external to us is determined by the categories and preconceptions, the rites and rhythms and favorite stories of our particular cultural environment. We have no access to external "reality" that is completely unshaped by these cultural constructions. At the same time, our encounter with the reality external to us is not completely determined by those constructions. Some who use constructivist language push it to an extreme— as if there were no reality other than the socially constructed. I always wonder how they deal with having stubbed their toes. Our cultures do indeed shape our perception, but no culture that lasts more than a few days can be mere sleight of hand. It has to make contact, however imperfectly, with something deeper.

Nevertheless, culture does not monopolize reality. There are tensions between our cultural and social constructions and our lived experience—tensions that play a key role in all significant social and cultural change, as well as individual and personal change. For quite apart from the solipsistic absurdities of certain hypertrophied forms of constructivist theory, the language of "construction," if used carelessly, misrepresents an important range of human experience and reflection. I mean, specifically, the way in which we sometimes discover the inadequacy of the constructs we have inherited and find ourselves forced to try to peer behind them or past them in an effort to find or create a new construct that will more adequately represent what we previously could not express. This is the experience, for example, of many gay and lesbian people in the modern world—the discovery that inherited constructions of sexuality did not match experience. This does not mean that lesbian and gay life in the twenty-first century is therefore a form of direct access to a reality unmediated by social constructs. Not at all. It is immediately brought into relation to other existing constructs in our efforts to understand and speak about it. But the existing social constructs of sexuality proved to be in error, and we discovered a more powerful reality behind the veil that they constituted.

If we discover a reality behind the constructs, we will inevitably incorporate it into new or revised constructs. At the same time, the simple fact of discovery produces in at least some of us an ongoing awareness of the distance between culture and the "reality" of world or self to which society applies its constructive talents. Such a consciousness may express itself in philosophical, reasoned efforts to get "behind" the available presuppositions in an organized way (e.g., the natural sciences); in a passion for reform of cultural norms (e.g., prophecy); in a mysticism that, even if expressed in language, is always held to be beyond what language can express; or simply in an ironic awareness of the distance between *all* cultural constructs and reality. In any case, the person who has discovered that there is something behind the scenery of social construction has come into touch with a different sort of reality—one that cannot be grasped conclusively, even though we do our utmost to communicate it in socially constructed terms or in revisions of them and plays on them.

Truth

A further dimension of this subject has to do with a term closely related to "reality"—"truth." For some time, it has been conventional among academics to dismiss all talk of truth. In part, this may be a salutary revolt against the tendency of the powerful to define as truth whatever they can use to support their assumption of power. The structures of power treat such truth as an objective quantum that they can and do possess. The antonyms of "truth," in this sense, are "heresy" and "error." There is another sense of the word "truth," however, that is more important to this discussion. A character in Cathleen Schine's novel *Rameau's Niece,* speaking of life in Czechoslovakia before the collapse of the Communist bloc, says:

> It is fashionable now to say that truth is just a convention. . . . But in Prague, where people have had to live a lie for so long, truth is no convention. It is a moral reality.[20]

"Truth" as antonym of "lie"—such a notion is deeply bound up with the experience of discovering the reality behind the scenes, the reality disguised or ignored by the official cultural constructs. Such experience does not suggest that truth is a possession. It is rather a discovery. Truth is the chink in the steel helmet of our preconceptions, through which we catch an unexpected ray of light. It is the disconcerting (and perhaps happy) moment when you find that part of what you were told can be peeled back to reveal something quite different underneath. This is "truth" not in the sense of "something I was told on authority," but in the sense of "something I have stumbled across."

The lie that truth exposes is not always a deliberate intention to deceive. Even if it began as that, it may simply have become institutionalized as a cultural norm. Every human culture lies to some extent, not only because most (if not all) cultures have their guilty secrets, but because every culture is the development of only a selection of human possibilities. Each culture is a selection; and yet each culture inevitably says, "This is what it is to be human." The desire to make good this claim, I suppose, is the reason why cultures and societies that are under deep stress tend to throw up various fundamentalisms. Since the culture is not experiencing the stability that its claims to perfection imply, some members of it try to enforce stability in order to save appearances. Paradoxically, the imposition of cultural stability is always doomed. Ironically, such imposition is occasioned by its own impossibility. Thus, the fundamentalists who have taken over the Southern Baptist Convention try to save their heritage by abolishing a crucial part of it—the independence of congregations. Fundamentalism of every sort is invariably a betrayal of what it claims to preserve; by enforcing its principles, it actually reveals its complete lack of faith in the power of the traditional order.

Perhaps every culture unconsciously longs to be left alone in its sense of completeness and inevitability. This typically proves impossible for physical reasons (such as climate change or plague or environmental degradation) and historical ones (such as war or trade or migrations or imperialism). It may also be impossible because each culture carries within it the seeds of its own change. One suspects, for example, that the virtual identification of the young male body with the divine in classical Greek culture made the revulsion toward the body in the later Greek world almost inevitable. To put it another way, a Greek culture that turned pessimistic would not be free to express that pessimism in any way whatsoever; it would have to use its existing social constructs and revalue them. The ascetic anchorite of the desert in the fourth century C.E. is, among other things, the transvalued ephebe of the urban γυμνάσιον in the fifth century B.C.E.

I do not mean to say that this particular change was inevitable—always a dubious claim historically. Perhaps the change would not have happened without, for example, the increase of epidemic disease in the imperial period or without imperialism itself, which deprived the youth's body of its original social context in the polis. I mean only to say that the Greeks put the young male body at the center of their whole cultural construct and therefore sowed the seeds of its own questioning and eventual reversal. Strains showed early in the rise of the professional athlete, whose body was not securely located in the polis. Deeper yet, one could argue that this cultural construct was deeply conflicted from the beginning, since one principal purpose of the exercise in the γυμνάσιον was to prepare young men to be sacrificed in war. The culture had a lie at its very heart. Whether through external collisions or internal incoherences, then, cultures inevitably experience discontinuities, the kind of thing whose discovery is truth.

Writing has a certain odd and important relation to truth in this sense of "discovery." In many cases, written texts attempt to reflect the official truth of the culture; but in the process, by the very act of concretizing it, they offer it up for analysis and dissection—for the exposure of its incoherence. On the other hand, writing is also a means by which the one who has stumbled across truth in the sense of discovery tries to propagate it and to help others to see behind the scene. One thinks of Plato's earlier Socratic dialogues, which make the formal effort to initiate the reader into the process of discovery rather than present an official system of truth. Jesus' parables have a similar quality.

Ironically, however, as such a text grows older, what was originally subversive is sometimes pressed into the service of a new cultural consensus.[21] Plato becomes Platonism—even, in his case, within his own life and oeuvre: the Plato of the *Laws* is quite different from the Plato of the *Symposium*. Jesus' parables become not so much opportunities of discovery as moral examples. At best, however, the preserved, written text of discovery will carry with it a subversive message: truth requires discovery and cannot be handed on purely as a prefabricated, systematic unity. Even at its most debased, such a text may still insert the moment of discovery, the possibility of truth, into the new cultural consensus as an element of incoherence that can alert future generations to the need and possibility for such discovery on their own part. The interpretive conversation is concerned with texts not just for their own sake, but for the sake of truth.

The Points of the Interpretive Triangle

Text

A "text," as the word is used here, is not a simple object. On the contrary, a text has many dimensions and cannot be confined to any one of them. It is, for one thing, a sequence of words, themes, or thoughts that occupy a more or less fixed relationship to each other. This may be preserved orally—with varying standards of consistency—or in writing. The critical thing constituting it as a text rather than an occasional utterance, is that it can be repeated and, when repeated, can be recognized by those who have previously encountered it.[22]

Given the dependence of oral texts on a stable social environment for their preservation, most texts that survive for long eventually take the form of a physical object, recorded in writing or by electronic means—a process that makes them both more and less accessible than oral texts. They can circulate independently of their creators or tradents; but they demand investments of time and energy in the acquisition of literacy, the physical reproduction of documents, and their decoding or awakening from encoded form. Moreover, until the time of Gutenberg or, still more so, the invention of cheap papers, such documents were relatively expensive and inaccessible for the ordinary person.

In addition, the written text is less easily adapted to changing needs. The tradent could make each recitation of an oral text relevant to the moment. With the written text, however, references eventually become obscure, the social and historical context of the original writing fades from memory, and even the language becomes first obscure and eventually unintelligible ("dead"). As a result, the written text becomes the preserve of specialists trained to study and understand ("resurrect"?) it. Their task is to mediate the text to the larger community; and they therefore exist in relation to the larger group. But their training also separates them from the community and makes them a distinct guild, with potentially different interests and concerns.

One most basic form of interpretation is translation, which produces parallel versions of the text in other languages. The resulting texts are hybrids, rooted partially in the culture of their earlier composition and partially in the culture of the new language and the time and place of the translation. Even for us who read the text in its original language, our own immersion in the culture of our own day and place means that, to some degree, we are still translating it to ourselves even if we do not literally change the words. Thus, a beginning student in NT Greek, who already knows the text in translation, will unconsciously treat the text in its original language as if it were a retranslation of the more familiar modern version. The more advanced reader of Greek still falls back, from time to time, on specific correlations of words rather than comprehending the text entirely within the ancient language.

The existence of interpreters does not mean that the larger community has surrendered all concern for its classical or canonical texts to the small coterie of specialists. The community maintains its connection with its texts in a variety of ways: for example, by housing them in libraries, by honoring them with adornment and using them in ritual contexts, by citing them as the authority for the usages of the community, whether those usages are in fact clearly related to the text or not.[23] The community may retain a strong attachment to its texts even when the original-language version is widely unintelligible and the physical books containing them largely inaccessible.

In these ways, any text that survives long comes into relation with ever-changing groups in ever-changing cultural and social and historical contexts. This means that its interpretation will change, too. In modern times, those who have handed on the Bible have often attempted to control the way it is interpreted in new settings, among new Christian communities—

for example, by publishing annotated translations. They have not found it easy, however, to retain control. On the contrary, the reading of the Bible has never been more diverse than it is today, a consequence of its transportability through time and space as a physical object.[24]

We cannot speak of texts as physical objects, pure and simple, however, since we will then fail to distinguish them from natural objects. One fundamental distinctive of texts is that they are human productions (even if sometimes ascribed to beings other than human). They are not natural objects, existing prior to or apart from human interest. They exist in the human medium of language as a result of human effort. Even when a divine influence is claimed or acknowledged (as may happen even in relatively secular contexts in the language of the "muse"), there is no text without human involvement in its production. If nothing else, the mere use of human language means that no canonical text escapes its human ties. If no human element, then no text, and therefore, no text that is not limited by its humanity.

This is not to minimize the importance of natural objects in the human world, only to distinguish an essential element of texts. The black meteorite of the Great Mother at Pessinus may have functioned, as a ritual object, not unlike the way books can function in some other religious contexts; it was an object of veneration, a sign of the interaction between divine and human spheres. Yet it was indisputably from outside the human world. And it had the advantage, compared with texts, of being mute. It was an object that had great human meaning, built as it was into a web of cultus and belief. But it was not language.[25]

The human element in texts, whether conceived as full authorship or mere stenography or something in between, means that texts connect us with other human voices. Of late, it has not been fashionable to recognize this. The "death of the author" and the text's subsequent independence have become almost unquestioned axioms.[26] In some respects, they constitute an appropriate warning. A text may say both more and less than its author intended; and in any case the process of interpretation that takes the text in charge is not limited to divining what the author intended. Our interest as readers is never limited to the author's meaning, but always broadens out to include the larger reality that environs the whole process of interpretation. This acknowledgment, however, should not blind us to the importance of the human element in the production of texts, for it is precisely this human involvement in the text that interests us. Through the text, we expect some communication, perhaps even some communion, with another human mind and heart. We hope to hear something we will find accessible in our humanness but which we may not have perceived on our own. We expect, in other words, a conversation.

To say that there is an author or, at any rate, some human presence shaping the text is to reaffirm that the text is indeed the product of a particular place and time. (In the case of highly traditional or heavily redacted texts, the time in question may have been a fairly extended one—but not infinitely so.) This, in turn, is to say that the text represents a grappling with reality as contemporary to it, whether in agreement with the cultural definitions available at the time or, to some degree, in an effort to question, revise, or otherwise subvert them. Every text begins where it originated, not simply as if it were automatic writing from the *Geist* of its time and place (zeitgeist), but as arising out of particular positive and negative experiences of that world.

The later reader will encounter the text initially in terms of one's own cultural location. Careful attention to the text, however, makes one aware of an alien quality in it that demands explanation. As already suggested by the example of Philo's reading of the Torah, this may be explained in a variety of ways, but it cannot be simply dismissed. For Philo, it was most easily understood as an allegorical concealment of the message. In the world of today, with our strong and often quite immediate awareness of cultural difference, it would be difficult to avoid assuming historical and cultural distance as one likely reason for our difficulty in understanding a text.

The author's cultural location does not settle the question of the author's meaning. It is generally a mistake to assert that Jesus or Paul or any other NT figure believed X because he was a first-century Jew and all first-century Jews believed X. Culture does not settle such questions. Only texts, finally, can do that—and never completely. The importance of the culture of origin is not that it settles such questions but that it provides the arena for the author's wrestling match with reality, whatever form it may have taken—affirmation of a cultural norm, subversion of a norm, refocusing of attention, insistence on the importance of seeing behind the scene, reversal of existing expectations, or whatever. No one's encounter with reality is culture-free, but neither is any culture one hundred per cent successful in closing off all other possibilities of constructing reality. The author's situation, in other words, is not unlike that of the reader today. It is a situation in which there is incompleteness, uncertainty, questioning. Any move toward finding and constructing meaning encounters these challenges by its very nature. The internal tensions of every culture, every society, and every historical moment guarantee that there will be disintegration and renewal, failure and change. But the exact character of those changes will not be the same from one cultural context or historical moment to the next.

When we speak of a text as participating in a triangular conversation of interpretation, then, we mean that it conveys a human voice, contextualized, like every human voice, by the realities of time, place, and culture. With Plato, of course, some readers will object that a text cannot engage in conversation at all. Plato's Socrates complains that if you ask a written text a question, all it can do is to go on repeating the same thing.[27] More recent objectors may argue (or, more likely, just assume) that the text can never be more than a passive object, the victim of its readers and interpreters: it means whatever someone takes it to mean. There is a truth here, but it is incomplete. True, the text does not make the writer present. It cannot answer questions put to it—at least not directly or in the questioner's terms. Still more to the point, it cannot interrupt a person who is imposing some quite alien set of interests on it and say, "You are not listening. That is not what I said at all." The text is almost defenseless against the boorish reader.

The text can, on the other hand, carry with it a wealth of human experience and reflection for the attentive reader, who will be looking in it for clues to these. Not every reader, of course, is attentive in this way, just as not every participant in an ordinary conversation bothers to listen to the other people in the conversation.[28] It is possible that a reader may try to silence the text or reverse it, just as one may silence or ignore or distort a living voice. Yet the text, because it is a human artifact, has a voice and is *capable* of entering into the broad human conversation. Whether it succeeds in doing so is largely a result of how interpreters and readers engage with it.

Any text is infinitely complex.

Community of Readers

The second apex of the interpretive triangle is composed of those who interest themselves in the text. While this may be an individual reader or hearer, here I am primarily thinking and writing of communities of faith and of individual readers who belong to such communities. Without some such community, without someone for whom or to whom the interpreter interprets, interpretation itself is at most a fleeting, isolated event. Interpreters also interpret for themselves, to be sure, taking on the role of reader, too, and wishing to understand what has so far eluded them. But the roles of reader and interpreter, even though they can be internalized in this way, are first and still foremost social. Without a community taking interest in certain texts, the interpreter has no standing.

The exact nature of the community and of its relationship to the text can range widely. A literature class has its texts, a nation its constitution; and the character and duration of the commitments implied in either case are likely to differ. Both a newspaper column and a canon of sacred scripture command certain readerships, though the two groups may not have exactly the same investment in the texts that define them. Communities of readers may be evanescent, brought into being entirely by a shared interest in a text—a few people, say, gathered around a flyer posted on the street. Or they may be of long duration, as in the example par excellence of the major world religions.

In any case, the community regards some text or body of texts as important to its existence, partly because it helps define the community, but still more so because it is thought to illuminate the world in which the community lives. The community has an *interest* in its texts; they are part of its self-understanding in the world. For long-running communities, we speak of such texts as "classical" or "canonical." Texts so recognized are more likely than others to receive formal, intentional interpretation since they remain as a focus of interest long enough for institutions to grow up for this purpose.

Canons, of course, are not unchanging, particularly in periods of social transformation. And they change, as we have already observed, in a variety of ways, one being recontexualization. Early Christianity retained various forms of the canon of the Scriptures of Israel, the inherited diversity still apparent in the varying Old Testament canons of modern churches. Over a period of a few centuries, it also added works of specifically Christian provenance to its inherited canon, thereby contextualizing the Scriptures of Israel in a new way and changing the character and focus of the older texts even if it did not change their specific wording.

Canons may also change through competition and the consequent removal of some works or their replacement by others. In twentieth-century China, the Confucian classics have been challenged by texts associated with other traditions, such as the writings of Lenin or Mao Tse-tung. It remains to be seen what shape the Chinese classics will take in the future as a result of the ensuing competition. The same kind of uncertainty hovers over the classics of Western culture in recent debates about what literature deserves to be read and studied in schools and universities.

Canons may also change by the blurring of their boundaries. Christians may assume that our canon is now fully stable. But Protestants are increasingly used to seeing Bible translations that include "apocryphal" books rejected by some of their sixteenth-century Reformers: e.g., Wisdom of

Solomon or Judith. And the recovery of the Gnostic library at Nag Hammadi, particularly the *Gospel of Thomas,* and of the Dead Sea Scrolls has sparked at least a curiosity about other writings contemporary with early Christianity and the use one might make of them. Such works are not entirely inside the canon, nor entirely outside it.

Communities, then, have some power of decision in relation to their canons. On the whole, however, they prefer not to exercise these powers consciously unless perhaps during periods of significant cultural upheaval and change. The texts that are important for most communities most of the time are those whose canonicity they have inherited. They have authority partly because they seem inevitable; it takes a wholesale revaluation of cultural principles as found in the Reformation period to prompt a conscious, intentional revision of them.

In quieter times, revision of the canon may proceed more subtly in the effort to let texts speak afresh during more slowly changing circumstances. But such revision tends, for the most part, to be done internally and unobtrusively—through shifts in what portions or aspects of the canon are particularly emphasized and how they are interpreted. Such relatively subtle revisions of canon may, at times, have a more substantive effect than wholesale revisions. Luther, as we have noted, changed Western Christianity as much by his emphasis on Paul and his way of interpreting Galatians and Romans as through his more overt questioning of other books.[29] American Protestant Fundamentalism's fascination with Revelation has had a similar effect in more recent times, rewriting the whole of Scripture, for all practical purposes, in apocalyptic terms.

Since a community values its connection with its canonical or classical texts, it is apt to assume a kind of ownership of them. This may express itself in reverence paid them, in a tendency to appeal to them to justify attitudes and decisions, and in the creation of libraries and institutions where they can be interpreted. Acknowledgment of specific canonical texts or of specific traditions in interpreting them may become an important boundary issue for the group, as in Islam or in Evangelical Christianity. The community often assumes, as part of its "ownership," that the values found in the canonical texts will be the same as those held most dear in the community as it presently exists. In modern American discourse, the claim that "the Bible says X" often means no more than "This is what our community has always believed" or even "This is my interpretation of what our community has always believed." Those who claim to speak for the Bible in this way cannot always be bothered, it seems, to engage in attentive reading of it. One suspects that the authority of the canon, in such cases, is symbolic of received dogma rather than rooted in the actual texts.

Such flat-footed appeals to the authority of the text, as I have already noted, are often misleading. In reality, classical or canonical texts are as likely to introduce mixed messages as simple prescriptions into the interpretive conversation. They tend to open space for reflection more than to close it, precisely because they were not composed in terms of the culture that is reading them. What is more, the community that claims the authority of the text can be relied on to contain its own contradictions. Since no one culture at any one point in its history can realize all human possibilities, each contains its own particular incompleteness and inadequacy. Each has gaps in its carefully crafted armor. The reality behind and beyond social construction keeps intruding on reality as socially constructed and disrupting it.

A living community is one that exhibits both continuity and change. Or, to put the idea in negative terms, it is neither fossilized nor totally chaotic. Those who see themselves as particularly the advocates of continuity will appeal to the culture's classical works for validation of the status quo. Those who advocate change may sometimes attempt to overthrow the classic works and replace them with others, but, alternatively, they may appeal actively to them as grounds for change by arguing that the culture is not living up to its own principles. Thus, appeals to the canonical texts commonly appear on both sides of serious conflict.

In both cases, there is a temptation for communities of readers to override any independent voice on the part of the text itself. The urgency of the situation seems to justify a claim that God—and therefore the sacred or classical text—is on one's own side. For example, it is not unusual for right-wing political and religious groups to insist that the Bible mandates mid-twentieth-century American patterns of family life, though it is virtually impossible even to find such patterns in the Bible, much less to find them commanded. The interpretive conversation collapses at such moments because the text no longer has a meaningful voice. And the community, though it may insist on, or even pontificate about, its canonical texts, actually becomes divorced from them. It reads them not to listen, but only to make use of them. The conversation is reduced to a monologue. There is no opening for the kind of surprise that the voice of the text might offer.

In such contexts, fraught with urgency to make the text speak in a particular way, the work of the interpreter becomes particularly important. It also becomes dangerous. It is politically dangerous because different sides in the dispute want the canonical texts in their camp. (This may be true even for those who reject the authority of the texts. Engels and other early Communists, for example, though they rejected Christianity, sought to claim Jesus and the earliest Christian communities as their own forebears.)[30] People appealing to the canon to validate their claims in a conflict will not be patient with the interpreter who disagrees with them.

The work of the interpreter, as a result, also becomes spiritually as well as economically and personally dangerous. The interpreter who maintains some neutrality may well be concerned for personal well-being. If the interpreter does belong to, or sympathize with, one of the factions, however, the temptation is not only external, but internal as well—the temptation to sacrifice one's role as interpreter to one's role as partisan. In an insistent way, all this raises several questions: How do we maintain personal integrity? What does the actual work of the interpreter demand of us? What is our responsibility to the text? What is our responsibility to the community that interests itself in the text and for which we interpret it? Certainly, we must take the concerns of the community seriously since they, too, are an essential aspect of the interpretive conversation.

Before moving to deal with the role of the interpreter, however, I think it is important to specify one other aspect of the community that enters into the interpretive conversation. Just as it was important to insist that the text being interpreted is, in some important sense, a human artifact, it is also important to insist that the community taking interest in the text is a human community. No community, even if it claims to have been graced with the ultimate revelation of God, can claim to be other than human. It will continue to be, as history has richly demonstrated, a community filled with sin, arrogance, error, and fallibility alongside its moments of insight, goodness, and joy. Many communities are quite resistant to this notion and wish to regard themselves as exceptions to the human norm, unique by reason of their virtue, their purity, their history, their religion, or whatever.

To transform a text into a direct manifestation of the divine, of ultimate truth itself, is, from the perspective of classical Christianity, a form of idolatry; it makes the text a kind of graven image. Idolatry is an enduringly powerful temptation, as suggested by its prominent prohibition in the Ten Commandments. The same temptation is also at work in relation to communities, tempting us to see our community as distinct from and superior to other communities, which are therefore entitled to less consideration. We apply the promise of the text to ourselves and its threats to others.

From Nazism onward, the recent history of the world is replete with moments when one human community has decided to treat its neighbors as if they were not human—not of the same category as themselves. Whether it is Hutu versus Tutsi, Serb versus Croat versus Bosnian Muslim, the Chilean military versus their suspected political opponents, or any other example that comes to mind, we cannot avoid recognizing that the process of dehumanizing others or superhumanizing ourselves is one of our most fundamental temptations to evil.

Religious communities, in particular, are tempted to identify themselves with God—never, of course, in so many words, as the impiety would then be too obvious to be maintained, but by cloaking themselves in divine ultimacy. When a religious community begins to suppose that its interpretation of the text and of the human, this-worldly reality to which the text speaks, is perfect and absolute, it has fallen into this kind of idolatry. In practice, it can no longer participate in a real conversation with the text because it already knows everything there is to know. At most, it will comb the text for further demonstrations of how perfectly it comprehends the will of God. But it should be self-evident that no human mind can contain the mind of God. Classical Christianity does not make such a claim even in the case of the Incarnation, but asserts that the incarnate Word is as truly human as he is God. In the Gospel of Mark, Jesus actually specifies limits to his knowledge (13:32). The church cannot claim to have more perfect access to the mind of God than the incarnate Word. If it does claim this, it has no further need of Scripture, which then serves only as a source of proof texts to hang in the church's shop windows for a kind of window dressing. Scripture fulfills its reason for existing only when it serves to facilitate the community's fallible, searching approach to the God we shall never fully understand.

What does it mean for the interpretive conversation when we insist on the humanity of the interested community? This is not a surreptitious way of intervening in discussions about the superiority of one religion to another or about the profound theological issues of describing ultimate reality. It simply means that no community has a right to exempt itself from what it shares with all humanity—everything from our wisdom, imagination, and beauty to our stupidity, hostility, and fascination with our own evil. Even if it understands its scriptures to be uniquely inspired, they are still relevant to the community in question only insofar as they offer something of value to humanity as such. One's own community, after all, is one human community among others. We are no longer in a world where one community alone can pretend to settle for all people what is good and right and true. If we should wish to make such a claim, we can do it only by commending our faith, not by imposing it.

Our humanity also means our incompleteness. If we grant that any particular body of scripture is indeed the unique word of God, it does not follow that the community having custody of it is therefore correct in understanding it. Since it is a human community, we can be sure that it is at least partly wrong. This means that a canonical text that cannot surprise us and lead to further learning and deeper understanding is of limited value. A canonical text that cannot reprove its own readers is worthless. A canonical text that cannot discourage its readers from dehumanizing others is worse than worthless; it is treacherous and demonic. But even when the text itself is not subject to such criticisms, it is easy for the community, in its arrogance and self-idolatry, simply to override the voice of its texts.

Every community that is human is also fallible. Every community, being human, is finite and subject to change, whether from without or from within. Every community stands in need of learning new possibilities and rethinking familiar presuppositions. Every community stands in need of both celebrating the gifts it enjoys through its cultural inheritance and repenting the evils that go along with them. Without recognizing these things, we cannot have an honest or fruitful conversation with our classic texts.[31]

Interpreter

Interpreters may, at times, be part of a conversation between community and text from its first moment; the Federalist Papers, for example, were interpretations of the United States Constitution offered before it was even ratified. But in any case, the interpreter necessarily becomes a part of the interpretive conversation as the aging of the text engenders the need for specialized knowledge in understanding it. It is not only the passage of time, however, that gives rise to interpreters; it is also the fact that communities normally act through their members rather than as collectives. As in Paul's image of the church as the body of Christ in 1 Cor 12 (itself indebted to earlier Greek reflection on the nature of the body politic), every community relies on a diversity of gifts and vocations among its members. Accordingly, the community's conversation with its canonical texts largely takes place through particular people, some of whom have specialized roles as interpreters. Few, if any, human societies manage without people who enjoy particular recognition as interpreters of the culture's texts.

In the case of an oral text, the tradent, the person most intimately familiar with it, is also its principal interpreter, adapting it in recitation to the
needs of the moment. In the case of a written text, another type of interpreter arises—the scribe or scholar. Early writing systems were difficult to
read, perhaps deliberately so. But even without the intricacies of Egyptian
hieroglyphs or Mesopotamian cuneiform, the existence of written documents invites the rise of scholarly specialists who know and reproduce
them, who can find things in them, read them to the unlettered, and
explain them to the inexperienced or inexpert.

What distinguishes the scholarly interpreter is the employment of specialized knowledge (often knowledge that no longer has any direct productive value in the contemporary culture, such as the ability to read
"dead" languages) in the service of knowing and understanding a community's significant texts. To make such an undertaking possible, the community assigns resources to it in the form of schools, libraries, and other
venues in which the interpreter labors and brings the results of that labor
to the larger community.

People come to the role of interpreter and are recognized as fitted for it
by a combination of desire and ability. The interpreter has to master the
skills required in the given culture—skills ranging from good memory and
a clear manuscript hand to the mastery of diverse languages and some
affinity for computers. The interpreter also needs to experience a desire for
the text and for learning, whether it takes the form of piety (particularly in
the case of sacred texts) or of the curiosity that can draw the interpreter
ever deeper into the text. Piety alone may not be the best motivation for an
interpreter; an inappropriate reverence, as I shall suggest below, can dis-
tract the interpreter from the work of interpretation. But neither is curiosity enough by itself, since the community expects its interpreters to work
with what is defined by the culture as significant, not simply to follow
their own noses.

The interpreter is normally a member of the community whose texts are
being interpreted, though this is less inevitable now than it once was. When
human cultures were more isolated from each other, the scholars of one did
not often concern themselves with the texts of another. The imperialism of
the West changed that by making such texts more widely accessible, and
Western scholars began the practice of learning and interpreting the canonical texts of other cultures, even as the West introduced the canonical texts
of Christianity and other Western classics into new cultural contexts.

I do not intend to make this sound like an innocent process. It was
not. While there indeed were scholars with honorable intentions, who

approached the texts of other cultures with respect, much of the attention devoted to them looked at them as curiosities from more "primitive" cultures, collected much as trophies and objects of art were collected for Western museums. Interpretation could be an intellectual aspect of imperialism, a way of wresting control of other cultures away from their own interpretive agents. Still, the history of imperialism created a situation in which we have come to accept that a person might become an interpretive specialist in relation to texts that are not canonical in that person's own community.

Christians who studied, for example, with Samuel Sandmel, a prominent Jewish scholar of the NT, never found it odd that we should learn from him. We might conceive such an interpreter from outside one's own group in terms of what classical Greek called a ξένος, a guest-friend, in the community that is invested in the text. The interpreter as ξένος brings a perspective to interpretation that those more fully identified with the community are not likely to have, but does so in a spirit of friendship, not domination.[32] Indeed, as human communities become increasingly multicultural, it may well be that we do not have the luxury of restricting our canonical literature in the ways possible in the past. We may need to cultivate the vocation of interpreter as ξένος quite deliberately.

Yet interpreters will continue, for the most part, to be drawn from the communities they serve. Cultural and community boundaries do not become irrelevant in a multicultural world; indeed, they may become more important. This is, to some degree, in conflict with the presuppositions of the Western academy. The political imperialism of the recent Western past encouraged the academy to treat the texts of all cultures as if they belonged not to their own communities but to the academy itself, just as their artifacts now belonged to Western museums. And the academy functioned as a community of scholarly interpreters whose principal objective was to gain one another's good opinion. This element in academic work has gone hand in hand with the quasi-scientific objectivism of modern academics to create a context in which any significant cultural and religious engagement of the interpreter with the text or its community seemed suspect.

Now, if the interpreter's religious engagement is such as to predetermine the interpretation of the text, it does militate against critical thinking; but the exclusion of such connections may be equally harmful. In the West, scholars have, in effect, applied the same imperialist mentality we used on other cultures to our own past. We have learned how to treat the canonical texts of the West as curiosities, too—as quaint objects drawn from the primitive culture of our own past, suitable only for distanced, "objective" academic study. Specialists in the Bible, the Greek and Roman classics, and ultimately the whole Western literary tradition are tempted to behave as if these texts are museum exhibits, the property of the academy, of no continuing public importance, suitable only to be strip-mined by the latest analytical methods. The idea that they are a trust of the culture at large or of specific communities of faith has often disappeared as anything more than a piety trotted out for commencement ceremonies.

The academicizing of scriptural studies works, in effect, a redefinition of the community to which the interpreter belongs and for which the interpreter employs her or his skills. Where the Western interpreter once worked in relation to a larger community that included political and religious leaders and creative artists, this same figure now increasingly works in relation to a community composed only of other interpretive specialists, an intelligentsia set apart by education and distinguished by a social formation and linguistic impenetrability that emphasizes its apartness. If this sounds claustrophobic, it is. Such a restriction of the community to and for which the scholar interprets attenuates the interpreter's connection to the rest of humanity. It focuses interest on purely intellectual and analytical issues, in community and text alike. What is lost is an earlier and more vital sense that the interpreter is integral to a larger community's conversation with its texts and therefore part of how it encounters that larger reality in which it lives and which it can never entirely tame or subdue or predict.

As Wilfred Cantwell Smith has observed, the interest of a culture in its canonical texts is typically quite different from the interest of modern scholars in those same texts.[33] Many Christians—and not just Fundamentalists—find twentieth-century biblical scholarship, insofar as they encounter it at all, irrelevant to their reading of Scripture. And this is true even though a great many biblical scholars are themselves Christians. Similarly, many Christian biblical scholars, even though convinced that their scholarship and their faith interconnect, are inarticulate as to how this happens or what it means. I suspect this represents an internalization of the more public dichotomy between the academic community that imperializes and the "primitive" communities of faith that are colonized, with the Christian scholar trying to live on both sides of the line.

This is an impoverishment first of the interpreter, who is deprived of his or her full humanity, and second of the community, which loses important elements from the interpretive conversation with its canonical texts. Remember that the text itself is not the point of that conversation. The ideas in the text are not the point. Ideas *about* the text are certainly not the point. All these are means, not the end. The goal of the conversation is

Not dependent on scholarship

illumination of life, of reality, of all the "out there" of our existence, which we understand in large part through our culture's construction of it, but which always remains also, to a significant degree, undomesticated by our cultural constructs and ready to break them.

The contemporary opportunity for interpreters to cross existing community boundaries is useful only insofar as it can be thoroughly decolonialized, so that it does not represent an act of imperial condescension by cultural, religious, or academic outsiders. A respectful crossing of boundaries, the work of the ξένος, or guest-friend, may contribute to the ability of every community to perceive the humanness of others. Perhaps it will help in the constructing of peaceful interactions in our increasingly diverse local communities. But this can happen only if the interpreter is indeed connected to larger human communities by bonds of respect, affection, and integrity—connected to the interpreter's own community as well as the one to which the texts in question belong, whether the two are different or the same. If the interpreter interprets only for an academic community, the questions and issues of the larger world will typically be lost, and that apex of the interpretive triangle where the interpreter resides will become an increasingly void and sterile locus because there is no meeting there between text and community.

In short, whatever works to reduce the active engagement of any one voice in the interpretive conversation threatens to impoverish the whole and make it irrelevant. The voices of the community can cause this by overriding the voice of the text or silencing that of the interpreters. The interpreters can do the same if we quit speaking with the community on behalf of the text, or take the part of the community against the text and so help to silence it. In some ways, the interpreter is the key element, developing an intimate conversation with the text in the process of getting to know it and understand it, sharing some kind of community with the group that has canonized the text—even if as a ξένος rather than a native or a naturalized citizen—and bringing the two together by listening to both. Still, the interpreter is always just one point of the triangle. The interpreter is never the sole conduit or point of contact between the text and the community. Text and community are always in some kind of interaction with each other, with or without the presence of the interpreter. Indeed, sometimes the interpreter may have to exercise some social ingenuity to be accepted as part of the conversation.

At the same time, the interpreter, to be faithful to the other partners in the conversation, must not only be related to them but also maintain a certain distinction from both. If interpreters could manage to disappear into the text, as it were, living so much inside the text as to understand it without any distance, they would no longer be able to put to the text the questions of their own time and place, of the community for which they interpret. They could not, in other words, *interpret* any more. Or, if interpreters become simply immersed in their communities, then they will no longer have any helpful insight into the text, with the consequence that the community will be trapped inside its own space and time without the benefit of the text's ability to open up its boundaries.

The interpreter, then, must remain both connected and distinct. And this, in turn, means that the moral and spiritual position of the interpreter is difficult, dangerous, and replete with its own particular temptations. One is the temptation to disappear into the community of readers, carefully appeasing its leadership and assuming its prejudices as camouflage. The other, made easier where academic institutions are relatively independent, is the temptation to crawl inside the text and not reemerge. This has become almost a norm in modern biblical studies insofar as academic guilds have taken as their task purely the elucidation of the "original meaning" of the text, without regard to the possible relevance of that meaning in other contexts. The academic community has even taken the further step of suggesting that its interest in the text is purer than that of others and that only its questions are of real importance. This has helped modern criticism not to notice its own investment in the control of the text or its tacit claim of ownership. Indeed, it defined the academic community as a noncommunity, a community without its own "slant," interested purely in the text itself.

Postmodern critiques of modern biblical studies have helped somewhat in overcoming this tendency. We have learned, at least in theory, that scholars, too, have a social location, complete with presuppositions deriving from culture, class, and other social factors. Unfortunately, the ideological critics who have revealed the problem often fail to apply their critique to themselves. In the process, they fall prey, themselves, to the temptation to disappear into a particular community, academic rather than religious, and read the text only as that community wants it read. This is particularly a problem with ideological criticisms. Feminist criticism, for example, at its most creative, has been a key element in opening up new ways of questioning the text and retrieving obscured voices; the task I am embarking on here is unimaginable without its influence. At the same time, feminist criticism at its most mechanical can be merely a form of tendentious reading that knows the answer—patriarchy—before it asks the question; in the process it thus imposes a reductionism on the text by omitting other important human concerns. The same temptation waits on every form of academic criticism if it divorces itself from diverse human communities. As a result, the interpreter who is completely immersed in an academic community is as useless for the task of interpretation as the one who is completely immersed in a community of faith.

The temptation to read tendentiously is not new, of course. But it is not on the wane, either. It is inherent in all textual studies precisely because human beings cannot help being members of communities, whether we like it or not, whether we are even conscious of it or not. My intention is not to find fault with the methodologies and basic insights of such modalities as sociological criticism or feminist criticism or queer hermeneutics. I wish rather to find fault with some of their applications. The true value, for the interpreter, of all methodologies is heuristic. They teach us to ask new questions and to see things we might not otherwise have sought. When academic guilds use them to prescribe results, however, they become the interpreter's tempter, just as the church is a tempter when it makes a comparable move based on the current (and always transient) state of its tradition of doctrine and life. Interpreters can interpret only by maintaining both the independence and the connectedness of our particular point in the triangular conversation.

These reflections on the role of the interpreter and its inherent temptations can also serve as the foundation for more positively framed thoughts on the character of the interpreter and the spirituality of reading. I will return to these topics in this work's concluding Epilogue.

Practicing Interpretation

The interpreter seeks to understand a text in order to make it clearer for others who are interested in it. A good interpreter will generally have a personal passion for such understanding in its own right. It is part of what fits one for the task of interpretation. But the passion to understand is not, in itself, enough. One becomes an interpreter only insofar as one also looks outward to the larger communities interested in the text. If one wishes to interpret for them, one must know their language—which is a shorthand expression for knowing their life. The interpreter is seeking to facilitate a conversation between text and community, a conversation in which each side needs to "listen" as well as speak to the other. On the one side, this means that the interpreter is particularly responsible for ensuring that the community does not simply run over the text in its eagerness to make it say what the community wants it to say. The interpreter is always on the alert for tendencies to force the text, whether they are creations of the moment or take the form of a long tradition of mistranslation. On the other side, it also means that the interpreter will need to bring the realities of the community into dialogue with the text and invite the text to shed light on them, not by forcing the text to give precise and direct answers to modern questions and problems, but by allowing modern realities to reveal complexities in the text, bringing into relief elements that might previously have been neglected, and allowing the text to respond in unpredictable ways.

It is a matter of cultivating the art of listening. The interpreter listens to the text in order to maintain its integrity in the act of translation. And the interpreter listens to the communities of readers or hearers today in order to discern what large issues the text might or might not speak to. In neither case can we achieve this in a reductionist way by dismissing whatever does not correspond to our theory. Only when complexity can speak and listen to complexity will the interpretive conversation go forward effectively.

Notes

1. See the collection edited by Fernando F. Segovia and Mary Ann Tolbert, *Reading from This Place,* 2 vols. (Minneapolis: Fortress, 1995).

2. These are now conveniently summarized in such works as Steven L. McKenzie and Stephen R. Haynes, eds., *To Each Its Own Meaning: An Introduction to Biblical Criticisms and Their Application,* rev. ed. (Louisville: Westminster John Knox, 1999); and A. K. M. Adam, ed., *Handbook of Postmodern Biblical Interpretation* (St. Louis: Chalice Press, 2000). As Adam notes in his preface to the latter (viii), the appearance of such works may well be a sign that methodologies that not long ago seemed new and radical are already being domesticated in the scholarly guild.

3. Joel B. Green has noted that, as the failure of the modernist project became evident, "the response for many was to rotate the discussion by 180°, to forms of study for which there are thankfully no facts, only perspectives"; "Rethinking History (and Theology)," in *Between Two Horizons: Spanning New Testament Studies and Systematic Theology,* ed. Joel B. Green and Max Turner (Grand Rapids: Eerdmans, 2000), 238. This only replaces one reductionism with another.

4. My own early experience of structuralist exegesis, for example, was that it consisted of little more than the tedious splitting of a text into two columns to prove that Claude Levi-Strauss was right about the workings of the human mind. The work of Daniel Patte, however, makes genuinely interpretive use of the method, for example in *The Gospel According to Matthew: A Structural Commentary on Matthew's Faith* (Philadelphia: Fortress, 1987).

5. Mary Ann Tolbert, "The Politics and Poetics of Location," in Segovia and Tolbert, eds., *Reading from This Place,* 1:305–17; and "When Resistance Becomes Oppression: Mark 13:9–27 and the Poetics of Location," ibid., 2:331–46.

6. I find a parallel in the Peircean notion of "musement," as described by Michael L. Raposa: "Musement requires a 'casting aside of all serious purpose' so that no concept or belief will be imposed by the Muser as an explanation in order to satisfy some preference or achieve some end. Rather, in Musement . . . beliefs literally come into play; they are themselves played with, tried on for size, always regarded hypothetically, as imagined possibilities"; *Boredom and the Religious Imagination* (Charlottesville: University Press of Virginia, 1999), 99.

7. Sandra Schneiders, *The Revelatory Text: Interpreting the New Testament as Sacred Scripture* (San Francisco: HarperSanFrancisco, 1991), 95–199.

8. I could make a long list of contemporary biblical scholars who are fully aware of the creative element in our work and make significant contributions to it. My point here is not to say that we never perform this function, but that the intellectual presuppositions and social institutions of biblical interpretation in our time do not recognize or support it. Those who do it, do it against the grain of our discipline, not with it.

9. Even in physics, this is proving more difficult; Sharla A. Stewart, "The Complexity Complex," *University of Chicago Magazine* 95/2 (Dec. 2002): 38–45.

10. The reductionist habit has become a kind of tic that shows up even where it is irrelevant. Cf. Ruth Anne Reese's reduction of writing to "black marks on white paper" that she expects to evoke "their chemical reaction in some other reader"; *Writing Jude: The Reader, the Text, and the Author in Constructs of Power and Desire* (Leiden: Brill, 2000), 152. The motif harks back to her earlier discussion of Richard Rorty, in ibid., 47–49.

11. A significant exception is Marcus Borg, *Jesus, a New Vision: Spirit, Culture, and the Life of Discipleship* (San Francisco: Harper & Row, 1987).

12. Papias, cited in Eusebius, *Church History* 3.39.15; trans. Robert M. Grant, *Second-Century Christianity: A Collection of Fragments* (London: SPCK, 1957), 68–69. The founders of form criticism of the Gospels, Martin Dibelius and Rudolf Bultmann, recognized the importance of placing oral tradition in its social context, but they never explored this issue in any depth. This left the analytic discipline of form criticism floating in air, as it were, with no clear connection to the social dynamics that controlled and animated oral tradition in the first place.

13. "Resorting to 'an alien expertise' to solve an immediate problem is often evidence of a 'quick-fix mentality' rather than a long-term, integrated solution. Though different contexts create different problems, there are six common problems," including distortion, decontextualization, borrowing out-of-date theory, and overreliance on individual theories, among others. Julie Thompson Klein, *Interdisciplinarity: History, Theory, and Practice* (Detroit: Wayne State University Press, 1990), 88.

14. With regard to religion, modernism and postmodernism in ordinary academic use are more alike than different in this respect. "At this point, postmodernity is simply realizing the modernist dream of sundering itself from a past that belongs to other people." Joel B. Green, "Rethinking History," 239, n. 2.

15. I am thinking particularly of his *On the Creation of the World according to Moses.*

16. E.g., John A. Sanford, *Mystical Christianity: A Psychological Commentary on the Gospel of John* (New York: Crossroad, 1993).

17. E.g., Jeffrey L. Staley, *Reading with a Passion: Rhetoric, Autobiography, and the American West in the Gospel of John* (New York: Continuum, 1995).

18. Countryman, *Biblical Authority or Biblical Tyranny?* 83–103.

19. Wilfred Cantwell Smith, *What Is Scripture? A Comparative Approach* (Minneapolis: Fortress, 1993), 223, speaks of the religious reader's "focus on interpreting (on understanding) the universe and human life—with the texts as mediating, and in effect secondary."

20. Cathleen Schine, *Rameau's Niece* (New York: Ticknor & Fields, 1993), 52.

21. In some respects, they can virtually be reversed; cf. Tolbert, "When Resistance Becomes Repression," 334–46.

22. L. William Countryman, "Tertullian and the Regula Fidei," *The Second Century* 2 (1982): 208–227.

23. See, for example, the excellent, interdisciplinary work of Harry Y. Gamble, *Books and Readers in the Early Church: A History of Early Christian Texts* (New Haven: Yale University Press, 1995), for the development of early Christian book forms and reverence for the text as physical object.

24. E.g., Jonathan Draper, "Confessional Western Text-Centered Biblical Interpretation and an Oral or Residual-Oral Context," *Semeia* 73 (1996): 59–77.

25. This was the cult object brought to Rome during the third century B.C.E. John Ferguson, *The Religions of the Roman Empire* (Ithaca: Cornell University Press, 1970), 26–28.

26. It is refreshing to find them being questioned again; e.g., Ruth Anne Reese, *Writing Jude* (Leiden: Brill, 2000), 122–52.

27. *Phaedrus* 275D–E.

28. Listening is critical to every aspect of the interpretive process, as Tolbert points out; "Christianity, Imperialism, and the Decentering of Privilege," in Segovia and Tolbert, *Reading from This Place,* 2:350–55.

29. For an interesting assessment of the effect of retaining James in the Lutheran canon, see Robert W. Wall, *Community of the Wise: The Letter of James* (Valley Forge, Pa.: Trinity Press International, 1997), 3–4, 299–306.

30. L. William Countryman, *The Rich Christian in the Church of the Early Empire: Contradictions and Accommodations* (Texts and Studies in Religion; New York: Edwin Mellen, 1980), 1–18.

31. Though I have approached this issue from rather a different angle, I believe that it is essentially the same issue of the ethics of interpretation and the integrity of the interpreter that Daniel Patte has wrestled with eloquently in *Ethics of Biblical Interpretation: A Reevaluation* (Louisville: Westminster John Knox, 1995).

32. Two recent examples come to mind, both Jewish scholars who have written significant works on Paul: Alan F. Segal, *Paul the Convert: The Apostolate and Apostasy of Saul the Pharisee* (New Haven: Yale University Press, 1990); and Daniel Boyarin, *A Radical Jew: Paul and the Politics of Identity* (Berkeley: University of California Press, 1994).

33. Smith, *What Is Scripture?* 212–42.

2. First Steps in Interpretation
An Application to Jude

To illustrate how the model of interpretation I am suggesting works in practice, I turn to the Letter of Jude, convenient for our purpose because of its brevity and also because it has not yielded much interest (or, at least, has not sparked much interest) for scholarship in the past century.[1] The interpreter's first task is precisely the literal act of interpretation or translation—making the text as available as possible to contemporary conversation, presenting it as accurately as possible in the changed context of another culture, era, and language. This is the task that draws on the interpreter's arcane knowledge, the task that situates the interpreter closest to the text, and the task that often lies closest to the interpreter's heart—the task in which the interpreter is in conversation most deeply with the text itself. This short chapter will exemplify this work by looking at two particular issues of translation that can substantially affect our basic perception of the letter.

First, however, it will be worthwhile to point out something of what I am presupposing about this letter's origins. No interpreter of Scripture begins from scratch. The text carries with it some tradition of its study, and each person's understanding of the text evolves in relation to that tradition and may also enter into its continuation and transformation, becoming part of the presuppositions of others. These presuppositions remain open to question and should not be treated as definitive conclusions. But they are where we begin.

It is difficult to date the Letter of Jude, much more to assign authorship or to say much about its audience. For a long time, scholars associated it with second-century documents such as the letters of Ignatius of Antioch or the *Epistle of Barnabas,* treating it as a product of "Early Catholicism." This rather clumsy term covers the period when early Christianity was becoming more pervasively institutionalized and when the element that eventually became the mainstream of Christianity was evolving its ideas of orthodoxy and setting itself in opposition to heresies.

More recently, there has been some tendency to date the work earlier. There is little in it that demands a late date, and its close relationship with 2 Peter 2, which parallels Jude quite closely, suggests that it must at least be earlier than that document. I am increasingly persuaded by these arguments. One reason, as I will show, is that I think the author's devotion to orthodoxy has been overstated.[2] Another reason is that the letter does not have the normal features of a pseudepigraphical work, which is likely to be more explicit about the points it is making, as, for example, in 1 Timothy or Titus.

The milieu in which the letter originated was surely Jewish Christian. The name "Jude, brother of James" suggests it, regardless of whether one thinks of him as the actual author. In addition, the letter assumes wide biblical knowledge on the part of the audience and an active acquaintance with Levitical purity rules about sexual ejaculation. The community or communities addressed were probably wholly Jewish Christian, for there is no hint of ethnic tensions.[3] They probably resembled the churches we know from the *Didache*—dispersed town or village communities, functioning primarily on their own, with a somewhat vaguely defined group of elders in charge, and accustomed to offer hospitality to itinerant Christian teachers.

While there is no certainty, I now assume that the work dates from before 90 C.E. and possibly before 70. The author may well have been Jude "the brother of the Lord," though that identification is of little importance to my interpretation. He is addressing a community or communities in which itinerant teachers have appeared with an unusual kind of Christian praxis. The communities do not appear otherwise to be under any grave stress such as might arise from persecution or internal Christian conflicts.

Listening to Jude

Our conventional or traditional reading of Jude owes a good deal to two questionable translations that appear in all or most of the English versions of the letter. The first error is quite venerable, appearing already in the Authorized (King James) Version (AV), which translates Jude 3 thus:

Beloved, when I gave all diligence to write unto you of the common salvation, it was needful for me to write unto you, and exhort you that ye should earnestly contend for the faith which was once delivered unto the saints.

The thought of "earnestly contending for the faith" pervades the tradition of translating this passage. The NEB even intensifies it to "struggle in defense of the faith." The interpretation was already in place in antiquity, for the Vulgate has *supercertari semel traditae sanctis fidei,* where *supercertari* seems to mean "to struggle on behalf of."

This is perhaps the single best known line from this little document, summing it up neatly as a work of incipient orthodoxy. I had always taken the translation for granted and was surprised, on studying the Greek text more closely, to find that the foundation for this interpretation is fragile.[4] The more usual sense of the Greek verb in question is to "fight with the help of" rather than "on behalf of." This suggests that Jude is thinking of "the faith once delivered to the saints" not so much in terms of an endangered treasure that has to be protected as in terms of a fundamental resource that will help in the defense of the community's life.

Reading the verse in this way, it becomes no longer a battle cry, but an expression of confidence in the community's prior experience of faith. Jude expects that it will provide them with critical aid in the situation of division and uncertainty that he addresses. This reading may, at first, seem unlikely to some, if only because Jude's general tone of voice in this letter seems more combative than reassuring. Yet the same thought appears again near the end of the letter:

But ye, beloved, building up yourselves on your most holy faith, praying in the Holy Ghost, Keep yourselves in the love of God, looking for the mercy of our Lord Jesus Christ unto eternal life. (20–21, AV)

Here again, the faith is not something to be protected so much as it is something to rely on—indeed, build on.[5] Perhaps we should simply accept that there may be some discrepancy between Jude's "voice" and the content of his message.

One wonders why the more anxious interpretation of verse 3 has been dominant for so long, since it is not well supported either by standard usage or by internal evidence. One can understand, however, that it must have made a kind of "self-evident" sense from the second century onward,

given the widespread assumption of the age that Christians have to fight to
protect orthodox faith from heresy. Indeed, this reading of Jude is part of
what encouraged historical-critical scholars to categorize it as a second-
century document. And once it was so categorized, no one was surprised
that it would strike such a note. But the argument is circular because nothing else in Jude really suggests a second-century dating.

The result of this interpretation is a picture of Jude as a polemicist on
behalf of tradition, opposed to change of any kind. He may, of course, have
been just that. One verse, even in so short a letter, will not settle the matter. But this particular verse, contrary to previous understandings of it,
probably does not point in that direction. Some readers may like the
prospect of a "kinder, gentler" Jude; others, as I know from experience,
will be offended by it. The interpreter's job is neither to please nor to irri-
tate, but to represent the now-distant language of the text as accurately as
possible.

The second questionable translation I point out here is of much more
recent origin, but it has also become pervasive in English versions of the
NT. The AV translated Jude 7 thus:

> Even as Sodom and Gomorrha [sic, with the Greek spelling, not the
> Hebrew], and the cities about them in like manner, giving themselves
> over to fornication, and going after strange flesh, are set forth for an
> example, suffering the vengeance of eternal fire.

The punctuation of AV is misleading here, suggesting as it does that "in like
manner" refers to the other cities as following the example of Sodom and
Gomorrah; yet the syntax and structure of the paragraph as a whole suggest rather that the people of Sodom and Gomorrah acted in the same
manner as the angels of verse 6. In other respects, however, one can commend the AV translators. "Going after strange flesh" is not a clear expression in English, but it is a reasonable representation of the Greek ὀπίσω
σαρκὸς ἑτέρας.

The same cannot be said for the translators of the RSV, who represented
(or rather misrepresented) the passage thus:

> just as Sodom and Gomorrah and the surrounding cites, which like-
> wise acted immorally and indulged in unnatural lust, serve as an
> example by undergoing a punishment of eternal fire.

The RSV has improved the translation with "just as," but committed an indefensible error with "indulged in unnatural lust." Clearly, they took the passage as a reference to homosexuality, since that was the common understanding of the Sodom narrative in the mid-twentieth century—a period that has been described as perhaps the most intolerant toward gay and lesbian people in Western history.[6]

A little reflection might have suggested that "going after strange flesh" or perhaps more precisely "alien flesh," is not a reference to same-gender sexual intercourse.[7] In fact, it lays the emphasis on the difference between the participants, not their sameness. In isolation, one might read the passage as referring to the fact that the objects of the proposed rape were foreigners, wayfarers, houseguests of a resident alien. But since the RSV translators correctly tied this verse closely to the preceding one, they might appropriately have recognized that the real issue was sexual interaction between human beings and angels. This is the most literal meaning of the verse, however improbable it may seem to later readers.[8]

Perhaps we should not judge the RSV translators too harshly, given that the whole issue of homosexuality was so forbidden as to be virtually beyond discussion in their time. More blame attaches to their successors, the translators of the NRSV, who retained the RSV's translation in their text, even though they offered a more literal alternative in their notes. By the time they were at work, a number of scholars had called attention to the literal meaning of the verse.[9] Despite this, the RSV's translation has become the default option for subsequent English versions.

Since Christian communities of faith are currently embroiled in sometimes punitive conflicts about sexual orientation, one can understand this traditionalism. Scholars, being quiet people, prefer not to become embroiled in disputes, especially those that might threaten their livelihood. At the same time, this means that scholars and translators are conniving with powerful voices in their communities to suppress the voice of Scripture, which in this case is actually concerned with something quite different from homosexuality.

If we continue to verse 8, we find that Jude is concerned about contemporary teachers whose practice he describes as being comparable to that of the men of Sodom in the same way that theirs was comparable to the angels of Gen 6. This practice involves the defiling of the flesh and disrespectful behavior toward angelic beings. All of this points, as we shall explore in more detail later (see chap. 4), toward some kind of ritual practice understood as sexual intercourse with angels. If scholars have failed to notice this, it is probably because we have assumed that the fault of

Sodom, according to Jude, was male-male sex and so have missed the triple reference (6–8) to intercourse between human beings and angels.

The reader may be asking how this sort of concern for translation can forward the practice of interpretive conversation. Is it helpful to be told that Jude is concerned about something unlikely to be on the agenda of modern readers? Does it perhaps distance him from us so far that there is no further occasion for conversation? That is possible. Whatever claims Christians may have made in moments of enthusiasm, we have never really taken the doctrine of inspiration to imply that every word of Scripture is equally relevant to every succeeding age.

On the other hand, these quibbles about translation do reawaken a conversation that might once have seemed to be largely exhausted. They present us with at least two questions worth exploring. One has to do with Jude's role as a warrior on behalf of orthodoxy. If the tradition of interpretation has misrepresented him in this regard, we might raise the question of how and why Christians slip so easily from celebrating our faith as a source of freedom and intimacy with God, to treating it as a trophy to be defended by any means necessary. Even if we finally decide that the tradition of translation has not misrepresented Jude in this matter, the question remains in our consciousness, since we know it is a reality of our own experience. It brings complex issues of antiquity face-to-face with complex issues of today.

The second question has to do with Jude's interpretation of the Sodom story and our contemporary struggles over the place of homosexual people in the churches. The long-standing assumption that the Sodom story is self-evidently about homosexuality runs aground here. How odd that a first-century Christian writer could see it in terms so different from those that became standard, through complex historical processes, at a later time.[10] How odd, for that matter, that scholars and translators could so long simply gloss over the literal sense of the text of Jude because we assumed that we knew in advance what the text must be about. Either way, we become aware that the scriptural text is capable of saying something new and surprising to us when we keep returning to it with an openness to new insight.

Our conversation with Jude thus takes a new turn without our having quite intended it. (At least, it was not anything I expected when I began reading Jude more closely several decades ago.) We find Jude, whom we may have expected to stand for a kind of militant certainty on the part of people of faith, instead provoking us to question our self-assumed roles as defenders of the true faith (however we may define it) and our certainties about received interpretations of Scripture. Whether Jude has more to offer us, we can say only as we move, in a later chapter, toward a fuller appreciation of the complexities of the environment in which he wrote.

Listening to the Communities of Faith

We have already pointed out that conflicts within the churches have affected our reading of Jude. One does not need to be deeply immersed in a Christian church to know that such communities are profoundly troubled and divided in our time by issues of sexuality. Indeed, we have already observed how those concerns have affected translations of Jude and obscured the clear import of the Greek text. Perhaps it is not too much to point out that the conception of orthodoxy attributed to Jude from ancient times is also involved in these conflicts. It embodies a conception of the church as a community that already knows all it needs to know and has little left to do but fend off heresies. Both anxiety about sexuality and a certain conception of Christian doctrine as having been delivered once and for all in a completely clear and intact package, are important features of current debates within the churches. And both have some of their roots in our reading or misreading of the Letter of Jude.

At this point I do not propose to analyze these elements further. But it is worth pointing out that the strong element of either/or thinking that has become apparent among us conflicts with the abundant evidence of history that our understanding of Christian faith can and does change over time. The rigidity that ignores this is problematic for many reasons, not least that the person or community claiming to know everything in advance cannot engage in conversation in any meaningful sense. The reading of Scripture is then merely an exercise in confirming existing prejudices, and the potential of entering into conversation with God through Scripture is essentially negated. Conversation, by definition, depends on a willingness to listen as well as to speak, and it forbids the mere co-opting, or other suppression, of the voice of the partner in conversation. Only the person who is prepared to be surprised can actually enter into conversation.

Many Christians, regardless of their stance on the contemporary conflicts, assume that Jude is not open to conversation. He is seen as a champion of the Cultural Right and an opponent of any possible rethinking of Christian sexual ethics. This is possible, of course. At the same time, there is nothing to suggest that he has precisely our modern issues in mind or that he ever expected to address them. In that case, he deserves a chance to hear from us as well as to speak to us. To categorize him in advance as an absolutist is questionable not only in terms of the translational issues I have raised above, but also because it threatens to flatten out the complexity of his own life, faith, and context. In the hope of conversation, we need at least to posit the possibility of a Jude who is more complex and less of a caricature than the Jude we have been used to, the Jude who is simply against sex and for an unchanging tradition. It is partly my scholarly fascination with this little book that keeps me reading it. It is also partly an awareness of the questions thus posed by our contemporary conflicts that makes me continue asking whether Jude can enter into real conversation with us.

Notes

1. The past fifteen years, however, have been more fruitful for research in Jude, with several significant commentaries and monographs. I note particularly the following: D. F. Watson, *Invention, Arrangement, and Style: Rhetorical Criticism of Jude and 2 Peter* (Atlanta: Scholars Press, 1988); J. Daryl Charles, *Literary Strategy in the Epistle of Jude* (Scranton: University of Scranton Press, 1993); Jerome H. Neyrey, *2 Peter, Jude* (AB, 37C; New York: Doubleday, 1993); Anton Vögtle, *Der Judasbrief/Der 2. Petrusbrief* (Evangelisch-Katholischer Kommentar zum Neuen Testament, 22; Solothurn: Benziger Verlag; Neukirchen-Vluyn: Neukirchener Verlag, 1994); and Ruth Anne Reese, *Writing Jude: The Reader, the Text, and the Author in Constructs of Power and Desire* (Leiden: Brill, 2000).
2. E.g., Richard Bauckham, "Jude, Epistle of," *ABD*; Charles, *Literary Strategy*, 50–53.
3. The idea that the addressees must at least reside in a Gentile context because only Gentiles would behave in such lewd fashion strikes me as an uncritical acceptance of ancient Jewish apologetic; Vögtle, *Judasbrief*, 5.
4. The dative with ἐπαγονίζομαι normally indicates either the opponent against whom one is fighting or "the person or thing upon whom (which) one depends for support in rivalry" (BDAG, s.v. ἐπαγονίζομαι). Despite having acknowledged this, BDAG proceeds to claim that the term, in the context of Jude, "can only mean *for the faith.*" While a reference to Plutarch is offered, the usage remains odd. It is a good rule for the interpreter to be suspicious whenever terms in the NT are given unique or highly unusual meanings. It is often a sign that the tradition is troubled by, or dissatisfied with, the more usual or literal meaning.
5. Cf. Charles, *Literary Strategy*, 168.
6. "It is unlikely that at any time in Western history have gay people been the victims of more widespread and vehement intolerance than during the first half of the twentieth century"; John Boswell, *Christianity, Social Tolerance, and Homosexuality: Gay People in Western Europe from the Beginning of the Christian Era* (Chicago: University of Chicago Press, 1980), 23.
7. "Many have interpreted [the phrase] as meaning 'indulged in sodomy.' The Greek, however, does not tolerate this." J. N. D. Kelly, *A Commentary on the Epistles of Peter and of Jude* (New York: Harper & Row, 1969), 258.
8. C. E. B. Cranfield, *I and II Peter and Jude: Introduction and Commentary* (London:

SCM Press, 1960), 159–60; G. H. Boobyer, "Jude," sect. 912c in *Peake's Commentary on the Bible,* ed. Matthew Black and H. H. Rowley (London: Thomas Nelson, 1962), 1042; and Victor Paul Furnish, *The Moral Teaching of Paul* (Nashville: Abingdon, 1979), 56. Interpretations of the verse as referring to same-gender sexual intercourse take the statement that the people of Sodom sinned "in a way similar to" the angels loosely, for example as referring to a common "degradation of nature." See E. H. Plumptre, *The General Epistles of St Peter and St Jude* (Cambridge: Cambridge University Press, 1879), 205. This is possible, but such an interpretation still runs aground on its inability to give any normal meaning to the word ἑτέρας (7). Richard Kugelman understands Jude's imagery for Sodom and Gomorrah, like that of Genesis 6, as heterosexual, pointing out that the city names are treated as feminine nouns here; *James and Jude* (New Testament Message; Wilmington, Del.: Michael Glazier, 1980), 91.

 9. See note 4, above.
10. Mark D. Jordan, *The Invention of Sodomy in Christian Theology* (Chicago: University of Chicago Press, 1997), 29–44.

Part 2

Honoring

Complexity

3. Moving toward Synthesis

Attentive and Critical Reading

If we translate the conversational model of interpretation laid out in chapter 1 into practical terms of method, what will it look like? At base, it is simply a prescription for attentive reading. All the skills of philology, history, rhetoric, and theology developed over centuries past continue to be useful to us in this process; some more recent additions to the tool kit will also prove helpful. The goal is to read critically—in the sense of taking as little as possible for granted and of clarifying our conclusions in a way that makes it possible for others to confirm or question them. I do not hope to throw out existing methods of biblical studies or to replace them with a new one, but rather to refocus them in a way that will be more conducive to an ongoing interpretive conversation that once again includes the communities for whom we interpret.

For this purpose, we need to find more synthetic approaches to the material, approaches that can enable us to bring texts into the conversation as larger wholes and also acknowledge the still larger complexities of life and thought that their words convey. I emphasize the use of larger wholes because fragments of texts are particularly vulnerable to victimization by the more powerful voices of the present. This is an experience so common we have a term for it—"proof-texting." The isolated verse can be *made* to mean almost anything. The voice of the text is stronger and less easily distorted when it is long enough and complex enough not to be easily reduced to a single idea. By the same token, we strengthen the voice of the text if we can also achieve and maintain some awareness of the intellectual, spiritual, and social complexity of the world in which it originated. The text carries along much of that complexity, which serves to underline the text's distance from our own world.

The idea of a method that is both critical and synthetic perhaps is not familiar. We have tended to feel that only analytical methods are critical.[1] As I suggested in the preceding section, this is at least partly the result of our borrowing the model of physics, which deals with a more limited number of influences interacting in more predictable ways than any study of human realities. Human realities gain meaning precisely in their complex interactions with one another. The isolated date, the one word added or subtracted by a redactor, the abstract form of first-century Mediterranean miracle stories—none of these has any particular meaning in itself. Each acquires meaning only as it becomes part of a more complex web of human interactions. One implication of this complexity is that all interpretation will be somewhat tentative. To say that our method is "critical" does not mean that it will produce universally agreed conclusions any more than previous "critical" methods succeeded in doing so. Interpretation will be as diverse as the people who perform it and the environments in which they work. Still, conclusions are critical when they appear in a form that allows others to say, with some clarity, "Yes, I see how one can derive that from the text," or "No, I can't see that in the text at all," or "I can see this much in the text, but not all of what you are claiming to see"—and, in each case, to express their reasons. In other words, the idea of critical interpretation is a gesture of confidence in the human ability to converse and a commitment to the possibility of wide circles of discourse among those who share an interest in a common topic.

The idea of critical interpretation also implies that the variety of interpretations is not infinite. Interpretations can be compared and evaluated and, at times, found wanting. The readers are many and varied; but the texts, in the case of the NT, are few. The ability of a text to blossom interpretively in many contexts is one measure of its depth and power; and there is no reason to fear the resulting diversity of interpretation. A single text can mean many things, some of which will strike any one of us, given our finitude, as astonishing and unexpected. Still, the finiteness of the text imposes limits. A single text cannot mean anything and everything without meaning nothing. In the give-and-take of the interpretive task, there are some readings that will prove, given closer examination and broad discussion, to be little more than wishful thinking or the imposition of the prejudices of the interpreter or the community.

Some academics, to be sure, do seem prepared to deny the finitude of meaning. The banner of postmodernism is sometimes flaunted as a way of fending off all criticism: "Since many readings are allowed, you cannot criticize mine." To be sure, this is typically a plea of students or of scholars unsure of their craft—reminiscent of the semiliterate medieval English priest who, when reproved by his bishop for his misreading of the Latin Mass, protested, "My *mumpsimus* is as good as your *sumpsimus* [we have received]." Still, more advanced theoreticians are not without fault in the matter: they often seem to take the interpreter's basic willingness and ability to read carefully—to distinguish *mumpsimus* from *sumpsimus*—for granted, and they neglect to insist on it as a prerequisite for their more theoretical arguments about the wide variability of interpretation. In actual practice, the basic willingness and ability to read a text carefully is often nine-tenths of the task in interpreting ancient documents.

Without acknowledging that some readings are better than others, there is no way to explain the common experience of "coming to understand" a text, especially insofar as it includes the recognition that one had previously understood it only in part or even out-and-out misunderstood it. A reading that does not respect the text, that violates its letters and grammar and syntax, that violently excises a few words from their context or wrenches them into some other world, may qualify as a creative reuse of the text, but not as an interpretation of it in the sense in which we are using the term here. Creative reuse is not intrinsically bad. But it deserves to be judged on a different set of criteria, on the basis of the creative power embodied in it, and not as interpretation. The question for such works is not "Does this new text help me return to and understand the Book of Job?" but "Is this new text, building on Job, powerful and revelatory in its own right?"

Interpretation, in the sense of the term used here, must be able to respond clearly to the question "Where did you find that in the text and its world?" For the professional, academic exegete, this means the ancient text in its original language. Knowing Greek or Hebrew or Aramaic and learning the cultural contexts of the ancient texts—these are fundamental preparations for the interpreter. But they are not enough. Interpreters must also learn to read the text attentively enough to allow it to defeat our expectations. In this regard, attentive reading is by no means the private preserve of those with tertiary (highest) degrees. Any one who has taught introductory courses in biblical studies for long has probably had the experience of a student, with little preparation in the subject, pointing out something in the text that we had never noticed ourselves. Yet once it is pointed out, it seems perfectly clear and even obvious. While the specialized knowledge of the academic interpreter is valuable, it offers no guarantee that the specialist will read carefully—or that nonspecialists will not.

Above all, the attentive reader is looking for the places where the texts upset the expectations we have brought to them. The supreme challenge in reading is not learning ancient languages, important as they are, but cultivating the honesty, integrity, and equanimity to accept surprise. The ability to accept that the text is not saying what one wants it to is as difficult for the academic as for any other reader. Given the spiritual disposition to accept surprise, the gifts we bring to the reading—gifts rooted in the particularities of culture and experience and the quirkiness of the individual mind—are not simply dependent on one's education. (Indeed, there is always a danger that education may flatten out the alertness and distinctiveness of the student's mind.)

However difficult the interpretive effort may be, for specialist and nonspecialist alike, it remains worthwhile for the simple reason that nothing less can help us free the voice of the text. If we claim the right to make the text mean anything we want, that deprives us of the chance to hear a voice other than our own. That, in turn, is a prescription for a world that will be not only boring but also increasingly futile. It is a world where we cannot know even ourselves, for the knowledge of self and the other are correlative and mutually dependent.

Reading that is genuinely critical and attentive therefore calls us to know the other side of the interpretive conversation, too: ourselves, our world, and the manifold things that we bring to the task of interpretation, whether in the form of cultural baggage or as part of the interpreter's personal particularity.[2] While our education in disciplines focused on our own time and place may offer helpful insights here, our world is too complex to be reduced to the one or two strands that education typically emphasizes. We shall have to acquire a broader knowledge—an embodied and not merely intellectual one. That means that the interpreter has a need to be genuinely engaged not only with the text but with the larger world in which one lives. Learning the world around us and the communities for and with which we interpret, is the work of a lifetime. It is gained largely outside the boundaries of the academy, even though we take with us the helpful habits of critical thought learned there. One will learn as much of what is crucial to the interpretive task from the newspapers, the arts, the daily business of living, and involvement in our human communities as from anywhere else. The capable interpreter needs to combine academic expertise with human experience.

It is equally important to examine and to foster the growth of one's own soul and spirit. The scholar is no more a blank slate, a mere photographic film recording the text, than anyone else. Who we are as human beings and as people of whatever faith we profess, secular or religious, is critically important. There is a spirituality of reading and study, even though biblical scholars are not accustomed to calling it by that name—a spirituality that calls for the questioning of ourselves and our world as well as for our careful reading of the text.[3] It requires a willingness to be surprised when necessary. It assumes that we ourselves are capable of growth, of learning, of change. Such a spirituality is not learned solely in the study. Nor can it be defined fully in the abstract. It is acquired, assimilated, and created with the help of others in the context of everyday life. Without this spirituality, our scholarship is without an anchor, without any reality of its own. It is apt to become merely the hired servant—prostitute, attorney, archivist, antiquarian, whatever—of the groups to which we answer. That might be a minor failing in a community utterly insulated against change, a community that did not really need the voice of Scripture to help it engage with changing reality. But it is unclear that such a community has ever existed or can exist, even for the length of a generation.

Sometimes we have spoken as if a critical method must be detached and purely objective. Detachment is indeed a part of what I am advocating—in the specific sense of the willingness to be surprised, even unpleasantly surprised! But neither detachment nor objectivity is an unalloyed virtue. The instructor who teaches Shakespeare or Euripides with the flattened affect of the detached and objective observer has failed to communicate or even come to grips with either playwright. Critical method is not about exiling our humanity or our faith from our study. It is about being both passionate and self-critical. Above all, it is about maintaining conversation with other students. It is about expressing our conclusions clearly enough that others can see how they are related to the text. It is about encouraging a conversation not only of passions or preconceptions, but also of reasons as well.

Critical Method and the Analytical

Modernism and postmodernism (at least as it is usually practiced in the academy) are not altogether unlike each other. The corporate culture of the academy makes use of both to serve its attachment to the analytical and the reductive. Postmodernism is prepared in principle to accept a multiplicity of meanings, but still largely fails to see that meaning, in concrete human terms, is always more complex than any one theory or method. Historically, "critical method" has often meant no more than an agreement on the part of a certain academic community to confine its interests to a narrow aspect of its subject matter and its conversation to a narrow circle of scholars. Postmodernism may claim to allow more space for subjectivity than its predecessor; but many avowedly postmodernist scholars, in my own experience, have no more sense of human complexity than their modernist predecessors. Where the modernist might assume that a text had been fully explained by creating a history of its redaction, so that every apparent inconsistency was historicized into embodying a separate stage of development, the postmodernist may assume rather that everything is explained by identifying whose power is upheld in different aspects of the text and who is marginalized. Either type of investigation may in fact prove useful and informative. Neither can ever capture the full complexity and richness of the text.

It is common to distinguish modernist biblical scholarship from postmodernist by saying that the former assumed a single "original meaning," while the latter assumes the possibility of multiple meanings. Yet this newfound multiplicity is essentially without effect within the academy because various varieties of postmodernism have often segregated themselves into separate worlds of discourse and do not communicate actively with one another, much less with those they see as theoretically insufficient. In both modernism and postmodernism, the most interesting aspects of the texts are often precisely those no one is attending to. Yet such aspects of the texts are certainly of interest to the communities of faith: what does human life mean in this world, in relationship to God and to one another and to the rest of the created order? Where is the biblical scholarship that is reading the texts for that? In one sense, there can be no academic method for this purpose because the question is too broad for scholarly study alone. In another sense, however, it is *the* vital question, and scholarship must find ways to be open to it and not close itself off from it with protective walls of theory and method.

What I am seeking here is a form of critical and scholarly discourse in which those elements of human speech that do not lend themselves to the analytical language of scholarship do not merely disappear: poetry, spirituality, the compromises and insufficiencies of ordinary human existence, the emotional and approximative elements of rhetoric, the questions of human meaning. Scholarly language excels at expressing simplicity, not complexity. As a result, it is still lured by reductionism. This is the same tendency criticized by Amos N. Wilder in his 1955 presidential address to the Society of Biblical Literature, from which one of the epigraphs of this book is taken. Speaking of the "attempts in contemporary NT theology" by Rudolf Bultmann, C. H. Dodd, and Oscar Cullmann, he offered the following critique:

> The biblical theologians appear too often to impoverish the vital symbols so as to obscure their concrete diversity. This makes it possible, then, to discover a dominant theme to which these diversities may all be said to witness. We can recognize the value of generalization and of schematic simplification, and we can acknowledge how much we owe to such scholars as those named. But we believe that one or another misunderstanding of imaginative symbol has handicapped their contributions.[4]

Perhaps one could sum up the point less politely by saying that scholars too often seem to have a tin ear for the complexities of texts.

How else, for example, can one explain the long-standing debate over *the* purpose of Paul's writing of Romans or the equally long-standing preference for thinking of the letter as Paul's conclusive theological summary? Lurking behind these discussions lay the assumption that Paul was himself a kind of academic theologian who would write with the single-minded purpose of explicating his systematics and from whom a final grand statement, in summary of his career, might be expected. Otherwise, why assume that the writing of such a letter had a single purpose? And why assume that that purpose was primarily intellectual? In the process, interpreters wound up dismissing much of the letter from active consideration, since only chapters 1–8 (or, more generously, 1–11) could be read in terms of such a purpose.

A root difficulty here is that analytical methods tend to give reductive answers to complex questions and can seldom accommodate the manifold complexities of human experience. This does not mean that analytical methods are useless. They may reveal significant strands of what goes to make up the larger fabric of a text, a life, a culture. But they cannot reveal the larger meaning of those strands. And if they pursue them in isolation, they become unhelpful if not outright misleading. The work of Bruce Malina and Jerome Neyrey, for example, has been quite helpful in bringing some social and cultural strands in the world of early Christianity into better focus and livelier play for contemporary scholarship. The limits of the approach, however, become apparent in their book on Paul, which winds up giving us a picture of the apostle as a homogeneous product of a homogeneous cultural setting. As a result, it bypasses all the complexity that we know from Paul's letters and has no real explanation as to why Paul should have proved to be the creative and controversial figure that he was. Only at the end, in their gesture toward the category of "prophet," do they suggest a possible way of seeing Paul in tension with his environment as well; and they do not really explore it.[5] A more appropriate assortment of methods, including synthetic as well as analytic elements, might well have produced a richer, more fruitful study.

The study of the Gospel of John is equally rich in examples. Rudolf Bultmann's monumental commentary divided up the Gospel into short units, which he assigned to a variety of strata. He detected these by observing points at which he found a lack of rational continuity and explained them in terms of a history of gnosticism in the Johannine community—a theory that has not, in the long run, proved persuasive. What he did not do was explain how the text came to be fragmented into so many relatively small units in the first place or how such fragments then composed what could be (and was for centuries) read as a single, relatively coherent composition. As a result, Bultmann appears simply to have applied a fairly narrow conception of logical rationality in order to mine the text for history and theology without ever dealing seriously with it as written document, a work of rhetoric.[6]

Similarly, in a widely read work on the history of the Johannine community, Raymond E. Brown presented the Gospel and 1 John as made up of sedimentary deposits laid down in successive stages of that history. John 1, for example, reported "The Originating Group and a Lower Christology." John 2–3 recorded "The Admission of a Second Group and a Higher Christology," and John 4 gives us "The Gentiles and a More Universalist Church." This is the effective structure of his whole work, though it becomes explicit only in the latter part of it, when he dealt with 1 John. Again, there was no effort to imagine how such a process of literary creation could have occurred. A rational analysis was translated into a historical account without reference to the literary questions it implied.[7]

Since both Bultmann and Brown were brilliant and observant scholars, the value of these two books is not entirely vitiated by the analytical approaches they used. And yet, in each case, what they overlooked poses major questions for the value of their analyses. A rational analysis that ignores the rhetorical complexity of the text being mined in this way cannot be convincing in the long run; rather than making the text accessible to conversation with the complexities of the reader, it actually reduces its potential value.

In the postmodern era, the recovery of concern for the literary character of texts has questioned this sort of exclusive analytical focus on history (or social world or theology). But a single-minded focus on literary analysis, detaching the text entirely from its social world, is open to the same objection. Reader-response criticism at times seems to relieve the interpreter almost completely of any need to read the Gospel of John in terms of its own historical, cultural, and religious complexity. The text becomes only a stepping-off point for the reader's personal reflections. Personal reflections may offer a compelling entrée to the text, of course, as in the case of William Temple's meditations on John (though Temple's broad education kept him from ignoring the historical particularity of John). In the case of some more recent work, however, the reader comes away having learned far more of the modern academic reader than of the work read.[8] This, of course, risks a certain disappointment, since the community invested in the text may well find the modern academic psyche less interesting than Scriptures themselves.

If modern biblical criticism was wrong in its uncritical embrace of the analytical, however, it was right in its recognition that the world of the biblical texts was not our world. Reading ancient texts with a mind and heart as engaged as possible with the distinctive realities of the times and places in which they were written, will continue to be a desideratum for us. This is true precisely because such a reading honors *their* difference in the same way that we wish to have our own uniqueness respected. Indeed, there is little possibility of having a sustained and fruitful conversation with these texts, in our time, unless we accord them this sort of respect. It is a basic condition of sustained and fruitful conversation under any circumstances. Postmodern criticism also respects this difference in theory, but some of its expressions are in danger of a kind of solipsism, in which nothing but the reader exists and the text is simply fair game for whatever operations one chooses to unleash on it. What both modernism and postmodernism need is to cultivate a respect for the text as a distinct voice, at least as complex as that of the modern reader—and likely more so.

Such respect for the text is important not only in order to free its voice, but in order even to *have* such a thing as biblical studies. A shared respect for what we are reading is probably the only thing most interpreters of the Bible have in common. The respect does not necessarily take the same form; it ranges from the devotion of the most fervent believer to the skeptical acknowledgment of a thoroughly secular scholar who studies the Bible only because its importance in Western culture seems to make such study necessary. But both extremes have, at least in principle, the desire to read what is on the page. The increasing fragmentation of the academic world, especially in the humanities and social sciences, affects scriptural studies as well. Such a situation is particularly true among those who have committed themselves to what one might call "high-theory" approaches, where the theory is as important as, or more important than, the subjects, texts, or issues to which it is being applied. This raises the question of whether biblical studies as a field even exists now.

What emerges instead often seems much like an experiment in group formation through the creation of high boundaries of language and the defense of those boundaries by mocking outsiders. The phenomenon is common enough to have become a fairly standard topic of satire in novels with academic settings. Even in its more genial manifestations, I question its utility. Ruth Anne Reese's recent monograph on Jude, for example, is unusually readable for such a high-theory work and does not bristle in the way that too often characterizes the genre. But in the end, her reading of Jude, interesting and fresh though it sometimes is, does not justify her investment of time and energy in the discussion of theory. Perhaps that discussion justifies itself for those whose principal interest is the theory itself; but it will not help sustain conversation among those whose primary commitment is to the text—among interpreters, in other words. And such focus on the text becomes increasingly important precisely as the number and diversity of interpreters and methodologies increases.[9]

The naive reductionism of both modern and postmodern academic biblical studies will not be overcome simply by new exercises in the excruciatingly self-conscious and single-minded employment of yet more analytical methods. It can be met only if we learn to look to our texts for something more complex, not for a single original meaning but for an original *range* of meaning—agreed, contested, stretched, transformed; intellectual, emotive, spiritual, practical; individual and collective; expressed in the complexities of the text's rhetoric and rooted in the complexities of the community of origin and even of the specific author. Only a more synthetic approach can honor the diversity of the world in which the texts were produced and the dynamism that characterized it. Biblical authors were not simply handing on familiar, well-worn ideas, but using their culture and traditions to create expressions of faith and ways of living together in response to the challenges of environing circumstances. They may have succeeded less than perfectly; even at best, human language

> Not just many interps, but many voices w/in text.

succeeds less than perfectly in expressing our fleeting discoveries of reality and truth. Authors will have had regard for the difficulty of conveying new thoughts and perspectives to their audiences and integrating these with existing presuppositions. They have had to balance a variety of both intellectual and practical considerations. In other words, the text is a complex human artifact that carries with it much of the cultural and historical complexity in which it originated. Neither side of this complexity can be understood if severed from the other.

The cultural and social environment in which a text was written did not so much determine people's beliefs and responses as it determined a world of discourse: which subjects were deemed important, where conceptual and ideological shoes pinched certain groups and gave advantage to others, what vocabulary was considered essential to discussion of a topic and therefore what would be novel in that context, what assumptions would be broadly recognized and accepted and therefore perhaps also most vulnerable to challenge, reversal, or rejection. Any ancient text will conceivably have meant somewhat different things to different readers, even when they shared a common cultural context. One need only think of our own age, which tells us that abortion, for example, is an issue of significance, but does not tell us what it means—or, rather, tells us too many things for us as a community to achieve a unified perspective. Any pronouncement on abortion will carry a range of meanings intelligible in terms of our particular era, but not reducible to one another nor coordinated with one another. Indeed, there is always the possibility of saying something unpredictable. We should expect the same sort of range and complexity in writings of earlier eras, especially in those of the Hellenistic-Roman age, which was as cosmopolitan as our own.

Toward Synthetic Method

In speaking of our need for synthesis and synthetic method, I do not mean to suggest the creation of a single controlling "metamethod" for biblical studies as a whole or even for an individual text. The synthesis I have in view is not a systematic one: a place for everything and everything in its place. It will not lead the student step-by-step or achieve a single final form. It aims rather at a quality of richness, and it achieves its vitality by its embrace of human complexity. Synthetic methods cannot prescribe in advance what their results will be. They are heuristic, not ideological. More than theoretical, they are historical, in the sense that they respect the particularity of the other. They involve an element of the intuitive, artistic, and creative since they must emerge in the interpreter's encounter with the text rather than being shaped in advance by confidence that we know what we are about to find.

What are the basic characteristics of such a synthetic method? It does not exclude any human factor in advance. It takes the complexity of one's own, more fully known environment as an example of the kinds of complexity that might be present in the text, but not as a prescription to be imposed on the text. It looks for ways to let the text take some lead in the development of our interpretation so that we are not simply imposing our own concerns. It aims at the broadly critical goal of producing interpretive conclusions that are open to reasoned discussion, but without sacrificing the passion that is appropriate to conversation about great human and spiritual issues.

Synthetic method also implies the importance of the notions of reality and of truth, as we have examined them above. It is the irreducible complexity of humanity, after all, that makes such notions indispensable. The impossibility of summing up complex human experience perfectly in the ideals of a single culture or era means that the discovery of reality and of truth is an unending process. Because synthetic method acknowledges this complexity and seeks to grasp and convey some element of it, its conclusions must always remain open around the edges, gesturing, at least, toward a still greater complexity into which each individual interpretation is interwoven.

Range of Meaning

All this implies a need to look at meaning in ancient texts in terms not simply of a single meaning intended by an author or heard by an audience, but in terms of a common range or complex of preconceptions, concerns, and possible stances that held author and audience together in conversation—not necessarily in agreement—and which is brought into play by a particular discourse in a particular situation. What is more, this range of meaning is embodied in a text that is itself complex and not simply transparent to the purpose that first animated it. The text is not simply ideas—much less the academic ideal of ideas in logical sequence. It is also relationship, emotional appeal, a whole array of different uses of language, sound, rhythm, tradition, innovation. In an ancient letter, for example, this range of elements might emerge in a number of ways, such as these:

- reference to an assumed (but perhaps not explicit) issue of concern
- reference to presuppositions that the author proposes as shared by the audience
- a rhetoric by which the author seeks to change minds, build agreement, or impose a conclusion
- implied (sometimes expressed) alternative perspectives
- a history and prospect of relationship between author and audience
- a set of tensions between author and audience
- a group of ideas
- a play of words, rhythms, emotions

These involve both rhetoric (the organization and tone of the document) and the social world environing the document. We can separate the two spheres notionally; but we cannot understand either without its relationship with the other.[10]

Attention to an original *range* of meaning implies that we are interested in ancient conversations of all sorts, from the most irenic to the most hostile. And it is not simply the conclusion of the conversation that interests us, but its beginning points, the presuppositions implied, the disagreements expressed or hinted at, the compromises invoked to maintain the community. The interpreter's job is to find ways into those conversations, ways to hear them as distinctively embodying some of the complexity of their place and time. This immersion can help the interpreter give the ancient text a voice in the interpretive conversations of our own age. These conversations will not be brought to an end by identifying the text's original range of meaning. That is rather the starting point for what is actually the more engaging and potentially the more significant aspect of the interpretive process, the triangular conversation in which we hope to assist both readers and text. In this conversation the particularities of both the text and its modern interlocutors become more apparent, and the search for faithful human meaning begins to encompass both. Such a search must honor both difference and continuity. Above all, it acknowledges the hope for human community that makes such conversation possible across so great a distance. A kind of interpretation that respects human diversity here truly enters into its own, as it embraces both difference and continuity not only in the contemporary world but also in the larger human and (in the specific case of the NT) Christian community over the ages.

Complexity of the Environment

The dynamism and complexity of the text, of course, do not exist in isolation, but have always been deeply implicated in the complexity and dynamism of the world in which the text emerged. Every aspect of that world is potentially of interest: its ideas, its emotions, the presuppositions it encouraged, the tensions that mark where those presuppositions might have come to seem inadequate or oppressive to some, its basic social organization, its struggles for authority and power, its capacity for change, the play of individual against group (weighted more heavily, in antiquity, on the side of the group than in the modern West), the play of innovation against continuity, and so forth. All this is mediated to us primarily through the scriptural text itself. We seldom have independent testimony from archaeology or other ancient texts about the precise social locale of any NT document, though we do a little better in the case of the Scriptures of Israel. In a larger sense, however, we can expect to use other documents and artifacts as points of reference to expand our sense of the social and cultural context.

Naturally, reconstruction of a large, complex social, intellectual, spiritual, and relational framework is fraught with difficulty and will always be partial and fallible. But the alternative of trying to ignore or escape it is no more secure. Indeed, one can more or less guarantee that purely analytical approaches, focusing on one issue and one issue only, will be in error for the simple reason that nothing in human life and culture has anything like its full meaning as an isolated process or object. To explain to a first-century person why you stopped at the ATM to withdraw cash or why and how that process works in our culture would take you in a great variety of directions. To name but a few, you might need to explain why, in our society, banks think it is too expensive to have an actual human being help you in this matter; why caution is advisable, since there may be people waiting nearby in the hope of a handout or an opportunity to rob the unwary; why we routinely keep money in banks (with some asides on the insurance of accounts and changed attitudes toward interest); how electronic messages work to give access; why one may still need cash in an electronic age; what your personal purposes were in withdrawing money at this particular moment; why these purposes seemed important enough to you for you to turn aside from your other tasks. Some of these would be easy to explain, some would not. Explaining any one of them in isolation would not tell your interlocutor much.

Since every aspect of human thought and behavior is part of a larger web, we are most likely to discover grounds of conversation with ancient texts by looking at them in terms of their larger interconnections. This was already apparent in the work of ancient biblical interpreters, even though they operated under rules and preconceptions quite different from ours. I think, for example, of Gregory the Great's *Moralia*. This huge commentary on the Book of Job does two tasks. The first, which Gregory specifically states that he will do only in summary, is allegorical; that is, in the terms of his time, he will relate the text to Christ and the church. The second task, more important in his eyes, was to treat Job as a way of thinking about the complex issues of faithful living, particularly as they affected his audience of Italian monks living in Constantinople. This latter aspect of the work, a dialogue between the complexities of the text and the complexities of life in Gregory's own time, remains brilliantly impressive today. The allegorical aspect, which consists of little more than an analytical list of items with their allegorical equivalents, impresses us as tedious or absurd. Does one need to know, for example, that the camel is an allegory of the church of the Gentiles because it meets half, but only half, of the definition of a clean animal? Analysis eventually kills the subject it is interested in.

If we are indeed to understand the Scriptures, it is not enough for us to take them apart and organize the resulting data in lists of allegorical, sociological, psychological, or theological equivalencies. At this point, we have not yet entered into real conversation with the text. What we want to see in a scriptural text is movement and relationship: Job debating his "comforters," Jacob wrestling with God, Moses breaking the tablets of the law in his fury over the golden calf, David coming to the realization of his wrongdoing, Jeremiah protesting his prophetic calling, Jesus teaching and healing and submitting to crucifixion rather than betraying his gospel, Peter defending the conversion of Cornelius and his household, Paul laying out the universalist impulse that forms the integral counterpart of the particularism in the religion of Israel—and the full array of responses to these dynamics, whether explicit in the text or implicit. Without relationship and movement, there is no meaning.

Rhetoric and Life

As we have noted above, all this social and cultural complexity is mediated to us, in an ancient text, primarily through the text itself. This means that, as interpreters endeavoring to foster conversation, we do much of our work by trying to read between the lines of the text. This is never a foolproof operation, though it is one with a venerable pedigree and an openness to critical testing. Before one can read *between* the lines, however, one must first read the lines themselves with care, attention, and respect. They are never presenting mere information, mere content. They present everything they have to say in ways designed to encourage and make possible certain responses. The comprehensive term for this quality—and it is the norm, not the exception—is "rhetoric."

Simply to point out the ideas of a text about a certain topic is never enough. We also attend to how it positions itself in relation to the topic, how the author seeks to relate to the audience, where the argument seems to assume agreement, where it seems to be working at the construction of such agreement, what emotions are communicated, whether explicitly or through the less articulate modes of rhythm and sound. Much of our rhetorical work, whether as authors framing it or as audiences deciphering it, is done intuitively. Part of the challenge, then, in the model of interpretation I am proposing, is that we learn to read with the whole self. We learn to notice our feelings as well as our thoughts, to perceive the cues that may be evoking them, and in the process, also to learn how to be alert to where the feelings and thoughts of others might differ. As we become more aware of how the rhetoric of a text operates on us, we shall become more aware of its complexity, its power, and its limitations.

To practice a synthetic kind of interpretation, then, means to proceed on two related but distinct levels, rhetorical and contextual. We are seeking a relatively complex image of the context in which the text originally had meaning and, in seeking this, we must also seek an awareness of the complex ways in which the rhetoric of a text reveals itself. The text will never simply give us a straightforward, analytical account of the issues it is addressing. (Indeed, one might question to what degree such an account of human realities is ever possible.) Every text is a rhetorical construct, grappling with meaning in its particular context. When we begin to see this and read in this way, we also discover an increased capacity to enter into conversation with the text because we are conversing, in our own rhetorical turn, with our own issues of meaning in our own time.

The great challenge of approaching the interpretive conversation in terms of synthesis is precisely the question of how we can come to grips with the complexity of our texts. The biblical texts will reveal themselves as more equal and provocative partners in conversation when we see them as complex productions of rhetoric rooted in nothing less than the complex social and personal life of their author's and audience's time and place. While this is a daunting prospect for any student of Scripture, it is also the one most worth pursuing. It calls for a widening of our horizons, an inclu-siveness of vision, a transcending of disciplinary and ideological bound-aries. It looks toward the possibility that the conversation between ancient texts and modern communities may yet be full of surprise and discovery.

[handwritten: Ultimate goal.]

Notes

1. "The modern academic mind lives by analysis, is suspicious of synthesis if ever it pauses to notice it, and in this case [critical biblical scholarship] has left it long since behind"; Wilfred Cantwell Smith, *What Is Scripture?* 14. I find Daniel Patte's obser-vation that "critical exegesis" is simply ordinary, interested reading argued, to be clearly helpful, since it removes the assumption that critical exegesis *begins* as a mode of analysis; *Ethics of Biblical Interpretation: A Reevaluation* (Louisville: Westminster John Knox, 1995), 10–11, 27–29, 64–65.
2. Mary Ann Tolbert rightly calls attention to the danger that this kind of emphasis on attentive reading, itself a learned practice, may wind up excluding the voices of those who have been denied this sort of education—and may close off possibilities of inter-pretation for those who have been too thoroughly acculturated by it: "Reading for Liberation," in Fernando F. Segovia and Mary Ann Tolbert, eds., *Reading from This Place* (Minneapolis: Fortress, 1995), 1:275. This is precisely why I argue that the practice of attentive reading has to be combined with the cultivation of a certain spir-itual, cultural, and personal self-awareness, so that we remain aware of our finitude and open to the insights of others.
3. Schuyler Brown calls this "The Empirics of Interpretation." While acknowledging its subjective, emotional, and creative element, he rightly defends it against the charge of arbitrariness: "*All* interpretation is subjective, since its point of departure is the interpreter." Still, "it is governed by the laws both of language and of the psyche"; *Text and Psyche: Experiencing Scripture Today* (New York: Continuum, 1998), 30–57; quotations from 57.
4. Amos N. Wilder, "Scholars, Theologians, and Ancient Rhetoric," *JBL* 75 (1956): 6.
5. Bruce Malina and Jerome H. Neyrey, *Portraits of Paul: An Archaeology of Ancient Personality* (Louisville: Westminster John Knox, 1996).
6. Rudolf Bultmann, *The Gospel of John: A Commentary,* trans. G. R. Beasley-Murray, R. W. N. Hoare, and J. K. Riches (Philadelphia: Westminster, 1971).
7. Raymond E. Brown, *The Community of the Beloved Disciple* (New York: Paulist, 1979).
8. I have in mind Jeffrey L. Staley, *Reading with a Passion: Rhetoric, Autobiography and the American West in the Gospel of John* (New York: Continuum, 1995); and William Temple, *Readings in St. John's Gospel (First and Second Series)* (London: Macmillan, 1955).
9. Ruth Anne Reese. *Writing Jude: The Reader, the Text, and the Author in Constructs of Power and Desire* (Leiden: Brill, 2000).
10. Daniel Patte offers a good example of the way in which "modern" analytic methods tend to flatten the complexity of a text and the tensions within it, and of how a mul-tiplicity of approaches can help correct this; *Ethics of Biblical Interpretation,* 37–49.

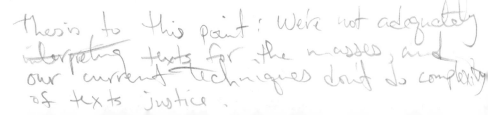

[handwritten: Thesis to this point: We're not adequately interpreting texts for the masses, and our current techniques don't do complexity of texts justice.]

4. Introducing Complexity
Further Exploration of Jude

If the interpreter's first task is to understand and re-present the words of the text as faithfully as possible, this leads on to the further work of discovering and displaying the complexities that the text carries with it. In practice, these two elements are, of course, not merely sequential. As one digs deeper into the complexities of the text, one's sense of the basic meaning of the words may well be affected. And any new insight into basic meaning may suggest different avenues for exploring the complexities—complexities both of rhetoric and of environment. Neither sort of complexity can be pursued adequately in isolation from the other. From the start, we encounter them as an intuitive whole embodied in the language of the text. While elements of intellectual analysis (grammatical, rhetorical, social, political, theological) will probably have entered into the creation of the text, they have merely been elements in a creative process that is larger and more complex than logical, analytical thinking alone could make it. What is more, the text does not particularly tend to reveal all these complexities to us. They remain largely implicit—to be teased out by attentive reading. They are not, for the most part, the "message" of the text; and yet they are what gives the message power, depth, and significance.

Reading Rhetorical Complexity

We will now move through the text of Jude, looking for indications both of a rhetorical structure that reveals movement in the text and of a social context that would give the rhetoric meaning and purpose. From the beginning of the letter, we want to see how Jude explicitly relates himself to his audience—and to what purpose:

> Jude, slave of Jesus Christ and brother of James, to those beloved in God the Father and called [and] preserved by Jesus Christ: mercy and peace and love be brought to the full for you. (1–2)

This salutation uses liturgical language—something that will reappear in the letter's closing doxology—and thereby suggests the Christian Eucharistic assembly as its environment. It lifts up the centrality of God and Jesus, the intimacy of the addressees' relationship to them, and the beneficent nature of the resulting gifts. Jude claims a relationship to the addressees by speaking of them as "beloved" and also claims an authoritative association with Jesus by denoting himself as his slave. This is a claim to exalted status as Jesus' agent as well as a declaration of personal humility.[1] He also calls himself "brother of James." This could refer to any James known to the addressees, but it may also be a subtle way for the author to identify himself as a "brother of the Lord," another claim to intimacy with Jesus.

The author now gives the first overt hint of the reason for his writing and moves quickly to attack his opponents:

> Beloved, exercising all speed to write to you about our common salvation, I've had a necessity to write you, urging you to continue struggling with the support of the faith handed on once to the holy ones. For certain people have sneaked in, people who were long ago recorded in advance for this judgment, impious people, turning our God's grace into license and denying our only master and Lord Jesus Christ. (3–4)

The problem, from Jude's perspective, is interlopers. Who are they? They are traveling Christian teachers whose message and pedigree Jude questions, much as others sometimes questioned those of Paul.[2] Since they are itinerants, he can describe them pejoratively by saying that they have "sneaked in." He also claims that they are already written down in God's book for judgment and that they are impious. These are rather general insults and do not tell us anything precisely about what they taught; but the next two insults are of a more substantive nature. At this point, we cannot say in what sense the new teachers could be seen as "turning our God's grace into license and denying our only master and Lord Jesus Christ."[3]

We are still, of course, in the realm of insults; but likely, in order to be effective, the insults had to make some connection with the addressees' perception of the teachers. We should watch for further indications of behavior that could be described as licentious and of a theology or spirituality that compromises the centrality or authority of Jesus in relating the Christian to God.[4]

Next Jude introduces a series of biblical warnings—examples of divine judgment on the wicked. The appeal to Scripture helps to define a framework within which he wants his addressees to evaluate both his own arguments and the teaching of the newcomers. Perhaps the examples are chosen at random, but they seem rather too well coordinated for that:

> But I want to remind you, though you know all, that the Lord, having once saved the people from the land of Egypt, the next time destroyed those who did not trust. And the angels who did not keep their own rulership but abandoned their proper dwelling, [God] has kept in eternal chains under gloom for the judgment of the great day. So, [too,] Sodom and Gomorrah and the cities around them, having committed harlotry in a way similar to them and having gone out after another flesh, afford a demonstration, enduring a sentence of eternal fire. (5–7)[5]

The general point here is to threaten punishment for those who oppose the will of God. Yet it is a quite particular selection of examples. Why not include God's rejection of King Saul? Or the destruction of Ahab? It is the character of the offenses in question that ties them together. The first offense was to doubt God's goodness. Since we have already seen, in Jude's salutation, a strong emphasis on the intimacy of the faithful community with God and a reminder to them to rely on the faith/trust they have already experienced, we may suspect that we are seeing a further example of that theme, this time in the negative. Trust in God brings us to stand before God with joy; rejection of that trust results in the destruction of those who do not trust.[6]

But how would failure of trust manifest itself among early Christians? Possibly by resort to other divine or quasi-divine powers, whether as replacements for Jesus or as auxiliaries. Indeed, the following two examples move steadily closer to describing just such behavior. The first is the example of the "Watchers," angelic beings mentioned in Genesis 6 and discussed at greater length in 1 Enoch (which Jude regarded as scriptural; cf. 14). These beings had sexual relations with human women and engendered giant offspring. According to *1 Enoch,* they also taught humans such arts as mining and metallurgy, which puts them in the position of quasi-divine benefactors but also disrupters of the earlier created order.[7] The angels were punished for initiating this transgression. The people of Sodom and the surrounding cities sinned "in a way similar to them," by trying, from the human side, to initiate sexual intercourse with angels. In this case, it is the human beings who were punished for attempting to initiate such an act.[8] These examples pick up Jude's reference to "license" in verse 4, but Jude does not seem to see the offenses in question simply as expressions of lust, but rather as an effort to establish connections between humans and angelic beings outside the original order of creation.

If we take Jude's choice of examples seriously, we have a sequence combining departure from trusting God with the practice of intimate relations with angelic beings. It is not immediately clear whether sexual intercourse is literally a part of this relation or a metaphor for it; but it will be a question to keep before us as we read on. For the moment, however, we can say that Jude probably sees the teachers as advocating a religious practice that entails intimate relationship with angelic powers and believes that this threatens the directness and intimacy of the community's relationship with God through Jesus and the Holy Spirit. It therefore constitutes a failure of trust in God. There is nothing inherently improbable about such concerns in early Christianity. We encounter something comparable in the church at Colossae, where the author believes that concern with elemental spirits threatens to crowd out the Christians' primary relationship with God in Christ.[9]

In the following sentences, Jude makes this explicit by comparing the new teachers with the people of Sodom:

> And likewise these people, too, pollute the flesh in their dreams and nullify lordship and blaspheme glories. But the archangel Michael, when he talked in debate with the devil about Moses' body, did not dare level a judgment of blasphemy, but said, "The Lord rebuke you." (8–9)

These sentences suggest two things about the new teachers: first, they do teach something they regard as sexual interaction with angelic beings; second, they feel that this gives them power to interact with the angels as equals or superiors.[10]

Jude's reference to polluting "the flesh in their dreams" suggests that he thinks of their praxis as involving ejaculation and visionary experience. The pollution could, of course, be metaphorical, but of what? It is easier to take it here as a reference to literal pollution, such as male ejaculation causes according to Lev 15:16–18. Jude seems to assume that his audience knows the purity law of the Torah. If, as suggested earlier, the addressees are living in Jewish-Christian communities, they will be practicing the Torah in some form or other as a matter of course; it is simply the normal conception of cleanliness in their community. If one reads the passage literally, then, it appears that the teachers are somehow encouraging dreams in which men have sexual emissions. That these dreams have specifically to do with angelic beings is clear from what follows: They "nullify lordship and blaspheme glories." "Lordship" (κυριότης) is used elsewhere, including the Greek remains of 1 Enoch, to refer to a particular class of angelic beings.[11] "Glories" seems to have a similar significance here, in contrast to the singular "glory" characteristic of God.

Sexual intimacy with angels might be interpreted as implying equality with the celestial beings—or even superiority to them.[12] Jude objects to this abrogation of the hierarchy of the creation. The Watchers' crime was to "leave their rulership." The men of Sodom, where the angels had appeared in male human form, apparently intended to humiliate the visitors by forced anal intercourse. To some extent, Jude may, from these biblical parallels, merely be deducing that the new teachers seek dominion over the angels. With or without any warrant from their own teaching, however, he depicts them as upsetting the hierarchy of creation itself and contrasts the behavior of Michael, who would not even rebuke an equal of his (if we assume that the devil started out as an angelic being) on his own authority.[13]

Jude does not debate the possibility of sexual congress with angelic beings (which he may well have accepted) or the new teachers' claim to have achieved it. Instead, he reverses their claims: they are not possessors of secrets, but blasphemers; they are not like angels, but like animals:

> These people blaspheme all the things they do not know; and all that they do understand—by instinct, like irrational animals—by these things they are being corrupted [or destroyed]. (10)

Jude goes on to place them in a long line of people who propagated religious error and received due punishment:

> Too bad for them! because they have proceeded down the road of Cain and poured themselves out for pay in the error of Balaam and been destroyed by the opposition of Kore. (11)

All these dire examples involve specifically cultic errors. Cain's sacrifice was not accepted, and he responded by killing his brother (Gen 4). Balaam tried to curse Israel for pay.[14] Kore (or Korah) led a rebellion against Moses and Aaron by offering incense, for which he and his comrades were punished with fire and by being swallowed up by the ground (Num 16). The examples all suggest that Jude's objection to the new teachers focused primarily on their ritual observances.[15]

Jude continues with a spate of rousing invective:

> These people are the hidden reefs in your love-feasts, fearlessly feasting with you, shepherding themselves, waterless clouds carried past by wind, fruitless trees of late autumn, twice dead, uprooted, wild waves of the sea foaming with their own shames, wandering stars for whom the gloom of darkness has been kept for ever. (12–13)

One can admire the vivid, even poetic quality of some of these images and their headlong pacing. Perhaps one should not press them too hard for information about the objects of their vehemence. Still, they do evoke themes we find elsewhere in the letter, suggesting that these invectives, too, are rhetorically coordinated with the rest of what Jude has to say.

The term translated "hidden reefs" (σπιλάδες) is etymologically related to the term "soiled" in 24 ("the garment soiled from the flesh"). Since reefs may become visible as discoloration of the water over them or disturbance of wave patterns, the term may in fact have connoted something like "blotches." The term hints, then, at the theme of sexual pollution, made still clearer in the subsequent reference to waves "foaming with their own shames." "Foaming" (ἐπαφρίζοντα) makes the hint quite broad, in fact, since the element —αφρ— that appears in this word is also part of the name of Aphrodite, who was born of semen from the severed genitals of the god Uranus (Οὐρανός) after they were cast into the sea. The parallel between semen and sea foam would be easy, since semen was understood medically as a kind of foam whipped up from the blood.[16]

Jude's images of waterless clouds and fruitless trees suggest to the addressees that association with the new teachers will bring no benefits. The claim that the teachers shepherd themselves tags them again as interlopers with a disregard for proper hierarchies and no real position in the existing Christian community.[17] It thus prepares the audience for the further claim that they are "wandering stars," or "planets." Here the term "wandering" (πλανῆται) carries connotations of "error" (πλάνη, as in "the error of Balaam," 11); but the word's denotation refers specifically to "planets," thus linking the new teachers in an unfavorable way to the celestial beings with whom they claim to be on an intimate footing. In late antiquity, after all, people increasingly conceived of the planetary beings as controlling earthly fates in ways either malign or indifferent toward human beings. Since these "wandering stars" were identified with either the gods of the Greeks or with angelic powers among the Jews, Jude is suggesting that they are doomed to punishment like the angelic powers already condemned for engaging in sexual intercourse with women.[18]

This makes an easy transition for Jude's return to *1 Enoch* to quote a prophecy of judgment:

> And Enoch, seventh from Adam, actually prophesied to these people, saying: See! the Lord came with his holy tens of thousands to do judgment against them all and to test every soul for all the works of their impiety that they committed and for all the hard things they said against him—impious sinners that they are. (14–15, quoting *1 Enoch* 1:9)

In itself, this quotation has little content beyond the threat of judgment. It comes, however, from the opening section of a book deeply interested in the Watchers and their influence on human beings.

After the series of attacks on "these people," Jude then offers two contrasts between the new teachers and his addressees, characterizing the latter positively in terms of their attachment to tradition:

> These people are grumblers, faultfinders, proceeding according to their own desires; and their mouth speaks bombast, as they astound people for the sake of gain. But you, beloved, remember the words that were spoken to you before by the apostles of our Lord Jesus Christ—that they said to you, "In the last stretch of time, there will be mockers, proceeding according to their own impious desires."
>
> These are the dividers, people who belong to the level of mere soul, not having spirit. But you, beloved, building yourselves up on your most holy faith, praying in Holy Spirit, keep yourselves in God's love, expecting the mercy of our Lord Jesus Christ for eternal life. (16–21)

Jude characterizes the new teachers as antisocial individuals, seeking only their own gain—a common enough accusation in early Christianity and one for which Jude has prepared his audience by comparing the teachers to Balaam (11). The accusation was no doubt true at times; both the *Didache* and Lucian of Samosata's *Death of Peregrinus* make it clear that the early Christian communities, with their tradition of traveling teachers, were vulnerable to charlatans. By citing an apostolic prediction, Jude indicates that tradition has already given the readers a category to accommodate this danger, and they should be prepared to deal with it.[19]

By way of contrast, Jude characterizes the new teachers as people without real understanding. He has already compared them to irrational animals (10). Now he consigns them explicitly to the level of soul (ψυχή), the subrational life force that humans share with other living things. In contrast to Jude's addressees, the new teachers do not have "spirit" (πνεῦμα), a necessity for anyone who would teach about God.[20] Jude thus takes their claim of privileged access to celestial realities and turns it on its head. It is not the new teachers, but the ordinary members of the existing community, who have privileged access to God. And they have it not by means of unusual religious practices or through the power of intermediate celestial beings, but by God's own gift of direct access in Jesus, manifest in their enjoyment of the Holy Spirit.[21]

It is not for the new teachers to offer something, then, to Jude's addressees, but for the readers of the letter to consider how to confront the teachers with minimal danger to themselves. The teachers are a problem in the senses that association with them might cause uncertainty on the part of some, that acceptance of their teaching would exchange the direct access to God that the community already enjoys for a questionable connection to beings of lesser status, and that dealing with them may threaten others with unnecessary physical pollution.[22] Hence, Jude's final appeal:

> And on some take pity as they dispute [*or* as they waver *or* as you dispute], and some save, snatching them out of the fire, and on some take pity with fear, hating even the garment soiled from the flesh. (22–23)[23]

This sentence confirms that there is internal disagreement within the community. Jude encourages his addressees to adopt an assertive posture and dissuade those who are attracted by the other side in the dispute. He regards the position of the wandering teachers as gravely compromising the faith that the addressees have known—so much so that, if any can be brought back from their teaching, they will have been saved "from fire." Fire is a common image for punishment in early Christian writing. It stands in sharp contrast, then, to the joy mentioned in the following doxology, which

is characteristic of those allowed to stand in the presence of God's glory.
Jude sees the opponents' teaching as posing a threat even to those who
resist it. He phrases this danger in purity language. The people are to treat
the opponents in a gingerly way, like garments soiled by physical uncleanness, which might render anyone touching them unclean. Of this much we
can be certain: Jude feels that the doctrines in dispute are critical to Christian faith and that they will divide the church if they have not already done
so.[24]

Finally, the closing doxology celebrates the intimacy of the congregation's long-standing relationship with God, soon to be vindicated by their
hoped-for rejection of the new teaching:

> But to the one able to protect you from stumbling and to have you
> stand blameless, with joy, in the presence of his glory, to the only
> God our savior, through Jesus Christ our Lord, [be] glory, majesty,
> might, and authority before every eon and now and to the eons of
> eons. Amen. (24–25)

Jude treats this as a kind of liturgical summary of what the congregation
has heard and enjoyed from the beginning. They have no need for sexual
intercourse with angels or those who teach it. God has already entered into
direct relationship with them through Jesus.

Contextual Complexities Carried by the Letter

There is a range of concern here centered on the issue of confident and
direct access to God. It was a widespread issue in early Christianity, perhaps because, in an imperial age, God must have seemed as remote as the
emperor. Early Christianity reiterated, in a great variety of ways, a sense of
God's having drawn near in the ministry of Jesus. Converts presumably
found a sense of intimacy with God through their identity as Christians.
That would not, however, mean that the question of access to God was
entirely resolved for them, or that they would cease to look for other
means of guaranteeing access to God and the heavenly court. The very fact
that the earliest Christians were converts would mean that they could
imagine hearing yet a newer message that would carry them further along
their path.

Jude's tone is quite polemical; at the same time, he repeatedly emphasizes a kind of simplicity and security that the addressees already enjoy in
the presence of God. Next to his phrase about the "faith once delivered to

the saints," the doxology is probably the best known and most repeated element of the letter. Yet this emphasis seems to pull in the opposite direction from the author's polemical tone. If we look to the rhetoric of the letter alone, we might see a combination of threat and promise: "You already have something good. Don't associate with these people, or you will lose it." On a basic level, this is accurate. Jude writes a letter of warning and uses whatever devices he thinks will deter his audience from moving further in the direction of the new teachers. The question, however, is why he believes that precisely this combination of devices may produce a desirable result. He does not threaten a personal visit, for example.[25] Is that because he does not want to make one? Because he does not think it will have the hoped-for effect—or, alternatively, thinks it unnecessary? Or because it is important to him, for some reason, to leave the matter in local hands?

We can at least consider the latter possibility since he gives specific advice to the local group (probably with its leaders primarily in view at this point) about handling the matter. In verses 22–23, he names several courses of action, which would leave them with some latitude as to how they handle individual cases. Moreover, part of his argument is that they already have the resources they need for this purpose—in the form of the "faith once delivered to the saints" and in the intimacy of their relationship with God in Jesus. What he does, above all, is recall them to their experience of conversion and the sense of right relationship with God that follows upon their experience of faith/trust. A more direct intervention on his part would disconfirm these expressions of confidence.

Still, Jude seems confident of his authority and exercises it without apology. The letter as a whole is cast in terms of "I tell you what to do about *them*."[26] However much Jude appeals to the experience and confidence of his addressees, he does not leave the larger issues of interpretation to their discretion. Should we give more weight to the content of his words in this respect or to their manner? Perhaps they are not entirely in conflict. If we consider the parallel conflicts of Paul with itinerant teachers in churches of his founding, we can see that, in earliest Christianity, issues of belief and praxis were often inseparable from issues of personal authority. Apart from his initial self-description, Jude never works overtly to establish or defend his own authority in the letter. In this, he contrasts not only with Paul but also with the author(s) of 1 and 3 John. Yet his authority is certainly being questioned.

Given that the letter was written at all, we can assume that the congregation addressed was still undecided about some aspect of the situation. If they had fully accepted or rejected the teachers of sex with angels, no letter would have been required—at least, not one in this vein. The leadership of the addressees is presumably still trying to evaluate the situation and determine their course of action. They must decide whether the new praxis is compatible with the faith they have previously professed. If not, they must decide whether the problem is serious or not. If serious, they must decide how to respond to it. The power these decisions represent is significant.[27] Jude's exercise of his authority depends on how the addressees exercise theirs.

Theologically, the matter of sex with angels in Jude is comparable to the interest in angelic powers in Colossians, where the author responds by insisting that Jesus has already triumphed over these beings in the cross (2:15) and that God has reconciled them through Jesus (1:19–20). In a general way, Jude's response is comparable to that of the author to Colossians and also to those of Paul and John, when they are concerned to rule out theological developments that make new or additional demands on the faithful. Jude presents the situation as one in which an existing Christian community has been visited by teachers who propose to improve on the existing faith/trust of the community by a ritual practice that leads to intimacy with angelic beings. They may keep this experience to themselves to establish their religious superiority, or they may teach it to others. We cannot tell. Jude's objections to this practice are framed partly in terms of the impurity it occasions—not, presumably, because he thought sexual impurity intrinsically wrong, but because it should be kept separate from the Holy.[28] Yet he is more particularly concerned that the practice involves a transgression of fundamental cosmic boundaries between human beings and angels, and that it shows a lack of faith/trust on the part of people who have already been introduced to the most intimate possible relationship with God in Jesus.

Similarly, Paul, in Galatians, does not object to circumcision in itself, but only when it is sought out by believing Gentiles after they have already accepted Christ (5:1–12). For Paul, there can be no added requirement beyond Jesus himself. Similarly, the author of 1 John encounters prophets who claimed that their spirit possession gave them insights and status superior to that of ordinary Christians (4:1–6). In response, he insists that the ordinary Christians have their own anointing and need no further instruction (2:26–27). It is precisely for this reason that he also insists on the priority of the tradition that began with those who saw and touched what had to do with the "word of truth" (1:1) because it is this tradition that vindicates the status of the ordinary faithful.[29]

In arguing here that the letter of Jude has a sustained theological purpose, I do not mean to deny the modern reader's perception of anger. Much
of the letter reads as a collection of threats and insults. Jude's expressions
of confidence in his audience somehow come through less persuasively for
us than his denunciations of the new teachers. How can we explain this? It
is at least partly a function of stresses in early Christian social structure,
with its multiplicity of itinerant prophets. It is also partly a result of the
openness to the new that must commonly characterize communities composed largely of converts. Having experienced one profound change of
perspective, they will not automatically reject the possibility of another.

The fact that the addressees have welcomed itinerant teachers will not
in itself have violated their existing connection with Jude, and Jude does
not fault them for having received the teachers in the first place. Rather, he
salutes the addressees, in a familial style common in early Christianity, as
"beloved" (ἀγαπητοί, 3). And he includes them with himself in references
to "our common salvation" (2), "our God," and "our only master and
Lord Jesus Christ" (4). Yet he can scarcely avoid recognizing that, if the
addressees should opt for the new teachings, his own authority would
have waned. Persuading his hearers to reject the new teaching, then, goes
hand in hand with preserving his own relationship with them.

By characterizing the new teachers in terms of biblical transgressors and
the existing congregation in terms of a tradition of intimacy with God,
Jude is canonizing the community's past and therefore also his relationship
with them. He persuades his readers that to accept the new teaching would
actually mean a radical break with their past faith, virtually a "denying of
our only master and Lord Jesus Christ." Instead, he insists that they must
deny the new teachers, excluding them and any followers they may have
gathered from the ongoing community. Ironically, he contrives to throw
the blame on the new teachers by calling them "the dividers" (19).

Jude, then, is a traditionalist, associating his position with the past, with
the authority of Scripture and of earlier itinerant teachers known to his
addressees ("apostles," 17). This makes it easy to read him, in rather
straightforward patriarchal terms, as saying, "I know what is best. Do as
you are told." At the same time, his defense of the tradition is not based
solely on its age or on assertion of personal authority. He insists, rather, on
the power of the faith/trust (πίστις) already familiar to his audience and on
the sense of joyful intimacy with God that they have already experienced.
He not only rejects the opponents' program of intimacy with angelic powers
on the grounds that it involves unclean and anti-hierarchical behavior; he

also places their intimacy with angelic beings in contrast to the intimacy with God that the faithful have already known through Jesus.

All this serves to underline the complex range of meaning to be found in this short letter—a complexity that is at once rhetorical, theological, and social. This complexity, in turn, marks the letter as a worthy partner in the kind of conversation that we shall pursue further in chapter 6.

Notes

1. For an explanation of the function of this language, see Dale B. Martin, *Slavery as Salvation: The Metaphor of Slavery in Pauline Christianity* (New Haven: Yale University Press, 1990), 50–60.

2. Paul responds to such criticism in 2 Cor 10–12. D. F. Watson assumes that Jude's opponents were sectarians; *Invention, Arrangement, and Style: Rhetorical Criticism of Jude and 2 Peter* (Atlanta: Scholars Press, 1988), 30. But this is an overstatement. Jude accuses them of proceeding on their own authority (12), not of deliberately setting up a rival community. They are more likely to have been itinerant "apostles" or "prophets" of the sort mentioned in *Didache* 11–13.

3. Since the new teachers are functioning within the Christian community, the "denial" of Jesus is presumably not an outright rejection, but some kind of diminishment of Jesus' importance in relation to the faithful; cf. Jerome Neyrey, *2 Peter, Jude*, 56–57.

4. Some take the closing phrases of v. 4 quite literally and assume that the teachers are "Antinomians"; e.g., Richard Bauckham, "Jude" in *HBC*, 1297. But it is unclear that the term "antinomian" tells us anything concrete about them; it is simply a charge brought against those who, like Paul, violate existing mores for some religious or theological purpose they conceive as compelling. It does not, then, tell us what laws the teachers were violating or on what principle.

5. This is a somewhat difficult passage to convey in English, and a few comments on the translation are in order: In v. 5, I have translated πιστεύσαντας as "trust." "Believe" is also possible; but the events to which Jude refers seem to be less a failure of formal, propositional belief than failure to trust that the God who led the people on the Exodus would continue to sustain them. In v. 7, I have used the archaic "committed harlotry" to translate ἐκπορνεύσασαι for the sake of the connotations it has acquired, courtesy of King James's translators, of engaging in foreign worship. It is not simply a human sexual transgression that is at stake here. As explained above, in chap. 2, I have kept to a word-for-word translation of ὀπίσω σαρκὸς ἑτέρας as "after another flesh," i.e., a flesh other than human.

6. The word I translated "faith" in v. 3 could equally well be translated "trust." The addressees are to depend on the *trust* that they have received as a gift.

7. *First Enoch* 8.

8. See above, chap. 2.

9. Col 2:8–23. Note that the service of the elemental spirits (στοιχεῖα) in Colossians appears to take ritual form (2:16–18, 20–23).

10. Their teaching may have been related to ideas in the Gospel of Philip; see Jorunn Jacobsen Buckley, "A Cult-Mystery in *The Gospel of Philip*," *JBL* 99 (1980): 569–81.

11. In this sense, it is often translated "dominion." Interestingly, some textual authorities, including Codex Sinaiticus, read the plural "lordships" in this verse, confirming that some ancient readers surely understood the passage as referring to celestial beings.

12. The importance of status inequality, whether of gender or age, to sexual relationships in the ancient Mediterranean world has become something of a commonplace among classical scholars.

13. Jude is relying on extra-biblical Jewish tradition here; cf. M. Eugene Boring, Klaus Berger, and Carsten Colpe, eds., *Hellenistic Commentary to the New Testament* (Nashville: Abingdon, 1995), 546.

14. Jude is following extra-biblical tradition, which saw Balaam as having succumbed to the temptation that he resisted in Numbers; J. N. D. Kelly, *Peter and Jude*, 266–67.

15. Jude's reference to Balaam as having received pay also serves to cast doubt on the new teachers' motives.

16. Aline Rousselle, *Porneia: On Desire and the Body in Antiquity*, trans. Felicia Pheasant (Oxford: Blackwell, 1988), 13, 19.

17. E. H. Plumptre, *The General Epistles of St. Peter and St. Jude* (Cambridge: Cambridge University Press, 1910), 209.

18. Note the repetition of ζόφος "gloom," in vv. 6 and 13, referring to the punishment of the Watchers and the teachers. The term appears in the NT only five times, twice in Jude, twice in the parallel materials in 2 Peter, and once in Hebrews.

19. Paul's language in 2 Cor 11 suggests that the same charge had been leveled at him; he implies that it is in fact true of his opponents.

20. Characterization of the human being as existing on three levels (body or flesh, soul, and spirit) was widespread in early Christianity; cf. 1 Cor 2:11–3:4. Those who failed to understand the Christian message adequately could be stigmatized as belonging to the level of soul or even body/flesh.

21. A similar argument is found in 1 John, where the author undercuts the claims of prophetic individuals by telling the audience at large that they have no need of such leaders since they all have an anointing and, with it, all needful knowledge (1 John 2:20–27).

22. The pollution may also be metaphorical, meaning to characterize their teaching as "belonging to the flesh, not the spirit." But if the addressees are indeed Jewish Christians living in a thoroughly Jewish environment, they probably maintain Levitical standards of physical purity as a matter of course and would be disturbed by cavalier disregard of them.

23. The text of these two verses is uncertain in several respects. Indeed, some ancient authorities omit them altogether, though their inclusion in Sinaiticus and Vaticanus seems to validate them sufficiently. Some authorities relate the participle of διακρίνομαι to the object of the main verb, others to the subject. In addition, διακρίνομαι itself is ambiguous, meaning either "to dispute" or "to waver." Since the word also occurs in Jude 9, where it must have the sense of "dispute," I take it that way here, too.

24. Some commentators have seen in verses 22–23 directions for responding to three distinct groups within the community: the new teachers (the "disputers"), those leaning to their teaching (the ones "in the fire"), and those who have fully accepted it (whose garments are defiled). See Plumptre, *The General Epistles*, 214; Kugelman, *James and Jude*, 104–5. The uncertainties of text, however, make this kind of detailed explanation weak. Bo Reicke, *The Epistles of James, Peter, and Jude* (AB, 37; Garden City, N.Y.: Doubleday, 1964), 214–16, infers that these verses are no longer related to the false teaching and its partisans, but give general instructions about admission of catechumens; he offers insufficient grounds, however, for assuming so major a shift in subject matter.

25. Contrast Paul in 2 Cor 13 or the Elder in 3 John 13–14.

26. J. Daryl Charles, *Literary Strategy*, 168.

27. Ruth Anne Reese, *Writing Jude,* 160–61.

28. Jonathan Klawans, *Impurity and Sin in Ancient Judaism* (Oxford: Oxford University Press, 2000), 22–26.

29. Kenneth Grayston, *The Johannine Epistles* (New Century Bible Commentary; Grand Rapids: Eerdmans, 1984), 14–27.

Part 3

Reading
Other People's
Mail

5. The Challenge of Interpreting New Testament Letters

To some extent, every reading is de novo, as any regular reader of lyric poetry can testify. We may return to a poem long familiar, expecting that it will once again produce in us the same response it has before, only to discover that, in one case, it has gone quite flat or, in another, it reveals new and quite unexpected ranges of meaning. This, of course, is a reflection of the nature of human language, which does not work through individual, discrete, logical connections like computers, but is capable of quite surprising leaps and evasions and novelties. Indeed, one of the distinctive capacities of human language is the ability it gives us to say and hear something *new*, however great a struggle that may require and however poorly we may manage it at first. There is, then, a quality of synthetic reading that one can only call "intuitive," which does not mean that it is beyond critical discussion, but does mean that it is not reducible to analytical method. How do we incorporate and describe this element of synthetic method? I am not sure that there is a general, comprehensive answer; but I offer one case as a way of getting at the issues involved.

Reading Other People's Mail

Scholars do not, in fact, have to create all our synthetic methods from scratch. We already have a basic synthetic model for reading at least one type of NT document—a model drawn from an experience widespread among literate peoples, the experience of reading other people's mail. This is not, as I hope will become apparent, a flippant proposal. Sophisticated reading is not an invention of the academy; it has been around a long time.

There is nothing in most NT letters to suggest that their authors had any audience in mind other than immediate contemporaries, primarily their specific addressees.[1] (Pseudonymous letters such as the Pastorals may be a partial exception, but even there the issues are those contemporary with their actual, as distinct from their nominal, composition.) When we read such letters, whether purely out of curiosity or to contribute to the ongoing interpretive conversation, we are reading something addressed to people other than ourselves. Recognition of this is as important for Christian readers as for any others.

High doctrines of biblical inspiration may seem to imply that the Spirit foresaw a larger and more distant audience. But any genuinely orthodox Christian understanding of scriptural inspiration must take, as its model and its limit, the doctrine of the Incarnation, which insists that Jesus is and was genuinely human and therefore genuinely a part of his own place, time, people, and culture.[2] The Spirit's larger, more ecumenical message is incarnate, then, in the particulars of the text, in its actual ancient specificities. It is not expressed in ageless abstractions, nor can it be. If the Spirit spoke to every age in the same words, it would be equally unintelligible to all. The Christian reader expects that conversation with God will be part of every process of learning, discernment, and interpretation—and also that conversation with other people will be part of the conversation with God. Some of these people are our contemporaries; some, including the writers of the NT letters and their addressees, are our predecessors.

Still, when we read these documents, even if they have become canonical, we are reading what was originally other people's mail. And a taboo normally interdicts this practice, thus placing it outside the normal circle of reading. When we do read others' mail, we are forbidden, ethically, to read it for such illicit purposes as would impose our interests in preference to the interests of the legitimate recipient. Scholars are, of course, no more immune to temptation—and no more doomed by it—than other human beings. To avoid the temptation to unethical reading, however, any reader of another's mail must practice a certain detachment, a willingness to let the letter belong to another more than, and prior to, ourselves. Doing this involves a spirituality, a basic stance in relation to the world, not just a craft or an art. It is founded in the respect that allows others to speak, as much as possible, for themselves. A basic test of our willingness to do so is that they are allowed to surprise and perplex us. If we insist that they answer our questions directly, respond to our concerns, validate our theology or other ideological stance, we are reading them in bad faith and in violation of the ethical mandate against reading other people's mail.

When does it become ethically permissible to read other people's mail? Under three circumstances: when we are invited by the addressee; when we become responsible for the addressee's affairs, as in the case of a trustee appointed on behalf of a person who can no longer conduct her or his own business; or after the addressee is dead.

Can we claim, in the case of NT letters, to have been invited? Perhaps, in a sense. The preservation of these letters (presumably, in the first instance, by their addressees) may be seen as a kind of invitation; certainly the practice of copying and circulating them constituted one. Their inclusion in the canon is indeed an invitation, coming from the larger community that sees itself as continuous with the addressees. This does not confine the readership to members of that community, but it does assert a claim that the letters be read in relation to that community. Just as Native American peoples, for example, sometimes protest the piecemeal and irresponsible (or, to put it another way, imperialistic) adoption of their sacred traditions by Americans of European descent, so too with the biblical canon; to read it responsibly means that one enters into some sort of relationship with the community that created and preserved it.

In addition, modern members of that community have an ongoing role as trustees of the community's inheritance. Insofar as we share some responsibility for the community's affairs, we may reasonably allege a need to be initiated into conversation with the earlier members through access to their correspondence. Such a claim implies that our reading will be not only out of curiosity, but part of a larger concern for the welfare of the community at large. Merely determining what the letter may have meant to its original writer and addressees will not, by itself, achieve that goal; it is only a step in that direction.

In any case, reading the letters of the dead is a not uncommon pastime in the modern world, where the letters of authors, public figures, and so forth are routinely published after their demise. Why do we read them? Partly out of curiosity about difference: What made this person distinctive? Partly out of a hope for continuity: What does this suggest about my own life? Neither of these interests can operate without the other. Difference without continuity is so alien as to be unintelligible; continuity without difference is too familiar to be illuminating and generates only boredom. This suggests a key element for the paradigm of reading other people's mail. We read the letters of the deceased in the hope of understanding both them and ourselves and in expectation that the two kinds of understanding might well be linked. If we commit the absurdity of reading these letters as if they were addressed directly and solely to us, they become useless to us. Yet, reading them as other people's mail, we may indeed hear, in them and through them, voices that speak to our condition.

How much of this do we articulate to ourselves when reading other people's mail? For the most part, very little. In the contemporary world, reading other people's mail may well be something we do—licitly or illicitly— before we begin to think about it. Yet there is a process involved that we begin to master well before it becomes fully conscious. It is a process both analytical and synthetic in character, a process in which the analytical and synthetic elements are inevitably wedded to each other. Indeed, the intrinsic relationship of difference and continuity to one another demands that we be engaged both synthetically, in seeking common ground as a context for difference, and analytically, in seeking difference as a way of giving new texture and meaning to common ground. Neither of these processes can advance far without the other.

Even on the most basic levels of reading, there is a necessary interrelation between the fine details of reading and the larger picture. And the choice of larger picture is itself open to debate. Consider, for example, an odd proposal by a distinguished NT scholar of the nineteenth century with regard to the opening of Paul's First Letter to the Corinthians.[3] The scholar argued that this letter, concerned though it emphatically is with local problems in the church at Corinth, was really a kind of encyclical letter. Why? He appealed to the phrase "with all those who call upon the name of our Lord Jesus Christ in every place" (1 Cor 1:2). He took the phrase, with the translators of the Authorized Version, as referring to additional addressees—"to the assembly at Corinth . . . along with all those. . . ." Alternatively, one might relate the phrase to the verbal adjective κλητοί ("called"), so that it defines the Corinthians as "called to be saints together with all those. . . ." (RSV). Our commentator resolved the question according to the analytical rules of Greek grammar, which would ideally forbid a prepositional phrase of this sort to be attached to an adjective, even a verbal adjective, without the intervention of a definite article. What the scholar missed, however, was that precisely this construction, grammatical or not, occurs a verse earlier, when Paul refers to himself as "*called* [κλητός] to be an apostle of Jesus Christ *through* the will of God" (AV, emphasis added).

On either interpretation, the phrase gains meaning only as it is placed in the context of a larger background. The question is whether to choose, with Lightfoot, the background of general Greek syntactical usage or, with later translators, the background of Paul's own usage in the passage

itself. Neither choice is inevitable a priori; and yet it would certainly be a
challenge—and probably not a productive one—to read 1 Corinthians,
with all its specific local references, as an encyclical letter. In either case,
the central point is that reading attentively is a process in which we move
back and forth between detail and big picture, between difference and continuity, between analysis and synthesis, between taking the text apart and
trying to see it as a whole, both in itself and in relation to its time and place
of origin. It is rather like looking at a large painting in a museum. You cannot see everything you might want to see from a single location. You move
forward to see detail and back to get the bigger view. And moving back, if it
is an interesting painting, prompts you to move forward; and moving forward prompts you to move back.

My reason for proposing "reading other people's mail" as a model for
the scholarly study of NT letters is not only that the documents are appropriate materials for it—they really were written for addressees other than
ourselves—but also that it captures the notion of a process that combines
the analytical and synthetic, a process that has not yet even thought of separating them. Taken as a model, then, it reminds us to aim at creating an
ongoing conversation between the analytical and synthetic that can, in
turn, support a conversation between the text itself and the modern interpreter and community. Such a conversation is possible only when it honors both difference and continuity, when it takes neither for granted, when
it accepts that the result of the conversation lies in the conversation itself
and in the lives of its participants, not in the identification of a single
meaning for the text.

What We Look for in Reading Other People's Mail

Real-Life Context

When reading other people's mail, we are always looking for a real-life
context for the correspondence. I do not mean to suggest that "real life" is
self-evident, a known quantity simply waiting to have the text held up
against it. We often know or guess bits and pieces of the circumstances in
which the letter was written; we then revise and add to this by reading
between the lines and comparing one passage with another. The dialectic
of continuity and difference means that we can read—and sustain our interest in reading—only if the writing has some element of the familiar and recognizable or, in other words, is related to something larger, including an
element already known, already given. Unless we can connect it with a

larger world, the writing, whether in familiar or unfamiliar characters, familiar or unfamiliar language, remains indecipherable. The most funda- mental form of connection possible is our sense that the writing refers to a world external both to the writer and to us—the world that forms the pri- mary context for human life. For all the contemporary enthusiasm for intertextuality, writing is not primarily about other writings—not, at least, outside the academic orbit. None of this is to deny the social constructions and psychological formations that intervene, as it were, between us and the irreducible realities around us—that, indeed, shape those realities for us in significant ways. It is simply to say that, when reading other people's mail, we keep looking for the world that formed their environment and interpreting it in relation to our own. Here are some things we look for:

Relationship

A letter normally arises out of an existing relationship, even if it is not a particularly direct or intimate one. In reading others' mail, one asks, "Who were these people to each other? What was their history? What were their prospects of future relationship?" The use of written communication also implies some distance in this relationship—at least a brief separation in space or the suppression of other forms of communication, as among pris- oners and schoolchildren. Not infrequently, it also implies distance in other respects, some matter about which writer and addressee are not in full agreement, some information not previously known to the addressee, some significant difference in circumstances that calls for encouragement or warning. Of all these, the letter is a momentary manifestation that can paradoxically survive its occasion. In most cases, the later, unexpected reader will have no direct access to the relationship or to its history and specifics apart from what appears in the letter. This means that one's knowledge is always limited—like all human knowledge. Still, one cannot refuse to ask these questions.

Occasion or Occasions

Letters are normally occasional documents.[4] The occasion may be in the life of the writer or in the life of the addressees or in both. Sometimes the letter may mention the occasion directly and explicitly. Often, how- ever, this is not the case. Some occasions are too well known to mention. In a letter to a relative, it may be enough to write, "Aunt Hilda is feeling less anxious about the bees." If the situation is already known to the addressee, the writer does not need to specify whether the anxiety arose from an attack on Aunt Hilda, on her uncertainty about what to do with an

inherited apiary, on her scientific concern about the disappearance of
native American species, on her professional concern about diseases of
honeybees or migration of Africanized hybrids, or whatever.

At other times, reference to the occasion of the letter is repressed or
veiled because to do otherwise would distress the addressee or even
threaten the ongoing relationship. One may write to express support without directly referring to the loss of a job or a grave public humiliation or
any sensitive topic. One may give advice about a threatened divorce without directly mentioning the more painful aspects of it. One may try to offer
a different perspective to an angry correspondent without directly mentioning the issue at hand for fear of stimulating the anger anew and making it harder for the addressee to think in new ways about the situation.

Problem and Proposed Resolution

As already implied, when the occasion is a problematic circumstance in
the life of the addressee, the writer is likely to address it and to offer some
approach to dealing with it. As later, unintended readers, we look for evidence of both, but must often reconstruct the problem from the proposed
solution. Even discerning the proposed solution can sometimes prove a
challenge. It may not be offered openly, but only implied. In any case, there
is a good chance that it will appear later in the letter rather than as the initial element. The problems of our lives carry a heavy emotional weight—a
weight that can make us less willing to consider new ideas. If the writer is
seeking to offer some resolution that the addressee might be inclined to
reject out of hand, without listening to it, the writer may argue for the proposal before actually revealing it. If the writer thinks that the best cure for
your depression and passivity would be to run away to the south of
France, the letter may well begin by praising the beauty of the place to
awaken your interest, not by making a bald proposal about flights and
lodgings.

Tensions on the Part of the Addressee or Writer

Even when the addressee is a single individual, letters often arise in circumstances where the person is undecided, being pulled in various directions by different allegiances, desires, or judgments. Such tensions are still
more common where the letter is addressed to a group. The writer, too,
whether communicating as an individual or on behalf of a group, may well
feel some tensions about the occasion—tensions that can become apparent
in the form of mutually contradictory passages within the letter. Thus, we
read for indications of ambiguity and uncertainty: "You seem clear that you

must accept this job offer; and yet your sense of what is ethical is holding you back." Or, "Those are my own thoughts on the subject, but I admit, too, to feeling that the damage the rhinoceros did to your cousin's dahlias demands some consideration."

Rhetorical Formation

If we assume that every letter has some real-world context, we also assume that every letter is essentially a rhetorical construct. By "rhetoric," I mean the attempt human beings make in speaking or writing, often quite unconsciously, persuasively to communicate ideas or perspectives that we fear may not be immediately intelligible or welcome to our audience. The letter, being constructed rhetorically, represents a compromise between a variety of forces or considerations. One is the point the writer intentionally wants to make. Another is the perceived limitation of the audience in accepting the point. Yet another is the need to find bonds of continuity that will encourage the addressee to remain in the conversation rather than terminating it. The writer may need to remind the addressees of their mutual relationship and keep them persuaded of his or her good faith; certainly, the writer needs to find a common language and perspective that will make it possible for the audience to see what the author proposes as an appropriate and faithful resolution.

To some degree, this is true of all human communication, spoken or written; to say, however, that a composition is "rhetorical" is to stress that this element is pervasive and essential to it. A philosopher might do well to pay some attention to rhetoric in the effort to initiate the reader into the author's peculiar vocabulary, ideas, and perspective. Much postmodern writing seems quite indifferent to this consideration; but some philosophers, particularly Plato and Kierkegaard, have given real attention to it. Masters of philosophical rhetoric as they were, however, they had a broader and more assertive purpose than that of the rhetorician—the goal of achieving not simply agreement on a particular occasion, but ongoing consent to the author's far-reaching construct of reality. While the rhetorical element is inescapably important for this purpose, it may well, for the philosophical reader, take second place to the ideas the writing embodies. The balance of logic and rhetoric in a letter is likely to be less one-sided. We read, then, for a variety of rhetorical devices and the traces they leave in the letter.

Movement within the Letter

The comments made above about occasion and problem suggest that the author is often trying to move the addressees in a particular direction. The "point" of a letter—that is, the issue that prompted the writing along with any proposed resolution of it—may often be found closer to the end than to the beginning. There are exceptions, particularly for the sharing of good news; but on more problematic occasions, the writer may feel a need to "prepare" the addressee. We read, then, for a sense of movement within the letter that corresponds to the letter's role in trying to move the addressee toward a resolution. The letter that begins "Sun and air and space are at such a premium nowadays . . ." may be moving toward "I hope you won't sell Granddad's farm for building tacky weekend cottages." Similarly, we have seen that Jude makes an early reference to the teachers whose work he opposes, but allows the nature of his condemnation of them to emerge gradually through characterizations (or perhaps caricatures!) touching on various aspects of their practice. His proposal for dealing with them is almost the last element in the letter.

The "point" will also, given the occasional nature of letters, almost certainly have to do with some quite specific, local, time-bound issue. If the writer makes larger, more abstract points, they typically serve a preparatory function. This is important to keep in mind, since we, at a distance in time and space, may relate more easily and obviously to the more timeless material in the letter. A letter may, of course, serve as a kind of essay or reflection, as in Seneca's *Moral Epistles* or Alan Paton's "Letter to a Young Boy Confirmed"; but that is far from the most common sort. Most letters respond to existing circumstances and draw more abstract considerations into play primarily to ground or commend a particular resolution or course of conduct.

Pacing and Variation

Since the writer wants to retain the addressee's interest, there is likely to be some variation in pacing. For example, solemn elements may be interspersed with lighter material, or exposition with exhortation. Sentence length can be varied in order to focus or refocus attention. Bits of particularly vivid expression or imagery serve to underline an idea or observation, drive it home, and render it memorable. Since human beings assimilate information by a combination of intellectual and emotional processes, as indivisible from each other as continuity is from difference or analysis from synthesis, the writer will be inclined, often quite without deliberate planning, to combine emotional and intellectual appeals. A principal tool of this—and a principal way for the later reader to recognize it—is through variation and pacing in the composition.[5]

This is partly just to acknowledge the everyday importance of "rhetorical figures." If the writer shifts into a more complex sentence structure, replete with subordinate clauses that add nuance and qualification to the ideas presented and encourage rumination on them in light of the addressee's own life and experience, it slows the reader down and requires a more active intellectual digestion of the thought. If, by contrast, the writer uses a series of short, clipped phrases, it focuses the attention, it underlines the point made, it drives home its importance. Questions put to the addressee try to engage the reader in a process of conscious agreement with the writer, do they not? Plays on sound (such as rhyme, assonance, rhythmic figures) help concretize a particular image or idea and render it prominent and memorable. Some of these are so effective that they become fixed phrases like λόγος καὶ ἔργον in Greek, which also works in English as "word and deed." In religious texts, liturgical language can make God a third party to the conversation. Blessings give a sense of completion and so tend to draw a particular section to a close.

Classical rhetorical theory developed a comprehensive catalog of such figures, but they were in use long before they were catalogued and are still used by people with no particular training in rhetorical theory. It will be useful to the modern reader of NT letters to know something of the classical catalog, since it emerges from the same larger cultural sphere as the documents themselves, but it is neither an exhaustive nor an exclusive list. We should not allow our curiosity to be limited by it.[6]

Identification and Distancing

Given the centrality of relationship to the letter, the writer has the opportunity to play on it. This often becomes particularly evident in the use of pronouns. The basic "I," "you," and "they" establish potentially overlapping circles of association, which can be handled with considerable subtlety. The first-person plural in Indo-European languages, with its fusion of "I-plus-you" and "I-plus-they," can be ambiguous and therefore highly flexible in creating a nuanced sense of who is inside the circle of conversation and who is not: "Your mother and I have talked about this, and we agree that all of us should spend Christmas at the farm." (Notice that in this sentence, "us" does not denote precisely the same group as "we," though the language implies that "we" have the prerogative of making decisions for "us.") Again, "I" can be used in contrast to "you" in order to set a distance between writer and addressees, while "they" are defined out of the conversation entirely: "I'm surprised to learn you've taken the same position as the people in the Omaha office, since we've always been more concerned about the integrity of the system, and they're only interested in the immediate bottom line." Sometimes these elements in a text escape our notice as unintended readers; in our own mail, we absorb their import almost without becoming conscious of it as a separate item of information.

Projections of a Continuing Relationship

The writer may be explicit about what she or he hopes for in the way of a continuing relationship with the addressee, since that is likely to be an issue of substance in the letter itself. Any such indications must, however, be viewed as an aspect of the rhetoric of the work as well and may have some end in view beyond simple communication of information. If someone writes, "I'm hoping to pay a visit to your area next month," it may be a simple expression of intent, an indirect request for an offer of accommodation, an implied deadline for accomplishing something the writer has suggested, or a reminder that the decorative urns sent you for Christmas (not actually mentioned in the letter) should be on display. For that matter, it may be all of the above. Even if explicit statements are absent, the letter may contain other indications of the writer's expectations of future interaction. Of course, the expectations of the writer are not conclusive. Only outside information could tell us, finally, whether they were in any sense fulfilled.

A Process, Not a Methodology

What I am proposing here is deliberately somewhat vague. It is a kind of mind-set that embraces both rhetorical awareness and alertness to the social, cultural, and personal history implied in a piece of correspondence. When we read letters addressed to others, we are reconstructing their world and we are paying attention to the way in which the writer is relating to the addressees through words, that is, to the rhetorical structure of the letter. Without doing both these things, we would not be likely to feel that we had understood the letters at all. But this is a process of trial and error, of hypothesizing and of confirming or relinquishing our hypotheses.

Academics find a certain attraction in methodologies that are so narrowly defined that we can know when we have completed our work. Unfortunately, such methodologies seldom yield truly useful results when pursued in isolation because they put blinders on us by the narrowness of their focus. This contributes, needless to say, to the familiar complaint of aridity in scholarly work. At their worst, such methodologies do little more than demonstrate that, if you chop a text up into squares that are three inches on a side, you will have a heap of paper squares three inches on a side to show for your labors. A methodology that tells you in advance what you should find is of limited value for reading ancient documents. Only a process that allows for surprise and encourages the most intelligent and self-critical reading of which we are capable can produce results of value.

Elements Specific to the Early Christian Context

Thus far, I have tried to describe the process of reading other people's mail in quite general terms, but we can be more specific when we turn to the NT letters. There was great diversity within the earliest Christian communities; the letters themselves offer good evidence of it. And the more one knows the first-century Mediterranean world, the more difficult it is—just as with our own world—to reduce it to a few elements. At the same time, some cultural elements were broadly characteristic of the first-century Mediterranean world. It should be helpful for me to sketch some of what I am presuming here about this background. The presuppositions shape the work to follow. They are not beyond debate, but I shall not attempt to justify them here, since they are well within the range of present scholarly opinion.

To begin with, I assume that the NT letters "worked." The preservation of the letters suggests that they were at least somewhat successful at what their authors aimed to achieve. Paul's letters seem to have been collected from his churches after his death, not derived from an archive of his own; and this implies that the recipients had preserved them.[7] One can at least guess that the same was true of the other documents. This is not to say that any given letter gained unanimous consent—or even that its addressees understood it fully. What it suggests is that the recipients of the letter (or a significant portion of them) continued to see themselves as being in a significant relationship with the author. The letter became a kind of physical representation of that fact.[8] The preservation of these letters is an external confirmation that they helped maintain a sense of connection between author and addressees; and they were, to that degree, successful examples of the letter-writing art.

Social Context of the Letters

I am also assuming some provisional images of the social character of early Christian communities—images of the sort that social history and sociological studies have produced over the last few decades. I do not want to suggest highly detailed images because we expect to ask each text to reveal to us as much as possible of its own specific, local, real-world context. But generalized images are useful in eliciting questions that might not occur to us if we had only our own modern experience to rely on. The images must themselves be open to question, but they do give us a starting point.

The single most important element is that the earliest Christian communities were voluntary organizations; they functioned like clubs. This means that there was less social "glue" to hold the local community together than in the case of groups defined more by inherited identity (like households and clans) or by economic interdependence (as in an ancient village). If one can make an adult choice to become part of a voluntary community, one can also make an adult choice to leave it. This would not necessarily be cost-free, but it was easier in antiquity than, say, abandoning one's household. The earliest Christian groups included households, but they had not yet, in the ambit of most NT letters, reached the second-generation stage, when Christian identity was something inherited by a significant percentage in the congregations. Members were converts who had made a voluntary act of identification.

I assume two broad types of early Christian communities. One consists of largely Jewish-Christian communities in villages and small cities of the eastern Roman Empire. These may have had a degree of stability often missing in their more urban and ethnically mixed (or entirely Gentile) equivalents. They may well have been centered in extended families; in any case, their environment was a well-known and relatively predictable group of townsfolk, not the more fluid metropolitan population. This small-town Christianity is described in works like the *Didache,* which is anxious about charlatans imposing on the good nature and innocence of local communities, but does not seem particularly disturbed about the prospect of schism within the community. Being composed of a largely Jewish-Christian population, such communities had the added advantage that their lives and mores were already reasonably well-defined for them by the continuity of their cultural and ethnic identification. To be sure, Christians taught a particular interpretation of Jewish identity and obligation, but at the beginning they remained a particular sect within the broad range of Jewish religious and ethnic culture and were only gradually faced with the choice of whether to conform to an emerging rabbinic consensus after the First Jewish War of 66–70 C.E.[9]

By way of contrast, Christianity in the larger Greco-Roman cities, from Paul's time onward, seems constantly exercised by anxiety about schism. In 1 Corinthians, Paul is concerned about the rise of parties owing allegiance to other traveling teachers. In 1 John, the community seems already to have suffered a secession—or to be in the midst of one. In 3 John, Diotrephes is separating his house-church from the others in the Elder's network. This tendency to schism, of course, survived long afterward, as one can see in the letters of Ignatius of Antioch, expressing his anxiety about the unity of the church he has left behind, or in the history of internal divisions in the Roman church over figures such as Marcion or Valentinus.

In addition, the members of metropolitan churches might be quite varied in cultural and religious background. The different presuppositions they brought with them could lead to substantial tensions over basic standards of behavior. Thus Paul, in 1 Corinthians, finds himself caught between those who feel it is right for women to prophesy and speak up in church and those who do not, between those who see nothing wrong with a Christian man's visiting prostitutes and those who object, those who defend a man's cohabitation with his father's wife and those who are scandalized by it, those who take it for granted that they can participate at a banquet in a Greek temple and those who are revolted by the very thought of it. It would take a couple of generations before Gentile Christianity emerged with its own basic and widespread assumptions about such issues of behavior.[10]

The character of earliest Christian teaching itself contributed to this variety and uncertainty. At first, teachers were largely itinerants. And, if the traditions of Jesus' teaching offer any indication, they focused more on producing an experience of conversion (μετάνοια) and creating a new sense of relationship with God than on detailed prescriptions for belief, conduct, or community organization. At first, contemporary popular Jewish practice continued as something taken for granted—insofar as anything could be taken for granted in the highly argumentative context of first-century Judaism. But admission of Gentiles called even this continuity into question. As Paul's letters show, first-century Christians were working out issues of belief, behavior, and community organization as they went along. Sometimes Paul had a clear-cut response to an issue; at other times, as with his curiously inconclusive argument about foods sacrificed to idols in 1 Corinthians, he appears somewhat uncertain himself. He argues first that idols are nothing (8:4–5) and foods sacrificed to them are matters of indifference except insofar as one's conscience is violated (8:7–8). Next he argues that the sacrifices offered to idols really do involve the worshipper in communion with demons (10:20–22). Finally, he concludes that one must avoid only what is publicly identified as sacrificial (10:25–29).

Given the fluidity of early Christian leadership, it was easy, especially in the cities, to find quite distinct or even mutually contradictory versions of what the movement was really about. In the first century, these seldom took the form of independent theologies (in the sense of carefully organized concatenations of ideas); they took the form rather of allegiance to different teachers and their distinctive teachings. Hence, the writer of a letter seldom enjoyed the possibility of debating different ideas without also addressing the pattern of allegiances and personal commitments with which they were entangled.

In either the town or the urban setting, then, the writer of a letter, particularly if touching on a difficult problem, had the challenge not simply of addressing the specific issue in hand, but of maintaining the very existence of the community. For those writing to urban churches, the unity of the community was often hanging in the balance, as Paul's frequent return to this theme suggests. For those writing to village and town churches, the unity of the community may not have been so much at issue; the fact that dissident groups would still have to continue living alongside each other would deter splintering. Still, there could be a threat to the community's continuing relationship with the writer, as we have seen in the Letter of Jude, and with other communities in the writer's orbit, as becomes apparent in 3 John.

This brings us to yet another significant and distinctive characteristic of first-century Christian communities. Even though local assemblies basically functioned much like Greco-Roman clubs, they also maintained communication with Christians elsewhere. No doubt some of the Roman government's anxiety about Christianity was fueled by an awareness of this network of communication. Without it, the NT letters might not have come into existence at all and would scarcely have been copied and recirculated. At the same time, however, there was little top-down authority at first among Christian communities. Local churches had a group, perhaps only vaguely defined, of elders. When Paul seeks to identify church leadership at Corinth, he falls back on the household of Stephanas, both because they were among the first converts there and because they have dedicated themselves to the service of the saints (1 Cor 16:15–16). Above the level of the local assembly, whether it represented a Christian village or an urban house-church, there were no formal governmental institutions or any formal power to compel agreement. There were only influential teachers and networks of congregations associated with them and with one another.

Since the earliest Christian letter writers were addressing a situation of great fluidity, they had to treat their occasions of writing in ways that would not only resolve a specific issue but also contribute to the stability of the group. In some cases, this may have meant accepting the reality of division and stabilizing the remnant (e.g., 1 John). In most cases, it meant trying to strengthen the bonds that united the existing community as a whole both internally and with the writer. The role of the early Christian letter writer is thus significantly different from that of, say, an Israelite prophet like Hosea. Hosea can denounce what he sees as evil in quite direct terms, since neither his own identity as a part of the people of Israel nor that of the people he attacks depends on what he says. The early Christian letter writer must actively maintain the existence of the community and will have to weigh carefully when, how, and what to denounce.

There is also a contrast with later periods in the history of Christianity when the relationship between writer and addressees could be formulated in institutional terms. A medieval bishop could give commands by virtue of his office, even though he would never be entirely free of political considerations. In earliest Christianity it was always more complex than that. Since authority was often defined in charismatic terms, it was dependent on constantly renewed recognition by the community. Competition for such recognition was intense. The connection between writer and addressees, even where the writer, like Paul at Corinth, was the founder of the community, was constantly being redefined and reinvented. As a rule, then, writers of NT letters also had to take renewal of their relationship with their addressees as a basic issue in writing to them.

In sum, letter writing in earliest Christianity tended to originate in situations of disagreement and tension. The writer, given the circumstances of life in voluntary communities, therefore carried certain inevitable burdens: the need to establish or renew the writer's own authority, to strengthen the sense of connectedness between writer and addressees, to identify some shared ground that could serve as a foundation for resolving the difficulties under consideration, and to strengthen or maintain the internal unity of the local community. None of these elements could merely be taken for granted. The writer could then proceed to construct an argument leading to a conclusion that might gain the general assent of the addressees—

"argument" here being understood in a rhetorical sense, not in a purely logical one.

The Element of Good News

We cannot understand early Christianity or its letters, however, as simply the working out of social and cultural givens. Christianity also, at the same time, constituted a novelty in its cultural context. It drew people away from familiar definitions of reality and brought them to embrace an understanding of God, self, and world that was significantly (though not, of course, entirely) different. Conversion was not only the basic initiatory experience of the first Christians, but also established a tradition that continued to be influential even in later generations, when an increasing percentage of their communities were born within the faith. This means that there was always a need for Christian writers to deal with the experiencing of truth. The possibility of discovering truth, of experiencing a reality that was not entirely what one had previously assumed or what one's culture had previously assumed, was a central element in their message.

They did not, of course, frame this element in the language I have just used—language that belongs to our time, not theirs. They phrased it rather in terms of a proclamation of good news. The truth they had discovered, the surprise they had to share, was fundamentally a positive one that deserved to be welcomed everywhere—though, of course, they soon came to understand that they could not rely on that happening. To welcome the good news implied that one became a part of the community that proclaimed it. Since the earliest Christian gospel was intent on bringing about this kind of discovery and conversion, any Christian leader writing a letter had a continuing responsibility to encourage this and help bring it about.

The centrality of conversion and the discovery of truth meant that these writers were not free to employ any means of persuasion whatsoever. If they were to maintain continuity with the basic message, they needed to confront their readers with the good news in ways that might turn out to be surprising and unexpected and so might provide an opportunity for μετάνοια, "change of mind." This concern stood alongside, and contextualized, the concern to maintain the life of the communities they addressed. The communities had meaning because they were places where human life might be transformed by the surprise of encounter with grace. They could not preach in one mode and conduct the business of their societies in an entirely different one.[11]

This gave the writers an additional reason to withhold direct reference to a problem or its proposed resolution until late in the letter. The first order of business was to give opportunity for renewing the addressees' minds and hearts. This meant reminding them of *what* they already believed, but also of *how* they believed, that is, through the process of conversion. The addressees often knew, of course, what the letter was likely to touch on, so much so that the letter itself, as we have seen in the case of Jude, might not bother to be explicit about it. Some of the addressees might be hoping the writer would deal with the issue at hand; others might already be rejecting what they thought the author likely to propose. Consequently, the larger portion of a letter would often be occupied with preparing the ground for the addressees to accept this proposal when it is finally made. Even Jude, brief as it is, offers a reminder of the addressees' past experience of conversion and trust in God before launching an attack on the new teachers. To omit such a preparation was to invite out-of-hand rejection by a portion of the group. The delaying of the "point" gave the writer time not only to build an argument but to revive the audience's sense of their conversion and what it meant for them.

The Rhetoric of the Letters

How far any of the NT writers might have experienced a full-fledged Greek rhetorical education has been a topic of conversation since antiquity, but the issue is not critical to my purpose here.[12] Rhetoric exists in practice long before it exists in reflection or in theory. As social, language-using animals, human beings found themselves practitioners of rhetoric, of speech used to sway others, long before individuals began to reflect deliberately on the process or construct a cultural norm for it. Thus the use of rhetorical skills was as characteristic of Hebrew culture, which did not develop a written theory of it, as it was of Greek, which did.

In rhetoric, the realities of social intercourse and the rich resources of language—not only the denotations of words and the guideposts of syntax, but all the musical, pictorial, and evocative resources of which speech is capable—are united into a human artifact of extraordinary complexity and density. In considering a rhetorical work, it is hard to tell what is most critical: the speaker, the audience, the occasion, the subject matter, the emotional appeal, or the music of language. Indeed, it is the combination of all these in support of one another that creates the power of the discourse. One can hope to analyze it to some degree without being limited to the predefined categories of a single culture or tradition.

At the same time, the influence of rhetoric was pervasive in the Greco-Roman world—almost to the degree that popular music and the cinema are in ours. This meant that any alert person absorbed some of the elements of what the culture defined as eloquence. It seems clear that Paul had enough exposure to Hellenistic rhetoric that he had picked up some of its ways. On the whole, however, the rhetoric of the NT letters is determined less by an educational process or a tradition of theory than by the exigencies of the immediate situation, by the tradition of teaching μετάνοια, and by the example of the common texts available to the Christian community, consisting primarily of the Scriptures of Israel in their Greek form. While it is helpful to know something of formal Greek rhetorical theory, the theory itself is not usually conclusive for our investigation. We are asking the texts to reveal their own rhetorical construction.

The reading of other people's mail is always and inevitably a complex and indeed interdisciplinary process. It involves literary, rhetorical, historical, psychological, social, and cultural dimensions. And it is a process that looks for surprises, not one that brings its conclusions with it. It is an engagement with the documents themselves, a conversation inviting them to reveal some of the particularities of their occasions, their worlds, their rhetoric.

Engaging the New Testament Letters

Rejection of the isolated use of analytic methodologies does not mean that the only alternative is to be totally intuitive in one's approach to the materials. This discussion of reading other people's mail and, more specifically, of the character and context of the NT letters, suggests a number of points that the reader can profitably hold in mind. None of these constitutes a self-executing method. They are rather hints about direction, signposts to look for, prospects to bear in mind, vantage points to try out. They can help train our vision and awaken reflection. They cannot and should not become rigid rules that try to determine, by their own constraints, the meaning that will emerge from the text.

I propose the following, then, as concrete methodological suggestions that put into practice the discussion thus far:

Read Back to Front

The letter is likely to be "in motion." That is, it is endeavoring to lead the addressees somewhere. The issue that evoked the writing, then, is likely to be addressed most explicitly near the end of the letter.[13] This procedure is roughly opposite to what has been most common in Christian reading of the NT letters. The more abstract and theological material of the body of the letter has been our preferred focus, and the concluding material has often been treated as a miscellany that is of little interest to the modern reader. We need to reverse this habit of reading. At the same time, one has to admit that the "end" of a letter is not always easy to identify. Is it the last line? The last page? The last rhetorically distinct segment? Or is it perhaps the last quarter or third of the letter, itself a complex construction? There can be no a priori certainty about this. As we shall see in the examples that conclude this work, we must remain open as we select what "end" constitutes our beginning point.

Look for an Issue That Prompted the Writing

Letters may, of course, be written on a kind of routine schedule, particularly in the modern world, where there are regular posts. But more commonly, they are occasioned by particular needs, events, or other stimuli. In the ancient world, the stimulus may have been no more than the availability of a messenger to carry the letter; but we must still ask whether the letter contains some indication of a particular occasion in the relationship between writer and addressees. This occasion may often be implied rather than overtly stated—and this for several reasons. For one, the occasion, if it arose within the orbit of the addressees, will have been well-known to them already. For another, if the writer wants to offer some kind of solution to a problem faced by the addressees, it may be politic to avoid mentioning it until the earlier portions of the letter have created a context for its resolution.

Look for a Proffered Resolution

Like the overt reference to the occasion of the letter, it may well be held back till near the end of the letter in order to avoid provoking possible objections before the writer has had a chance to create the desired context for the resolution—a context in which the writer hopes that the resolution can make sense to the addressees. This resolution may be phrased somewhat obliquely, a device that would serve several functions related to issues of honor in the society. There may be real social costs to some members of the community in accepting the proposed resolution, for there are always issues of relative status and maintenance of honor in resolving disputes. If the writer does not make a specific proposal, there is less risk that a decision against it will compromise the writer's honor and provoke an irreparable breach with the congregation. Moreover, by pointing in a relatively general way toward a possible resolution instead of laying it out in detail, the author leaves the addressees the freedom to tailor it to their situation. By leading the addressees right up to the point of the proffered resolution without specifying it in detail, the writer may save everyone concerned from potential loss of honor.

Look for the Variety of Possible Responses

There could be positive or negative responses to the proffered resolution. It is rare for any community as a whole to greet a proposed resolution to its local disagreements with unalloyed enthusiasm. The letter writer who is well attuned to the audience will be conscious of some possible reactions and will try to encourage or discourage them in shaping the letter. Sometimes our broader knowledge of the period and the culture helps us understand some of the background of those possible reactions.

Read the Main Body of the Letter as Preparation

Examine the main body of the letter as preparation for the proffered resolution. However interesting Paul's theological reflections in Romans or Galatians may be in their own right, they appear where they do for reasons beyond the simple delight of spinning out the theological implications of his own thought. (I do not deny that such pious and intellectual pleasures may have had a role, too.) The writer is weaving a theological context that accords with the writer's characteristic teachings, but is also calculated to gain the assent of a substantial portion of the audience addressed. By gaining their assent, the writer constructs a setting within which later references to the issue at hand and to the writer's proffered resolution are more likely to gain their approval as well.

Look for History and Future Prospects of Relationship

The letter emerges from, and builds on, some kind of relationship between the writer and the addressees, without which it would be meaningless. Even in a letter like Romans, there is a need to establish the existence of some relationship as a fundamental reason why the addressees might wish to pay some heed to the letter. A letter from a complete stranger carries no weight unless at least the possibility of relationship can emerge from it. All correspondence, then, gains its coherence at least partly from this larger context. We look at the letter to see what kind of relationship grounds its writing and what kind of new, revised, or strengthened relationship the writer hopes will emerge from it. It should be said that, while "relationship" tends to be a positive term in modern English, the reality so designated is as open to corruption as any other human reality. In considering relationships, the interpreter should be alert to issues of power and authority and to the possibility of abusive elements.

Look for Elements That Derive from the Gospel and Conversion

The reader needs to look for elements that derive from the gospel and the early Christian focus on μετάνοια/conversion, whether in the content or the presentation of the material. Since the NT letters are products of the Christian movement, we should expect to see the particular spirituality of that movement reflected in them in varying ways. This spirituality did not have a single expression; we cannot reduce it to any one version of it. Yet it remains a pervasive element. One is looking not merely for Christian motifs or ideas, but for a sense that God is doing new things and inviting humanity to be part of this renewal in unexpected and surprising ways. The dominant "tone" of early Christian speech is not command (though that is certainly not absent), but rather the offering of new opportunities of insight.

Pay Close Attention to the Persuasive Details

Carefully observe the details by which the rhetoric of the letter guides the addressees toward accepting the proffered resolution. As I have already suggested, I am using the term "rhetoric" here in a broad and basic sense. It covers the shaping of arguments, both rational and emotional, the use of pacing, the register of language employed, the subtle implications of pronoun usage, and so on. Particulars to look for include the following:

- Rational development of arguments. For example, what counts as authority? What prejudgments are assumed to be common to both writer and addressees? What chains of argument are employed?
- Emotional development of arguments. In what ways do the arguments touch on the addressees' basic fears, hopes, and loves?

- Use of conventional rhetorical structures at home in Hellenistic culture and/or in the Scriptures of Israel, whether learned formally or absorbed by general exposure. Look for traces of standard rhetorical genres and themes.
- Use of rhetorical figures as ways of governing the pace and emotional quality of the letter. Be conscious of the aesthetic consequences of shifts in language, of the choice of unusual vocabulary, of assonance, rhyme, and other sound-based figures, of asyndeton and polysyndeton, and so on. Issues of pacing may sometimes be best described in musical terms since they help separate sound from the sense of the words.
- Use of pronouns as ways of designating continuities and differences within and among communities. Become conscious of the effects of pronouns in suggesting different ways of relating the addressees to the writer, to one another, to the larger church and the world.

None of these suggestions, by itself, can guarantee an adequate reading of a letter. The chief goal is not to apply them mechanically or with the aim of creating a complete analysis of the letter in one particular respect. Instead, the main point is to awaken the mind of the modern reader and interpreter to some of the many ways in which we make connection with writings that were not originally directed to our own familiar orbit. No one is really likely to learn the basic concept of "reading other people's mail" from a list like this one. I am not trying to produce a complete definition of this process here but only to awaken some awareness of it in those who use it.

Theory and Practice

Theory and practice are twin siblings, essentially coeval, even if, in any given instance, one is necessarily born before the other. No complete theory of interpretation can be formulated in advance; it will always arise at least in part out of reflection on prior practice. And there is no practice of interpretation that does not immediately draw the interpreter to ask theoretical questions. Often enough, one finds that an interpreter's theory and practice actually diverge in ways the interpreter did not notice. We think we are doing one thing, but an astute observer, working only from our practice of interpretation, might form a rather different sort of theory and assume that we were consciously committed to it. While this can present a problem, it is also an ongoing opportunity for reflection and enrichment of both theory and practice.

In any historical discipline, theory and practice have to engage in an ongoing conversation in which each criticizes and refashions the other. The uniqueness of each moment in human history means that it could never have been predicted on the basis of theory. And yet the continuity of conditions and the finite (albeit quite broad) limitations on human creativity mean that there is indeed room to form generalizations about the past as in continuity with the present. A new theory will often reveal hitherto neglected aspects of the material. On the other hand, a new look at the material will often reveal the inadequacies of the current theoretical framework—and even suggest other theoretical approaches.

But how does one decide the value of such a proposal as the present one? What might constitute a demonstration that the ideas just presented are appropriate or fruitful in reading the NT letters? There will be no proof of indisputable validity, of course, because human intercourse is too complex to allow of the filtering out and separate analysis of all its details. This problem is exacerbated in the case of a small corpus of historical documents, such as the NT letters, where the number of "experiments" we can make to correct or confirm our hypotheses is limited. No one essay at interpretation is likely to produce a result that would make further interpretation unnecessary. If nothing else, the movements of time and language and culture will create a need for new interpretation. Still, one can reasonably ask how we recognize a competent interpretation or process of interpretation. The most important evidence that we can adduce in favor of any process of interpretation is its ability to honor the text in two ways: by acknowledging the text's independence and by offering an interpretation of it that is both economical and comprehensive.

In referring, first, to the text's independence, I mean to say that the text is a unique human artifact. To be sure, it shares with other texts the fact that it belongs to a particular place and time. And yet, given that human culture is never a perfectly unitary or exclusive reality, the text cannot be totally determined by that place and time. It is also determined by its specific circumstances, by the idiosyncrasies of its writer (and to some degree of its addressees), and by its distinctive way of reading and developing the available cultural corpus. The text then is significantly, though not totally, distinctive even within the world of its origin. In relation to the interpreter, then, the text is doubly independent, distanced by its culture and even from (or perhaps better, within) its culture. We cannot force it to give

Why does he use these words: "text" + "interpretor"?

answers to our own questions. And if we want a conversation with it, we must begin by listening to it respectfully in its own terms. A competent interpretation, then, needs to be focused on and led by the text itself, while also showing an ability to bring into play a knowledge of the cultural context as it is useful to the interpretation of the text.

Second, a competent interpretation needs to handle the text in a way that is both economical and comprehensive. To put this criterion another way, such an interpretation needs to be able to show the unity of the text (what holds it together) while also attending to the ways in which that unity is realized in the details of the text. An interpretation that makes admirable sense of one sentence will fail if it also makes nonsense of the surrounding paragraph. Sometimes, it may be possible to argue that the sentence in question ought to be interpreted in isolation from its literary environment; it is possible, for example, that some NT letters are in fact pastiches made up of originally independent elements. But barring strong arguments of such a kind, an interpretation that makes use only of a few elements in the text while ignoring much else is always suspect.

A competent interpretation of a text, then, is one that produces a reading of the text that is both comprehensive and specific. It will at least be aware of the document as a whole, and it will pay attention to its details as well as seek what holds it together. Furthermore, such an interpretation will draw its decisive arguments not just from the cultural or historical context but from clues within the text that suggest how the writer is in fact making use of the broader context.

Such an interpretation has a right to be recognized as competent, even when one does not agree with its results. To be genuinely fruitful in terms of the ongoing human conversation with the text, however, the interpretation will not rest here. A fruitful interpretation must recognize that it is we who are reading other people's mail. What do we get from this process for ourselves? This is not necessarily any easier to discern than the original range of meaning. It requires an ability and willingness to exercise, on ourselves and our world, a critical discernment at least as great as we are prepared to lavish on the study of the past. For precisely this reason, the conversation will always remain unfinished, open to new voices and insights. The particular interpretive effort always opens out onto the larger human and Christian conversation about meaning and identity, about God and the world.

For interpretation to be fruitful in this sense implies something more than an academic interest in the text. It does not have to be, in the present context, a specifically Christian interest, but it does need to be a concern for plumbing human values in the presence of the Holy. In other words, fruitful interpretation of any canonical text has certain spiritual implications for the interpreter and the interpreter's community. The interpreter is at risk of being surprised by the text and of having one's own preconceptions challenged by it. The interpreter must abandon the notion of making the text serve his or her modern purpose, whether that is to affirm some orthodoxy, ecclesiastical or academic, or to overturn it. Like all authentic conversation, fruitful interpretation must be open to genuine interaction, dispensing, as far as possible, with control, overt or covert, of the results.

The remaining portion of the present work consists primarily of three experimental readings. The first is a brief conclusion to the interpretation of Jude already begun. The others will focus on two letters different both from Jude and from each other: James and Romans. While I do not intend to drag the reader through every twist and turn of my own decades-long conversation with these texts, I will include enough evidence of my own changing perceptions to demonstrate the conversational character of the complex, analytical-and-synthetic method that I am proposing. It has been, throughout, a process of discovery and often of surprise.

Each of the three letters offers certain challenges and opportunities. The Letter of Jude has the advantage of being quite short and, having been relatively ignored in the past, of having fewer prior expectations attached to it (though it is not entirely devoid of them). The Letter of James, on the other hand, has the advantage of presenting a major challenge to the process I am offering here. James is often read as a miscellaneous collection of wise sayings. Even when exegetes do see it as having a certain amount of direction and purpose, their analyses differ enough among themselves that there is no consensus about rhetorical form or purpose. We shall see, then, whether the process I have laid out leads to a coherent reading of James that might qualify as competent in itself and give an opportunity for fruitful ongoing conversation.

The third and final example is Paul's Letter to Romans, which I treated briefly in my earlier book *Dirt, Greed, and Sex.*[14] I have long intended to explore the rhetorical character of Romans in more detail. My use of it here gives me an opportunity to do this while also going beyond it in trying to understand Romans as a whole and catch, in a new way, some of its enduring pertinence for modern Christian thought and life.

In each of these three cases, the approach I have proposed here will prove itself insofar as it can alert the practitioner of interpretation to new possibilities in reading the text and help us remain close to the text in the process of interpretation. Reading and interpretation will always remain unfinished. They are an expression of σωφροσύνη, of practical wisdom, rather than of logical or scientific necessity. Of course! They are, after all, an integral part of the life process of the reader and interpreter.

Notes

1. The copying and further circulation of such letters, however, was surely common from the beginning, sometimes with the express encouragement of the author; Harry Y. Gamble, *Books and Readers in the Early Church: A History of Early Christian Texts* (New Haven: Yale University Press, 1995), 97–98.

2. Paul Gibson, *Discerning the Word: The Bible and Homosexuality in Anglican Debate* (Toronto: Anglican Book Centre, 2000), 65–74.

3. J. B. Lightfoot, *Notes on the Epistles of St. Paul* (1895), 145, cited in C. F. D. Moule, *An Idiom-Book of New Testament Greek* (Cambridge: Cambridge University Press, 1971), 96.

4. Some NT letters may have originated as something other than letters, as is suggested, for example, with Hebrews, which could have originated as a sermon. When such a document was sent as a letter, however, there was presumably an occasion prompting the action, even if it was as minor as the happenstance that there was a ready means of delivery at hand—a rarer circumstance in the ancient world than in the modern.

5. This represents an intuitive and practical recognition on the part of speakers and writers that human beings learn and think with our emotions as well as our minds, something that is again coming to be recognized by psychologists; Daniel Goleman, *Emotional Intelligence* (New York: Bantam Books, 1995).

6. For the student, one ready point of access is the list of figures in Herbert Weir Smyth, *Greek Grammar* (Cambridge: Harvard University Press, 1959), 671–83.

7. Gamble, *Books and Readers,* 95–101.

8. This sense of connectedness could endure long afterward. Consider the example of the Scillitan martyrs, who, when asked the contents of their box, replied that it included "letters of Paul, a just man." It was not simply the content of the letters that was significant to them, but the sense of connection to their author. Gamble, *Books and Readers,* 150–51.

9. These communities remained close to the type posited for Jesus' own ministry by Gerd Theissen, *Sociology of Early Palestinian Christianity,* trans. John Bowden (Philadelphia: Fortress, 1978).

10. A good study of Paul's congregations is Wayne A. Meeks, *The First Urban Christians: The Social World of the Apostle Paul* (New Haven: Yale University Press, 1983).

11. "Here it is important to make clear what the formative element is in the largest as in many of the smallest units of the early Christian literature. We speak of it as the Good News. But it is Good News of a total and ultimate kind, and not only recited but effectively and dynamically demonstrated"; Amos N. Wilder, *Early Christian Rhetoric: The Language of the Gospel* (Cambridge: Harvard University Press, 1971), 29. Wilder stresses the "revelatory character of Jesus' parables" (72) and argues that Jesus' "world-dissolving vocation . . . accounts for the consummate shape of these sayings" (77).

12. Note, for example, two works casting doubt on Paul's knowledge of rhetorical theory: R. Dean Anderson Jr., *Ancient Rhetorical Theory and Paul* (Kampen, The Netherlands: Kok Pharos, 1996); Philip H. Kern, *Rhetoric and Galatians: Assessing an Approach to Paul's Epistle* (Cambridge: Cambridge University Press, 1998). As George A. Kennedy has noted, it may not make all that much difference whether a NT writer had formal rhetorical training, since rhetoric was so much a part of everyday Greek culture; *New Testament Interpretation through Rhetorical Criticism* (Chapel Hill: University of North Carolina Press, 1984), 9–10.

13. The very interesting exposition of Philippians by Cynthia Briggs Kittredge makes a similar observation about the importance of the appeal to Euodia and Syntyche: *Community and Authority: The Rhetoric of Obedience in the Pauline Tradition* (Harrisburg: Trinity Press International, 1998), 91–94.

14. L. William Countryman, *Dirt, Greed, and Sex* (Philadelphia: Fortress, 1988), 109–117.

6. Conversing with the Letter of Jude

The interpretive process suggested in the previous chapter will not necessarily change what I have already said about Jude. Most of what it advocates, I have already been doing. Indeed, as I suggested earlier, the process or approach I am advocating in this book has itself emerged in a kind of conversation between practice and theory over the years, and it should remain open to correction and improvement from either side. My impression is that we are never perfectly clear about either. Sometimes practice changes and makes theory rethink itself; sometimes the reverse happens.

We have looked at the Letter of Jude in terms of both rhetoric and the environment in which it initially arose. We have asked about the nature of the author's relationship to the addressees. We have read between the lines in an effort to see what sort of issue particularly prompted the writing of it and what resolution the author proposes. We have looked for elements of good news in a generally angry and polemical text. The one thing we have not done thus far is to read the letter back to front. It will be worth seeing whether this might add anything to our process.

Then there is the question of how this short document might enter, through the process of interpretation, into conversation with Christians in our own time. No one essay or book is going to exhaust that task or even encompass much of it, for the larger conversation between a community of faith and its sacred texts is much more diffuse and dispersed than that. Indeed, it has to be, because the community of faith is itself dispersed and varied and will approach its texts with a great variety of concerns and questions. Still, we can make a beginning by suggesting where the present reading of Jude suggests points of conversational interaction.

Reading Back to Front

Many commentators have found the Letter of Jude relatively formless and oblique.[1] It only hints at the issue that prompted its writing. It constructs no large theological arguments. It sounds angry enough that many readers may not expect rational argument in any case. Its brevity can seem more tantalizing than useful. It was precisely in my reading of Jude, however, that I first began to think that one might profit by reading such documents back to front. The moment when I began to take the closing benediction seriously made a critical difference in my perception of the work. There will be no need to repeat the whole interpretation of the letter given above, in chapter 4. We can simply look at the concluding elements to see how they participate in that changed reading.

The letter concludes (24–25) with a doxology in liturgical language. It is not unusual for early Christian writers to use doxologies or benedictions to signal that one is at or near the end of a work or of a major section in a work.[2] Sometimes later readers slide over them as a kind of formality; but liturgical language requires a particular kind of reading. The widespread notion among biblical scholars that it is merely prefabricated and only loosely related to its context is mistaken. Liturgical forms were not, by and large, fixed among early Christians before the third or fourth century. In the third century, for example, Hippolytus offered a prefabricated Eucharistic prayer, but noted that it was only for the use of those bishops who felt unable to create their own.[3] Liturgical language, then, was not simply a sacred space filler or a way of affirming the writer's piety. Nor was it merely the unthinking repetition of traditional elements. It was a distinct medium of communication into which a writer might shift as occasion dictated.

One should expect, then, that liturgical elements in early Christian writing typically have some specific relationship to the overall document. At the same time, one must recognize that liturgical language has a specific sort of relationship to speaker and audience. The speaker may stand over against the worshiping community in using such language—particularly, as here, in giving a blessing.[4] But the speaker is also identified with the community and uses language that the community recognizes as its own. Through the use of familiar vocabulary and forms (and sometimes through variation of them), the speaker evokes the community's sense of identity, which is deeply interconnected with its stance in relation to God. This is one reason for the apparently stereotyped nature of liturgical language, which is to say, its quality of being readily recognized. This did not prevent the early Christian speaker or writer from adapting it to the needs of the moment; indeed, it made the adaptations all the more recognizable.

Such adaptation is normally expressed through the choice of which elements in the liturgical tradition will be emphasized in prayer. In a period of social tension occasioned, for example, by war, a prayer that begins "O God of peace" will make one kind of point, while "Lord of Hosts and God of righteousness" will make quite another. Both expressions are thoroughly traditional; what the worshipping community listens for is the *selection* of traditional elements being employed in a particular setting. This selection must often operate rather subtly, for the context of prayer does not accommodate polemic. Prayer may allow polemic when the community is under grave attack or when there has been schism; a liturgical leader may then anathematize the opponents or pray for protection from enemies or for their conversion. But as long as the community is still intact, however precariously, liturgical language will typically avoid referring directly to internal tensions. Part of the purpose of common worship, after all, is to give concrete expression to the unity of the worshipers. When liturgical language does serve to exclude, it most often works indirectly. When the Nicene party in the fourth century changed the *Gloria patri* from the traditional "Glory to the Father through the Son in the Holy Spirit" to the form familiar today, this worked to exclude Arians from Nicene worship. But it made no reference to the Arians by name and thus avoided overt polemics.

It seems safe to say that the Letter of Jude is primarily a polemical work, given its whole catalog of insults and correspondingly meager theological development. Yet it is a document addressed to a religious community. If the concluding doxology has an integral relationship with the rest of the letter, we ought to look in it for precisely this kind of indirect exclusion of some point of view. This would be achieved not by direct refutation, but by emphasizing other elements in the shared faith of the community— elements incompatible with the views of the opponents. If so, what do we find?

The text of these two verses is somewhat uncertain. Given the propensity of liturgical texts to grow by accretion, however, we can probably accept the shortest and simplest version as close to the original. In translation, we have rendered it thus:

But to the one able to protect you from stumbling and to have you stand blameless, with joy, in the presence of his glory, to the only God our Savior, through Jesus Christ our Lord, [be] glory, majesty, might, and authority before every eon and now and to the eons of eons.[5] Amen. (24–25)

What, in particular, is being emphasized in this doxology? None of the language is particularly odd or individual to Jude. The term ἄπταιστος, "without stumbling," is found only here in the NT; but the imagery of falling as a symbol of losing relationship with God is common in early Christian writing.[6] Still, the text emphasizes a selection of elements from common stock. The language about "protecting you from stumbling," for example, suggests that the author wants the audience to remain, in some significant way, in their existing state, characterized metaphorically as an upright posture. Change would represent failure or regression.

To remain in their present, standing state means having direct access to God's own presence—"to have you *stand* blameless, with joy, in the *presence* of his glory." This may be understood in terms of future eschatology: God is able to do this in the last days. Or it may be understood in terms of the present life of the community, perhaps specifically of standing before God in the Eucharistic assembly.[7] In either case, the standing posture expresses freedom from fear and guilt, and it also implies dignity and joy. The presence of God is normally seen, in Jewish and Christian tradition, as fraught with danger. The author of 1 John thinks it a great thing if Christians can stand before God with παρρησία, "boldness, the ability to speak freely" (e.g., 3:21; 4:17). Jude goes a step further, promising that his audience will experience joy in God's presence.

This is, moreover, the presence of "the only God." Reference to the only God could serve to distinguish the God of Israel from the gods of the Greeks, but there is no obvious reason why Jude would be making that point. Greek religion does not otherwise seem to enter into this letter as a problem; indeed, its milieu seems to be thoroughly Jewish Christian.[8] Reference to the "only God," however, could also serve to emphasize God alone, as distinct from other supernatural beings thought to have power over humanity. If one dates the letter in the second century, one might think of the aeons (αἰῶνα) of gnostic thought or various kinds of angelic powers. But such dating is dubious at best, and a more broadly Jewish explanation is available. In ancient Jewish mysticism, one of the challenges facing heavenly travelers was the correct identification of celestial beings they might meet, beings sufficiently terrifying to be mistaken for God's own self.[9] Jude, then, may be emphasizing not only the ease and delight of Christian entry into the divine presence, but also that it is truly *God's* presence into which the faithful enter—not that of any subordinate being.

This God is described as "our Savior," a term also used of God else-where in the NT (e.g., Luke 1:47), but more often applied to Jesus. Jude's language, then, is not altogether strange, but the application of the term "Savior" to God serves to underline the doxology's emphasis on Christians' direct and joyful access to the divine presence. God is Savior; Jesus is the mediator rather than the originator of salvation. The phrase "through Jesus Christ our Lord" can be read either with "our Savior," expressing Jesus' role in God's saving of us, or with the ascription of praise that follows: "through Jesus Christ our Lord be ascribed glory. . . ." The position of the phrase allows us to read it in either way or, perhaps, in both. Jesus is both the mediator of salvation and the means by which we return praise to God. In either case, Jesus is a rhetorically subordinate figure here. The focus is on the one God.[10]

To God are then ascribed "glory, majesty, might, and authority." This is not an accidental accumulation of honorifics, but a list that covers all the bases of power and legitimacy. God's authority is, first, divine, as the term δόξα ("glory") suggests. In older Greek, the term meant "opinion, repute"; but ancient Jews and Christians often used it as designating a divine attribute, even though they could still use the term in its older sense as well and even play on the tension between the two. "Majesty" suggests an imperial image of God, normal for the period in which Jude wrote. "Might" specifies that God has the power to do whatever God wills. "Authority" asserts the legitimacy of God's exercise of that power. Again, we see a strong reaffirmation of the centrality and sufficiency of God. The closing passage of the doxology affirms that this centrality and sufficiency of God is eternal. It precedes all creation, is active now, and will continue in force forever. This emphasis on God's absolute priority works to exclude the possibility of there being any other powers that Christians must appease.

All in all, the doxology emphasizes, in ways appropriate to liturgical language, God's unique power and priority and the Christian community's directness of access to God. None of this would probably have seemed revolutionary within the community's liturgical context, but it was a sig-nificant claim (and a significantly *Christian* claim) in terms of the larger culture, which tended to assume that the great gods, much like the emperor, were difficult to access. And it serves to point to a particular direction. Why would Jude focus on precisely these elements out of the undoubtedly much broader liturgical store available to him? What might be challenging these principles in the context of his addressees? If we read the whole letter with these questions in mind, I do not think we will find different answers than we have already found. Indeed, we found reason to ask these same questions in the first few verses of the letter as well. But in my own experience, it was my reading of the letter back to front that first alerted me to look for rival divinities (in this case, angelic powers) and for elements that might interfere with the existing confidence of the congregation in the presence of God (by suggesting that they needed a further, angelic mediation).

Before leaving a back-to-front reading, however, let us back up a step further and look at the sentences immediately preceding the doxology. The "end" of any document may not be easy to identify precisely.[11] Many ancient Greek letters, though not Jude, send greetings to and from individuals in or related to the community addressed. Are these, when they appear, the "end" of the letter or just a postscript? In some cases, they might have significance; yet they are likely to appear whether they have any pressing relation to the other contents of the letter or not. Similarly, a religious writer might feel impelled to close with a doxology or benediction regardless of how closely it might be tied to the purpose of writing. In order to give ourselves a firmer sense of an "end" to use as a base for reading the Letter of Jude as a whole, it will be useful to look a little further back.

The sentence directly before the doxology runs like this:

And on some take pity[12] as they dispute [*or* as they waver *or* as you dispute], and some save, snatching them out of the fire, and on some take pity with fear, hating even the garment soiled from the flesh. (22–23)[13]

Here Jude's use of purity language can be taken literally, if we are right in assuming a fully Jewish-Christian context. But the reference to purity also has the effect of suggesting that the opponents who are thereby being marginalized carry with them the risk of alienating the community from God. Impurities such as those that attached to sexual intercourse were not, of course, intrinsically sinful; but the Torah assumes a sharp separation between the Temple, which is entirely pure, and ordinary human defilement. The two are to be kept apart. Insofar as the Christian community is a site of intimacy with God and therefore comparable to the Temple, it must be cautious about purity, taking care that it is always dealt with appropriately.[14]

If we step back one sentence further, to verses 20–21, we find elements that will reappear in the doxology:

> But you, beloved, building yourselves up on your most holy faith, praying in [the] Holy Spirit, keep yourselves in God's love, expecting the mercy of our Lord Jesus Christ for eternal life. (20–21)

The readers/hearers are to remain in continuity with the faith they have already professed, finding strength and stability in it. This is affirmed when they pray in the Spirit, which gives them an experience of intimacy with God, confirming God's love for them. By keeping God's love central in their faith, they can look forward with confidence to its full realization, through Jesus, in eternal life. The use of an early Trinitarian formula serves, like the final doxology, to focus all attention on God or God's most intimate agents.[15]

Interestingly, one early papyrus and a manuscript of the ancient Bohairic Coptic version of Jude omit Jude's directions in verses 22–23. Without them, the continuity between verses 20–21 and the closing doxology is more obvious. That is not to say that the directives are not original; the evidence is good enough to justify retaining them. But even a temporary bracketing of verses 22–23 gives us a sense of how they interrupt what amounts to a celebration of the community's intimacy with God in order to attend to something that the author judges a threat to it.

Our examination of the concluding three sentences in the Letter of Jude raises useful questions for a front-to-back reading: (1) Why does Jude stress the exclusive centrality of God (with Jesus in close proximity)? (2) Why does he present the relationship of Christians to God in terms of intimacy? (3) What is the "new" teaching that he thinks contradicts the readers' "most holy faith," and whence does it arise? (4) Why does he use purity language to warn his readers about the opponents? (5) Why does he feel that embracing the opponents' teaching would compromise a Christian's opportunity to stand with joy in the presence of God's glory? Our reading above, in chapter 4, has dealt with these questions. Reading Jude back to front would simply have made them clearer from the beginning.

To be sure, none of this would necessarily have alerted us to look for sexual intercourse with angels as an element in the praxis of the itinerant teachers. That is part of the unpredictable, historical specificity of the occasion. But neither is it the main concern of the letter. Jude is not engaging in a theological argument about the meaning or advisability of such activities. He assumes his theological principles rather than making them explicit. The letter aims rather at producing a certain action on the part of the addressees: the expulsion of the itinerants from the community and the neutralizing of their influence. Because he is clear about his own position and assumes that the addressees will understand and agree with it, he does not argue the case. He does not even need to make the position he is attacking completely clear.

Entering into Conversation with Jude

We have seen a variety of tensions and complexities in the Letter of Jude focused around such issues as the following:

- A teaching of direct access to God in Jesus versus a praxis of recourse to sexual intimacy with angelic powers as a means to heavenly access.
- A certain confidence in the stability of the local Christian community versus a sense of crisis that calls forth expressions of anxiety and anger.
- A polemical rhetoric enlisted in the cause of gospel peace and joy.
- And tradition being invoked in the name of freedom.

How are we to assist this complexity to become available to conversation with the equally great complexities of our own time?

Jude confronts us quite directly with the issue of boundaries in communities of faith. He seems to stand in direct contradiction to a modern mainstream Christian desire to practice openness and foster a variety of understandings of Christianity. Perhaps he summons us in conversation, then, to ask about possible limits to such a stance. For there can be no doubt that there are such limits, even for the most committed liberal. Mainstream churches would not be eager to give a platform to such as Fred Phelps, for example, or the leaders of the racist "Christian Identity" movement. Would we even reject such people if they were already among us? We should have to take the possibility seriously. Liberal Christianity, which originated as a softening of boundaries, sometimes consoles itself with the fantasy that, if everyone is allowed to speak, no one will say anything harmful. Jude at least confronts the possibility that speech may do harm and that not all teachings are in fact compatible with the good news, even when the speakers are self-professed Christians.

The Letter of Jude also challenges the common liberal assumption that tradition and freedom are necessarily opposed to each other. If the tradition is itself already a tradition of freedom, it may be that change will only mean a reduction of liberty. Let us assume for the moment that Jude's overall understanding of Christianity was close to Matthew's (we have no evidence to say either that it was or was not, but I account them both as Jewish Christian). Would the addition of a major role for angelic beings tend toward greater liberty? Or would it constitute a pulling away from what Irenaeus would later call "the brevity of faith and love"[16] toward an elaborate angelology with correspondingly elaborate rites by which Christians might seek access to God? A religion proclaiming "You shall practice intimacy with angelic beings" as a fundamental directive is of doubtful compatibility with one that places the love of God and neighbor, without reference to angels, in the foreground.

This is not a trivial issue. Christians have always felt a pull toward making our religion more precise, more definite, more quantifiable. Where the Jesus of the Synoptics seems to be breaking barriers between humanity and God, Christians have been adept at rebuilding them in the form of increasingly elaborated and more stringently enforced orthodoxies. The Athanasian Creed turned Nicene Christianity into the required pass for the gates of heaven. Western Christians long excluded one another from Communion over fine points of Eucharistic doctrine; many still do. Most Christian traditions still hold, in some form or other, that heterosexuals enjoy most-favored status in the reign of God. If my reading of Jude is correct, he would actually stand on an unexpected side of all these issues, on the side of spiritual freedom and simplicity rather than dogma.

This, of course, is the exact opposite of what most people have assumed—and of what I had always assumed before I began to take Jude's concluding doxology seriously. I am, indeed, almost embarrassed to be suggesting something that may strike my readers as bizarre. And yet such a reading of Jude is in harmony with concerns we know from other first-century Christian authors—and even, counting Irenaeus, some second-century ones. Jesus' ministry shocked the religiously punctilious because it deprived them of their assumed superiority over the religiously lax. Jesus associated with all alike and offered a more direct way to God. This has been a perennial embarrassment for Christians, particularly for the religiously punctilious among us; and we have repeatedly tried to remove it by multiplying requirements. The problem does not come from outside influences—from Judaism or Gnosticism or whatever—but from the nature of religion itself, including Christian religion.[17] Jude is neither a liberal nor a conservative in modern terms. He is a traditionalist dedicated to simplicity and freedom.

Part of the continuing difficulty many of us have with Jude, however, goes back to his polemical language. Modern scholars have long viewed

Jude as a champion of second-century orthodoxy. I have already suggested why I think that reading is mistaken. But his style was and is adopted by those who defend orthodoxies, whether of second-century or sixteenth-century or other origins. And polemical style has a tendency to beget polemical religion—religion that no longer needs to justify its hostility to dissidents by appealing to the centrality of gospel freedom, but can simply claim that, because the tradition is the tradition, it is automatically justi-fied in repressing any disagreement. Jude, of course, says nothing of the sort; and yet I cannot help feeling that there is a path, however circuitous, that leads from Jude to the Inquisition and to various contemporary Chris-tian fundamentalisms. The tool Jude chose to defend gospel freedom turns out to be better fitted to the purposes of the gospel's opponents. Conserva-tive or traditionalist Christians who draw encouragement from Jude would do well to think carefully about whether they are in fact betraying what he ultimately stands for. If one cannot connect the tradition one is main-taining persuasively with the joy of standing in God's presence—and that not just in one's own spiritual experience but in that of the people one addresses—one cannot claim to be standing in Jude's succession.

What redeems this letter for me, nonetheless, is Jude's repeated expres-sions of confidence in the Christian community he addresses. The central thread of his argument is not, finally, "Do this because I say so" or even "Do this because it is right." It is "Do this because you know what inti-macy with God you already enjoy, and you have no need to risk it for the sake of novelty." In short, Jude appeals to the spiritual experience of the Christian people, gained in their conversion to the way of Jesus, and their ability to reason from it and form judgments based on it. As long as that is the case, I am happy to remain in conversation with him. Indeed, I have gained by the conversation.

Notes

1. By contrast, Watson, *Invention, Arrangement, and Style,* 28–79, argues that it is a well-formed and successful example of deliberative rhetoric in terms recognized by ancient rhetorical theorists.
2. E.g., doxologies serve such purposes in Heb 13:20–21; Eph 3:20–21; and Rom 16:25–27 (though it may not be original); benedictions in Rom 15:13; 2 Cor 13:13; Gal 6:18.
3. Hippolytus, *Apostolic Tradition* 10.
4. The passage is technically a doxology, ascribing praise to God; but the reassuring connection it makes between God and the addressees makes it function also as a benediction.

5. I have translated the final phrases in this way instead of the more usual "before all time and for ever and ever" simply to leave open the possibility that Jude is reasserting his claim over language also used by gnostic Christians. I do not, however, see other signs of gnostic teaching in his description of his opponents.

6. Plumptre, *St. Peter and St. Jude,* 169, 215, points out that the usual English translation "without falling" is inexact and that "stumbling" is in fact a milder threat than "falling."

7. Justin Martyr reported that Christians stood for prayer at the Sunday Eucharist; *First Apology* 67.

8. Some later mss. do refer to the addressees in v. 1 as Gentiles; but the rest of the letter gives no support to such a reading. The one other suggestion of Greek religion is the allusion to Aphrodite in v. 13; but it is vague and general.

9. Gershom G. Scholem, *Major Trends in Jewish Mysticism* (New York: Shocken Books, 1961), 51–54.

10. Jude shares with the Letter of James this focus on theology rather than Christology.

11. Watson, *Invention, Arrangement, and Style,* 67–77, identifies vv. 17–23 as the *peroratio* of Jude's work, which he conceives more in terms of an address than a letter. My own approach leads to a similar conclusion, though without the prior assumption that Jude is following a specific contemporary rhetorical model.

12. Other mss. read, "And some test/reprove . . ." I incline toward "pity" not only from its appearance in Sinaiticus and Vaticanus, but also because it would be the more difficult reading from the perspective of later scribes, for whom heretics were more to be rebuked than pitied.

13. The text of these two verses is uncertain; see above, chapter 4, note 23.

14. We have no reason to think that Jude's community sought as complete a separation from sexual impurity as that at Qumran; but they can hardly have ignored the problem if acts that created impurity were being recommended as a means for entering the divine presence.

15. It is impossible to say exactly how Jude understood the relationship between God, Jesus, and Holy Spirit. But the threefold formula, in early Christianity, antedates any clear Trinitarian doctrine. E.g., see the second-century apologist Theophilus of Antioch, *Ad Autolycum* 2.10, 15.

16. "Not by the much-speaking of the Law, but by the brevity of faith and love, men were to be saved"; Irenaeus, *Demonstration of the Apostolic Doctrine* 87, trans. J. Armitage Robinson (London: SPCK, 1920).

17. L. William Countryman, *Living on the Border of the Holy: Renewing the Priesthood of All* (Harrisburg: Morehouse Publishing, 1999), 33–46.

7. Interpreting the Letter of James

Reading Back to Front

The Letter of James, like that of Jude, is difficult to locate precisely in the history of early Christianity. As with Jude, scholars over the last few decades have increasingly dated it early rather than late. The dating is not a matter of great moment for my reading of the text. I see it as written during a period, either before or after the First Jewish War, when there is no open warfare and as addressed to Jewish-Christian congregations scattered in smaller cities and villages, probably in the Syrian-Judean countryside.

The Letter of James presents problems of understanding similar to those of Jude. The contents seem miscellaneous and the language stereotyped. Just as Jude could seem to be little more than a collection of insults, biblical references, and liturgical phrases, James can be read as a rambling screed of good advice, erupting occasionally into ill temper. Such moral instruction, to which scholars have come to apply the Greek term παραίνεσις ("paraenesis"), may seem to have—and to require—no particular literary or rhetorical structure. And it has thus far proved impossible to achieve any great degree of consensus about the literary organization of the Letter of James.[1] Such apparent lack of organization may be thought to correspond to a lack of specific occasion as well. Paraenesis often, though not always, seems to take the form of generalized good advice rather than a response to a particular issue.[2] James is also thought of as a "wisdom" writer, belonging to a tradition that goes back to and through Proverbs to ancient Near Eastern roots. The Book of Proverbs seems to have only a minimum of intellectual or rhetorical organization.

Should we expect more of James? We should certainly be alert to the possibility that the whole process suggested in this work is ill-suited to some of the NT letters. They are a varied group of documents, and we cannot a priori reduce them to a single pattern.[3]

Still, we can at least be open to the possibility that the Letter of James had an occasion, a specific array of circumstances that evoked its writing, and that it therefore has a point to make—the kind of point that can help generate a rhetorical whole. The occasion might be broadly framed—a sense that the audience needed to hear anew what wise and moral behavior looked like for Christians in the circumstances of their time. Or it might be more specific—an occasion created by current events or conflicts among the addressees. The fact that the subjects touched on in the letter are in fact fairly limited in number may suggest a higher degree of focus than has usually been found here.[4] The Letter of James was sufficiently significant to its first readers for them to preserve it. While this might have been for general purposes of instruction, as with the Book of Proverbs or the "Two Ways" document that appears in both the *Didache* and the *Letter of Barnabas,* we should hold open the possibility that it played some more specific and critical role in the development of the community addressed. A back-to-front reading may then reveal what the challenges were.

The letter concludes with a series of reflections that circle around a common cluster of themes: patience/endurance, sin, sickness, prayer, healing/restoration, and confession. All these, one notices, touch on things that can go wrong in both the individual and the body politic and how they may be set right again. The way in which these themes are braided together is typical of most of the letter. There is no linear progression from one to another. At times, the links are not obvious, and we may well question which of the connections we identify are really there in the text and which are of our own creation. In the following discussion, I will try to remain close to what is explicit in the text in identifying the relationships.

It may be helpful to say a word about my translation of James in relation to current linguistic usage. I call attention to the presence of women in the congregation by translating ἀδελφοί as "sisters and brothers." This is a well-founded translation of the term, and one can scarcely doubt that there were women among the letter's addressees. James, in fact, shows his awareness of women in the early Christian community by using female imagery for God (1:18), by the phrase "brother or sister in need" (2:15), and by paralleling the example of Abraham with that of Rahab (2:20–26). James's awareness of women, however, does not mean that he has entirely reversed or overturned the patriarchal assumptions of the culture. He repeatedly uses the term ἀνήρ ("man, adult male")[5] in ways suggesting that he thought of his addressees first and foremost as males. This would hardly be unusual in the ancient Mediterranean context, where men were seen as being public persons, active in the community assembly, in a way that women generally were not. I have chosen not to conceal the male bias of the language here. The same may legitimately be said of Paul; and I shall use the same device (in chap. 8) in translating Romans.

Let us begin with the end of the work, the closing sentence:

> [5:19]My brothers and sisters, if anyone among you goes astray from the truth and someone turns him around, [20]let him know that the person who has turned a sinner out of his road of error will save his soul from death and "will cover a multitude of sins." (Prov 10:12)

In a way, this closing sentence seems quite unrelated to the rest of the work. The verb ἐπιστρέφω ("turn") has not appeared previously in the letter; πλανάω ("go astray") has appeared only once (in 1:16); the related πλάνη ("error") not at all. The association of sin with death, however, does appear in 1:15, the expression "to save a soul" in 1:21, and "truth" in 1:18 and 3:14—suggesting that there may, after all, be some connection between earlier parts of the letter and this concluding sentence.

Another problem with this final sentence is that it is internally ambiguous. Who is commanded to *know*? The sinner or the person turning the sinner back? Again, whose soul is being saved? The sinner's or that of the person who turns the sinner away from "his road of error"? Whose multitude of sins will be covered? None of this is made explicit. This may be the result of poor composition. The ambiguous antecedent is a problem that to some degree dogs every writer. On the other hand, writers may be inclined to be more than normally careful with their closing words. What if we suppose that the ambiguity is deliberate? Since we do see some connections with the beginning of the letter, we might guess that James is actually summarizing the purpose of his writing here. He is seeking to turn some Christians whom he sees as being on the road of error back to the community of the church. He presents this as a general goal for Christians, but it also fits the specific character of the present writing. He avoids claiming, however, that he (or anyone who turns another back to the truth) is a superior dispenser of grace. Indeed, he leaves open the question of who is the primary beneficiary of such action: the sinner who turns back, or the one who initiates the turning.

If we think of this sentence as a possible key to the rest of the Letter of James, we may expect the rest of the letter to be framed in a similarly self-abnegating manner, in which the author refuses to set himself over against the audience. James's frequent address to the audience as "brothers and sisters" reinforces this sense of fundamental equality. We shall also expect that the purpose of the letter will be to bring about significant change in at least some members of the audience. The change will be at least partly a change of behavior, since the reference to the sinner's "road" has connotations of "walking," a common rabbinic and early Christian term for "behavior." At the same time, the author also wants a change in perspective and understanding, for the sinner is said to wander away "from the truth" and to follow a "road of error." When we move to a "forward" reading of this letter, then, we shall want to look for behaviors the author wishes to change and the worldview he evokes for changing them. We shall also want to see in what ways the author either continues to place himself on a level with his audience or breaks with this pattern.

Preceding this final sentence of the letter is a short discourse on sickness, sin, forgiveness, and the power of prayer. At first glance, it seems quite unrelated to the closing sentence:

> 5:13Someone among you is suffering—let him pray. Someone is in good spirits—let him sing psalms. 14Someone among you is sick—let him call for the elders of the assembly and let them pray over him, after anointing him with oil in the Lord's name. 15And the prayer of faith will save the sick person, and the Lord will raise him up. Even if he may have committed sins, forgiveness will be extended to him. 16So confess [your] sins to one another and pray for one another so that you may be healed. The energetic entreaty of a just person has a great deal of strength. 17Elijah was a person who suffered like us. And he prayed with prayer for it not to rain; and it did not rain on the land for three years and six months. 18And he prayed again; and heaven gave rain, and the land sprouted with its produce.

The only significant points of *verbal* repetition between this passage and the final sentence of the letter are references to sin and the use of the verb σώζω ("save"). There are, however, other interesting elements of continuity.

One is the matter of equality. Just as James declined to set himself above the audience in 5:19–20, he stresses the great prophet Elijah's likeness to the audience, rather than his difference. And despite the special role of the presbyters, one comes away from the passage feeling that it is not primarily a matter of a few officials praying for the rest, but of a community of equals, who secure healing and forgiveness for themselves in the very process of extending them to one another. The ambiguous mutuality we found in the closing sentence appears here, too. The addressees will benefit one another by confessing their sins to each other and by praying for one another. There is a pregnant ambiguity in "pray for one other so that you may be healed." It reads quite differently from the potential alternative: "pray for the sick that they may be healed." The person praying is included in the healing as much as the person for whom prayer is made.

The connection made here between sickness and sin is potentially significant, like the connection made in the final sentence of the letter between sin and error. Like Paul (1 Cor 11:30) and other early Christians, James is prepared to accept a connection between sin and ill health. His emphasis, however, is not on the condemnation of the sick, but on the availability of God's grace for healing and forgiveness.

Directly before this passage stands an isolated sentence on what appears at first to be a completely unrelated topic:

> 5:12But above all, my sisters and brothers, do not swear—neither by heaven nor by earth nor with any other oath; but let your "yes" be yes and your "no" no, so that you do not fall under judgment.

Two things need to be said about this sentence. One is that it takes up, in general subject matter, though not in vocabulary, an earlier concern in the letter, the governing of the tongue. By interrupting here, it also has a marked effect on the pacing of the conclusion, which might most easily be thought of in musical terms as one final return to an earlier theme, introduced here in the middle of the letter's "coda." Its aesthetic effect on the forward motion of the passage is much like that created by Schubert when he interrupts the conclusion of the last movement of his *Octet* (D803) by reintroducing, just before the final *accelerando*, the relatively threatening bars that open the movement. While such a comparison is, of course, farfetched historically, I suspect that we can often express the relatively abstract issues of rhetorical pacing more clearly by such musical comparisons.

At the same time, the sentence is tied to what follows by its reference to judgment. For James, lying speech is a principal form of wrongdoing. It brings one under judgment of the kind that might well lead to sickness. It requires the prayer of faith to save the sinner and gain forgiveness. There may even be a kind of wordplay involved in this reference to judgment. In place of ὑπὸ κρίσιν ("under judgment"), some mss. have εἰς ὑπόκρισιν ("into hypocrisy"). While this variant is probably an error or a deliberate scribal "improvement" of the text to make clear that James is speaking of the sin of hypocrisy, it highlights the implicit wordplay that is already in the text. In Matthew's Gospel, which contains materials probably known to James either in writing or in the form of underlying oral traditions,[6] hypocrisy is virtually treated as the root sin of the pious, a fundamental denial of the reality of God. What one does with the tongue is a profound reflection of what is in the heart.

In one final "backward" step, before we turn to read James from the beginning, we find a short discourse on patience or endurance:

> 5:7So be patient, brothers and sisters, till the Lord's arrival. Look! the farmer waits on the valuable produce of the earth, patient for it till getting the early and the late rains. 8You be patient, too. Make your hearts firm, because the Lord's arrival has drawn near. 9Do not complain of each other, sisters and brothers, so that you may not be judged. See! the judge is standing at the doors. 10As an example of suffering and patience, brothers and sisters, take the prophets who spoke in the Lord's name. 11Look! we call those who have endured blessed. You have heard of Job's endurance, and you have seen the Lord's end [or goal], that the Lord is full of compassion and merciful.

This passage is tied to what follows in several ways: the reference to suffering, echoed at the beginning of 5:13; the agricultural references; the use of the prophets as an example, echoed in the reference to Elijah's prayer in 5:17–18; the reference to judgment, echoed in 5:12; and the mutuality of not complaining about one another, echoed in the later advice to confess to and pray for one another and in the ambiguity of the final sentence as to who benefits from the return of a straying sinner.[7]

To return to musical analogy, the complex use of recurrent motifs in James is not unlike Wagner's use of leitmotiv, in which short distinctive thematic elements are interwoven in new and varied combinations. It produces a rich texture and a sense of unity even when the text appears to jump without connection from one topic to another—from patient endurance to oaths to sickness and prayer and finally to the recalling of the straying sinner. Even through these changes of topic, certain elements of continuity show up. The author promotes mutuality among his audience—and includes himself, the prophets, and Job in that same mutuality.

The breaking of this mutuality, often through speech, is a serious sin and liable to bring one under judgment. Such judgment may already be manifest in sickness or other misfortune; but the addressees are to respond to such circumstances with patience, endurance, mutual confession, and prayer for one another. Above all, the great aim of the letter is to turn around some situation among the readers of the work, some sickness in their mutual life. If successful, the letter will save souls from death and cover a multitude of sins. All this is presented in the loosely organized and rather proverbial style of paraenesis, making heavy use of traditional (and therefore familiar) material and designed to encourage reflection on the part of the hearers.

Reading in Forward Motion

Endurance and Trust

With these ideas in mind, we now move to the beginning of the letter to see whether comparable concerns appear in the introduction and body of the work, to analyze how the author handles them rhetorically, and to look for more concrete indications of the nature of the issues that form the occasion of the writing. The salutation of the letter is simple, but rhetorically significant:

> [1:1]James, slave of God and of the Lord Jesus Christ, to the twelve tribes in the Dispersion, greetings.

The author's claim to be a slave is probably, like that of Jude, a claim to a certain intimacy with God and with Christ and to a role as their agent. It asserts the author's claim to be heard. At the same time, it subordinates the author to the shared faith that grounds the community rather than focusing on his personal authority. Similarly, James's habit of addressing his audience as ἀδελφοί ("brothers and sisters") suggests a certain basic equality with them.[8]

In the salutation, James defines the addressees as "the twelve tribes in the Dispersion." While the audience is probably Jewish Christian,[9] his reference to them as "the twelve tribes" is as much theological metaphor as a literal statement of descent. It emphasizes their identity as the chosen people of God and heirs of God's promises. It also suggests a reunion of Israel and Judah and may therefore hint at the presence of Samaritans as well as

Jews among the addressees. Yet, wherever the addressees may be located, they are presently to be understood, either literally or metaphorically, as living in the Dispersion, not in the promised land.

The addressees are thus in tension between God's promise and their present circumstances, and this points the direction of what follows:

> [1:2]Consider it all joy, my brothers and sisters, when you fall into various trials, [3]knowing that the testing of your faith produces endurance. [4]And let endurance have [its] work mature[10] (*or* perfect), so that you may be mature (*or* perfect) and complete, lacking in nothing.

The emphasis on endurance, as we already know, will also figure prominently at the close of the letter. It suggests that James is writing in a general context of social opposition to the Christian community, in which some are experiencing at least the threat of disadvantage related to their Christian identity.

James weds to this concern for endurance another concern for wisdom:

> [2:5]And if any of you does lack wisdom, let him ask [it] from the God who simply gives to all and does not reproach; and it will be given him. [6]But let him ask with trust (*or* faith), not wavering at all. For the person who doubts is like a wave of the sea, blown by the wind and tossed about. [7]For let that person not suppose that he will get anything from the Lord—[8]a two-souled[11] man, unstable in all his ways.

Again, we see how the conclusion of the letter echoes the beginning. At the end, James stresses how powerful is the prayer of a just man. Here it is the prayer of those who trust that is powerful, perhaps because trust reflects the wisdom of a correct understanding of God, who is not primarily judge or king here, but the one "who simply gives to all and does not reproach."

The following passage can be read as describing the behavior of Christians who are *not* doubters or waverers:

> [1:9]But let the brother who is poor rejoice in his exaltation, [10]and the one who is rich in his humiliation, because he will pass away like a wildflower. [11]For the sun rises with its heat and dries up the vegetation, and its flower falls off and the elegance of its appearance is lost. So, too, the rich person will wither as he goes.

Single-mindedness allows both the poor and the rich Christian to see that
their true worth is found elsewhere than in their social status. The poor
are exalted, perhaps by some special value assigned to them in the community James addresses (though 2:1–4 may contradict that possibility),
but certainly by the assurance that God gives equally to all. The rich are
humbled by recognizing that, for all their wealth, they are as mortal as
anyone else; but this, too, is a liberating realization. In short, poor and
rich are brought, in the Christian community, to a common level of self-
understanding, in which their social status ceases to be of primary importance. We should notice, however, that James devotes considerably more
attention to the rich here than to the poor. Perhaps they pose a more significant problem.[12]

This line of argument directly furthers James's call for endurance, giving
both groups reason not to take their trials with ultimate seriousness. It also
continues the theme of wisdom—this recognition of their relativity and
their common mortality being an aspect of the wisdom that will see them
through the trials. It also raises, for the first time in the letter, the theme of
rich and poor. Although we did not encounter this theme in examining the
conclusion of the Letter of James, it receives a quite emphatic treatment in
the passage just preceding that conclusion, where the rich are sharply condemned for withholding the wages of their laborers. Perhaps we should
have been more extensive in our "backward" reading of the letter. The
theme will also appear again at the beginning of chapter 2, making it one
of the recurrent themes of the letter as a whole. In the present passage, the
vivid simile of the wildflower, alluding to Isaiah 40:7, should serve to
lodge the topic securely in the reader/hearer's memory for future reference.

With this, James returns to speaking about trials:

> 1:12Blessed is the man who endures tribulation, because, once proved,
> he will get the wreath of life that [God] promised to those who love
> him. 13Let no one, while experiencing trials, say "God is putting me
> through a trial." For God is untried by (or inexperienced in) evils;
> and God himself puts no one through a trial. 14But each person is put
> through trials by his own desire, being drawn out and enticed [by it].
> 15Then desire conceives and gives birth to sin; and sin, when con-
> summated, gives birth to death.

James identifies the problem his audience is experiencing not with the
external events that prompt it, but with their own unwise desires. If a person's desire runs toward earthly security, it will make troubles hard to

endure. One becomes a waverer like the "two-souled" person, the opposite of the one who asks with trust, for the trusting person focuses not on social status, but on the reversal of that status implicit in Christian faith. The person who endures is blessed (as James will reiterate at the end of the letter, in 5:11) because endurance is founded on right appreciation of life and trust in God; such a person will therefore be garlanded, in a sign of victory. There is no occasion to reproach God for sending trials when it is really our own failing that turns events into trials.

If God does not give trials, what does God give? James returns to the theme of the God who gives freely:

> 1:16Make no mistake, my beloved sisters and brothers. 17Every good giving and every complete (*or* perfect) gift is from above, coming down from the Father of the lights, with whom there is no variation or shadow cast by turning. 18He has freely given birth to us by a word of truth, so that we would become the firstfruits of his creatures.

James associates God's complete reliability with that of the fixed stars. Astronomical imagery pervades the whole passage, beginning with Μὴ πλανᾶσθε ("Make no mistake"), which echoes the Greek term for "planets," the wandering or straying stars. God, by contrast, is one with whom there is no "variation" (παραλλαγή, a technical term of astronomy).[13] The phrase τροπῆς ἀποσκίασμα ("shadow cast by turning") is less clear, but probably has astronomical reference, too.[14]

James's reference to God as giving birth[15] to us provides a female image corresponding to the metaphor "Father of the lights." It also contrasts the earlier image of desire giving birth to sin and sin to death with God's giving birth to the Christian community to become firstfruits of the creation. This distinction is directly related to the addressees' ability to endure trials, since it defines their self-understanding. Desire can produce only disappointment and death. God—and therefore trust in God—can produce life. This demands a complete reversal of the usual worldly scale of values—the kind of reversal that can produce poor Christians who rejoice in their exaltation and rich ones who rejoice in their humiliation.

At this point, James moves to a discourse on listening and doing. It can be read as quite general; but since the context is a document that will be read aloud, it implies a suggestion to the addressees as to how they might hear the letter itself. Before moving on to take this passage up, however, we may suitably pause to ask how the beginning of the letter matches what we previously saw of the letter's conclusion. We noted that, in the conclusion, the author encouraged mutuality in the congregation's life, that he spoke of sin as leading to judgment and sickness, that he called on the congregation to respond with patience and endurance, with confession and prayer. The introduction to the letter is not identical, yet its concerns are related, sometimes rather closely so. It talks about the need for endurance, reversal of status between rich and poor in the Christian context (cf. the need for mutuality stressed in the conclusion), the danger of sin leading to death, the power of prayer, the dangers of wavering, and above all, the uncompromising generosity of God.

We still do not know whether particular circumstances in the community are being addressed and, if so, what they are. But the social disadvantages of being a Christian are at least a part of the overall background. We have a suggestion that some members of the congregation believe that God is sending their troubles as part of a program of testing the people. James, however, holds that their own inappropriate desires are the real problem.

Listening, Doing, Speaking

James now provides some extended hints about how to read this letter:

1:19Know [this], my beloved brothers and sisters. And let every person be quick to listen, slow to talk, slow at anger. 20For a man's anger does not accomplish God's righteousness. 21Therefore, putting aside with gentleness all filth and excess of evil, accept the implanted word that can save your souls.

22And become doers of the word and not just hearers, fooling yourselves—23because if anyone is a hearer of the word and not a doer, this person is like a man who contemplates his natural face in a mirror. 24For he contemplates himself and goes away and immediately forgets what he looked like. 25But the person who stoops to look into the full (or perfect) law of freedom and sticks by it, having become not a hearer of forgetfulness but the doer of a work, this person will be blessed in his doing.

26If anyone thinks of being religious without getting control of (literally, bridling) his tongue but deceiving his heart—this person's religion is empty. 27Pure and unpolluted religion with [our] God and Father is this: to look after orphans and widows in their trouble, to keep oneself unspotted from the world.

James is discouraging ready speech—for what reason? No doubt he is drawing this motif out of the general stock of wisdom sayings. Yet the strong emphasis he gives it here, throughout the body of the letter, and in his concluding admonition against oaths, suggests that it was a main concern in the context for which the letter is written. In this first reference, he links speech with anger, suggesting that he is concerned about contentious conversation within the community addressed.

The phrase "quick to listen, slow to talk, slow at anger" is a striking one in Greek. The language of this letter is relatively free of rhetorical figures based on syntax and word arrangement. Its vivid moments are created more often by similes and wordplays. This particular Greek phrase, however, makes striking use of homoeoteleuton (rhyme), parallelism (the first two adjectives are completed by infinitives), and asyndeton (lack of connectives). James (1:19) captures the hearers' attention by rhyming ταχύς ("quick") and βραδύς ("slow") and by omitting conjunctions. In a longer sequence, the figure of asyndeton can suggest that the series is infinitely extensible; in a relatively short series, like this one, it may suggest rather that each element is an aspect of a single reality. In the present case, the latter interpretation is preferable, especially since James avoids extending full parallelism throughout the sequence, but gives it a sharp sense of conclusion by replacing what would have been the third infinitive with the prepositional phrase "at anger."

Since the principal function of religious speech is the interpretation of our world and of events in relation to God, we might well compare previous examples of such speech in the letter itself. Those who pray without trust are warned not to expect answering gifts. Poor and rich Christians are told to rejoice in their reversal of status. Those who endure are pronounced blessed. Those who ascribe their troubles to God are reproved. We might suspect that the issue of appropriate and inappropriate speech is somehow connected with this triad of concerns: tribulation, social status, and the effectiveness of the readers' or hearers' relationship with God.

In any event, James's admonition to listen first and speak only after due consideration acts as a prescription for the hearing of this letter. The auditor is told to pay close attention, setting aside one's own position and not looking for an opportunity to be angry. Perhaps James expects some of his addressees to be in a potentially hostile frame of mind as they listen to the reading of this missive. By admonishing the whole group in the most general of terms early on, he avoids confronting them directly, but reminds them that they are responsible for how they interact with what they are reading or hearing.

There is also a further element in James's treatment of "listening." He insists that all serious listening is done not simply with the intellect but with the whole of one's life. Listening that does not find expression in action is of no great value, a fleeting experience without consequence for the future. Only listening that produces action is worthy of the name of religion. The term translated "religion" here is θρησκεία, which stresses the *cultic* element in religious observance. By the content he gives it here, James is redefining this familiar notion of "religion" away from the cultic realm and toward that of care for the needy members of the community. In this, he is following the example of the prophets of Israel (e.g., Mic 6:6–8).

James is also redefining purity, in a way not uncommon for NT writers, with his admonition to keep oneself "unspotted from the world." Earlier, he wrote of "putting aside with gentleness all filth and excess of evil" (1:21); in that context, "filth" could have its normal sense of physical uncleanness or impurity.[16] In 1:27, however, it is more likely that James is redefining purity and impurity not in Levitical terms of physical contagion, but in terms of doing good or evil to others. The key evidence for this is that there is no conjunction between the two infinitive clauses defining θρησκεία. They are not two items in series; rather, the second is in apposition to the first. Caring for the weak *is* the way one keeps oneself unspotted. In this, James shows affinity with the Synoptics' Jesus and with Paul, both of whom redefine purity in metaphorical ways so that it now applies to other moral qualities of action.[17]

In sum, James sets up two basic criteria for his model audience: they are to be receptive and patient listeners, not hurrying to express their own views, particularly not in an angry way; and they are to translate what they hear into practice, with acts of mercy forming a central concern of their religion.

The Occasion of the Letter?

By this point, James has sketched a picture of the model listener and introduced a coherent and related set of issues, all of which continue to be subjects of concern at or near the end of the letter. The conclusion, however, does not seem to represent any marked development of thought in comparison with the introduction. It affirms the power of the just person's prayer and praises the person who turns another back from error. It discourages oaths and encourages directness and simplicity of speech. It asserts the nearness of Jesus' Parousia. These seem to be variations on themes raised in the introduction more than developments of them. They serve more to remind us of the earlier themes than to bring their treatment to a clear conclusion. That may, in fact, be all the letter does—a kind of reinforcing, circular movement. If, however, James writes in order to move and guide his readers regarding some particular application of these topics, the evidence of it must lie in the materials intervening between those we have already examined.

In the central segment of the letter, James moves first to the issue of social status, reproving the community for its treatment of visitors:

> 2:1My sisters and brothers, do not hold the faith of our Lord Jesus Christ of glory with favoritisms. 2For if a man with a gold ring and fine clothes comes into your synagogue and a beggar in filthy clothes comes in, too, 3and you pay attention to the one wearing the fine clothes and say, "You sit here in this nice seat," and to the poor person you say, "You stand over there or sit on the floor by my footstool," 4have you not made distinctions among yourselves and become judges with evil thoughts?
>
> 5Listen, my beloved brothers and sisters. Has God not chosen those who are beggars in worldly terms to be rich with trust (or faith) and heirs of the kingdom that he promised to those who love him? 6But you have treated the poor without respect. Do the rich not lord it over you—and they drag you into courts? 7Do they not blaspheme the good name invoked over you?
>
> 8Now, if you are performing (or perfecting) the royal law according to the Scripture, "You shall love your neighbor as yourself," you are doing well. 9But if you are playing favorites, you are committing sin, reproved by the law as transgressors. 10For whoever keeps the whole law but falls short in one thing becomes liable for all. 11For the one who said, "Do not commit adultery," also said, "Do not kill." If you do not commit adultery, but you do kill, you have become a transgressor of the law.
>
> 12So speak and so act as people to be judged by a law of freedom. 13For judgment will be merciless toward the person who has not practiced mercy. Mercy gets the last laugh on judgment.

This unit is longer, more direct, more concrete, and more pointed than anything that precedes it. This, in itself, gives it a certain rhetorical force, rather as if a film shot in a hazy, soft style should suddenly come into sharp focus. The passage also gains power by shifting the way James addresses his audience. Hitherto, he has used the second person plural mainly in order to give rather general commands: "Consider it all joy" (1:2), "Make no mistake" (1:16), "Know this" (1:19), and so on. The only exception is in the subordinate clause "when you fall into various tests" (1:2). The vivid examples of the wildflower and the man looking at himself in a mirror have had no direct grammatical relationship to the audience. There has been little direct reference to the audience's situation. Now, quite without warning, James offers them a negative example framed in terms of their own community life.

Is the example an actual incident or a hypothetical problem created to illustrate a dimension of James's subject matter? There is no way to resolve the question. The one thing we can assume, I think, is that the readers/hearers are expected to recognize a possible aspect of their own community life in the story—and also a contrast with their basic, shared convictions. James tells them that their interest in social status is getting the better of the community's egalitarian principles, already referred to in the saying about social "reversal" of 1:9–10.

The group's interest in status may well be connected with the reality of their social disadvantage, already mentioned in 1:2, for James returns briefly to the theme of persecution or oppression in 2:6–7. If some rich people are among the persecutors of the Christian community, then the community's desire to show a rich visitor special consideration may arise from a wish to curry favor with a potential enemy. Perhaps the rich visitor has been invited in the hope of persuading him or her to become a patron rather than a persecutor of the community. In any case, the rich have power in this world, and the community's desire is to possess their goodwill.

The Christian community itself, however, does not appear to be altogether poor. There are chairs and footstools—not unlike the benches with footrests and the special seat for the patron in the synagogue at Dura-Europus.[18] By offering the rich visitor one of these good seats, the congregation immediately incorporates him into their number. In telling the ragged visitor to "stand over there or sit on the floor by my footstool," the speaker pushes the poor to the edge of the community or assigns them a low status within it. James's point, in this regard, has to do not so much with the effect on visitors—this is not an essay on church growth—as with the effect on the congregation itself. When you treat visitors in this way, he writes, "have you not made distinctions among yourselves and become judges with evil thoughts?" The experience of reversal on the part of the rich and poor brother, pointed out earlier as an example of the community's shared presuppositions, is now replaced with a new seriousness about social status.

Favoritism for rich visitors presumably implies favoritism for the rich within the community, too. In a community that James has persistently addressed as "brothers and sisters," it raises the possibility that other, external social values may supersede the basic Christian norm of equality. James has earlier used the unusual phrase "the law of freedom" (1:25)—a phrase that appears again in 2:12. In the present passage, he also speaks of the highly egalitarian commandment to love one's neighbor as oneself as "the royal law" (2:8). The latter phrase characterizes it as the law of God's kingdom, of which the poor are the heirs (2:5). In other words, the royal law is a law that recognizes the princely status of the poor. The alternative phrase "law of freedom" perhaps designates it as a law that knows of only one human status—that of free person. The phrase does not mean "law of emancipation," but rather a law that acknowledges the right of all to exist and to behave without subservience.[19]

According to James, the poor are not only the equals of the rich in God's sight. They are actually their betters. In language that recalls 1:9–10, where the poor are urged to rejoice in their exaltation and the rich in their humiliation, James now writes of the poor as rich in faith or trust and the true heirs of God's kingdom. The rich, on the other hand, are persecutors. Since we have seen that James's audience is not entirely poor and that James is concerned that they are reviving the importance of social distinctions *among themselves,* we can also hear his denunciation of the rich, persecuting outsiders in 2:6–7 as a kind of warning shot fired across the bow of the richer members of the Christian groups. There is a likelihood that these are significant leaders in their communities. James will need to approach them with circumspection, avoiding any irreparable breach. One way to do this might be to criticize not them, but their persecuting analogs in the larger society.

James emphasizes for them "the royal law" of loving one's neighbor as oneself. The Jesus of Matthew's Gospel asserts that this commandment (and the parallel one of loving God with one's whole self) is the peg from which all the rest of the law hangs (22:40). James makes a similar point in a somewhat different way by insisting that the whole of the law is so intimately integrated that the violation of any one commandment is violation of the entire law. Indeed, in what seems a curious and rather extreme move, he uses murder as his example, though one would scarcely like to think that murder could have been common in the Christian community. Even if his hearers are otherwise law-abiding, the committing of murder would mean that they have violated the whole law. To avoid the danger of violating the law, his readers/hearers must instead practice acts of mercy.

Perhaps James wishes to say that such acts satisfy the commandment to love one's neighbor as oneself. I have argued elsewhere that the early Christians were seldom if ever egalitarian in the modern sense. They did, however, esteem a broad and unforced generosity, which may have had the effect of relieving the poor of their perennial need to play up to their patrons—the kind of toadying that contemporary satirists like Juvenal sketched with devastating scorn.[20]

James, however, expects some skepticism on the part of his audience about the need for such generosity. And he seems to think they will use what sounds like a half-understood Paulinism to justify their tendency to pull back:

2:14What use is it, my sisters and brothers, if someone claims to have faith but does not have works? Can faith save him? 15If a brother or sister are [sic] naked and left without daily nourishment 16and someone from among you says to them, "Go in peace, be warm and full," but does not give them the things needed by the body, what is the use? 17So, too, faith, if it has no works, is dead in itself.

18But someone will say, "You have faith, and I have works." Show me your faith apart from the works, and I will show you my faith by the evidence of my works. 19You believe that God is one. You do well. The demons, too, believe—and quake.

20But do you want to know, you empty person, that faith apart from works is useless? 21Was our father Abraham not justified by works when he offered his son Isaac on the altar? 22You see that the faith was working together with his works and by the works the faith was brought to completion. 23And the Scripture was fulfilled that says, "And Abraham believed God, and it was reckoned to him for righteousness"; and he was called God's friend. 24You see that a person is justified on the basis of works and not on the basis of faith alone. 25And in the same way, was not Rahab the prostitute, too, justified by works when she received the messengers and sent them away by another route? 26For just as the body without spirit is dead, so, too, faith without works is dead.

Like the preceding passage about visitors to the Christian assembly, this is, by the standards of this letter, a long and coherent block of argument. It is tied closely to the preceding passage, where James had insisted that only mercy can get the better of judgment. The eternal salvation of his audience

is dependent on their doing acts of mercy. But someone may object by citing a teaching that James has himself already agreed to, though not in so
many words: the teaching that salvation is dependent on God's goodness,
not on human merit. Earlier in the letter, James had referred to "the God
who simply gives to all and does not reproach" (1:5). He had declared that
"every good giving and every complete (*or* perfect) gift is from above, coming down from the Father of the lights, with whom there is no variation or
shadow cast by turning. He has freely given birth to us by a word of truth,
so that we would become the firstfruits of his creatures" (1:17–18). The
primacy of grace is at the heart of all early Christian thought, however differently various thinkers may have interpreted it. James has no apparent
intention of disowning it.

What James objects to, rather, is the tendency of some of his addressees
to use one version of the teaching of grace to excuse their increasing
indifference toward the poor among them. They argue that grace is appro-
priated sufficiently in one's life by the simple act of believing the message
and that no further action is required. James may think they have drawn
this teaching from Paul. His quotation of Gen 13:6 ("Abraham believed
God . . .") is not particularly apposite to his own purposes, but it is precisely the quotation Paul uses in Rom 4:3 to support his own rather different contrast between faith and works. Paul, to be sure, did not understand
the primacy of grace to exclude or obviate the value of good works on the
part of the faithful. Quite the contrary, he insisted on them as the fulfilling
of love. The Paulinism that James attacks, then, is a half-understood one,
as adopted by members of the communities addressed.[21]

James argues that works of mercy continue to be essential in the Christian's relationship to God and neighbor. They are essential because they
give effect to faith. Abraham's experience was first to have faith, then to
offer Isaac on the altar. This act "fulfilled" the Scripture that spoke of
reckoning his faith *for* righteousness. James is apparently reading the
preposition εἰς (here translated "for") in its common purposive sense.
The faith, he is arguing, was not reckoned to Abraham *in the place of* righteousness, as Paul reads it, but rather *to produce* righteousness—a purpose
fulfilled in the offering of Isaac. This is of a piece with his earlier advice to
the reader/hearer that one must hear with one's whole life, not just the
mind (1:22–25).

The works that James has in mind are not primarily the legal requirements that served to preserve purity or to distinguish Israel from the Gentiles. Like Paul, he seems to bracket those. Notice that he described the

poor visitor to the Christian synagogue as a beggar dressed in filthy clothes and therefore probably not in a high state of purity. And alongside Abraham he sets as his other example of good works the figure of a Canaanite woman who was a prostitute. The fact that she gave the Israelite spies hospitality and sent them safely on their way is enough to make her unclean and accursed ethnicity and her slavish occupation irrelevant.

James's discussion of faith and works, then, is not really a new departure in the letter, as if he had swerved suddenly into an unrelated dialogue, but a continuation of the previous discussion of social status. The richer Christians must practice works of mercy in order to win their salvation. Such works will prevent them from practicing "favoritism" and will fulfill the "law of freedom," since they will thereby keep the poor free from subservience. They must not hope to secure their future either by saving their wealth or by currying favor with rich outsiders, but rather preserve a kind of life within the Christian community that makes for a minimum of social distinctions.

Teaching

There is at least one kind of social distinction within the Christian community, however, that James cannot well attack—the distinction that makes some people teachers. In writing this letter, he himself is functioning as a teacher of wisdom. The juxtaposition of this topic with the preceding suggests that others within his orbit are claiming some role as teachers, too. Perhaps they are the ones who are using the theology of Paul to justify a new kind of behavior within the community. This would not be unusual, given the mobility of early Christian teachers. James addresses the issue by warning, in effect, against presumption:

> 3:1Do not many of you become teachers, my brothers and sisters, knowing that we shall receive a greater judgment. 2For we all make many mistakes. If anyone does not make a mistake in speech, this person is a complete (or perfect) man, able to bridle the whole body as well. 3And if we put bits into the mouths of horses so that they will obey us, we actually guide their whole body. 4Look! even ships, big as they are and driven by strong winds, are guided by the smallest rudder, wherever the will of the pilot wants. 5So, too, the tongue is a little member and boasts great things. Look! what a little fire kindles such a lot of wood! 6And the tongue is a fire. The tongue constitutes the world (or ornament) of injustice (or unrighteousness) among

your members, polluting the whole body and setting on fire the wheel of becoming—and set on fire by hell. [7]For every nature of both wild animals and birds, both creeping things and sea creatures, is being tamed and has been tamed by human nature; [8]but not a single human being can tame the tongue—a restless evil, full of death-dealing poison. [9]With it, we bless the Lord and Father, and with it we curse human beings made according to God's likeness. [10]From the same mouth issue blessing and curse. My sisters and brothers, these things should not happen this way. [11]Does the spring pour fresh and bitter [water] out of the same opening? [12]Can a fig tree, my brothers and sisters, produce olives or a grapevine figs? Neither can fresh water produce salt water.

The danger of speech is hardly an unusual theme in ancient wisdom literature. Yet we encounter it here in the form of a long, sustained passage, suggesting that James has some specific issue in mind. If some relatively prosperous persons among his addressees are justifying a prudential line of behavior by appealing to half-understood bits of Pauline theology, they must have received those bits from somewhere. It is not likely that they picked them up directly from Paul's writings, since those took the form of letters addressed to specific churches and were not collected and published until the early second century. It seems more likely that they learned of these ideas from traveling teachers, some of whom may have heard Paul at one time or picked up scraps of his teaching in congregations he had founded.

There was an expectation, in early Christianity, that such traveling teachers were poor. But one can be poor in terms of personal property and still live fairly well, provided that one can rely on generous treatment by one's hosts. Traveling teachers might well be inclined to tell the rich leadership of a community what they wanted to hear, securing their own welcome at the expense of the patron's care for the local poor. Some such concern appears to pervade the *Didache,* where there are efforts to limit traveling teachers' opportunities to feather their own nests. They were allowed, for example, to order the preparation of a banquet under prophetic inspiration, but not to eat from it themselves.[22]

James tries to isolate such teachers and also to discourage "amateur" authorities from arising within the local community by making speech as such a problematic quality. There are only a few real teachers occupying this heady but dangerous role, and James is one of them. (Note the first person plural in 3:1—"*we* shall receive. . . .") Others are being warned off.

Since the true teachers are relatively few in number, they will indulge in no casual speech. Aware of a heavier judgment that awaits them and of their own human weakness, they will measure out their words with care. The letter, of course, exemplifies this.

James has another important concern in mind, too. He objects to the polemical element so common in early Christian discourse. The praise of God should not share space in discourse with the cursing of human beings. Jude might serve as an example! Or does James have Paul himself in mind, invoking anathema on his opponents?[23] In any case, the phenomenon was far from unknown. Or perhaps he is concerned about specific developments within the congregation or congregations that he is addressing. Is there a quarrel there that threatens to disrupt the life of the Christian society? Such tensions sometimes took theological form. James, however, as he will reveal in due course, thinks that the true source of conflict is not in ideas but in ungoverned desires.

First, however, he argues briefly that the prevalence of conflict itself shows that there is something not of God in the present situation:

3:13Who is wise and comprehending among you? Let him show his works by good conduct, with meekness of wisdom. 14But if you have bitter jealousy and strife in your hearts, do not boast and lie against the truth. 15This wisdom is not coming down from above, but is earthly, soul-level, demon-like. 16For where jealousy and strife are, there is upheaval and every evil action. 17But the wisdom from above is, first, dedicated (or chaste), then peaceful, mild, obedient, full of mercy and good fruits, not wavering, not hypocritical. 18And the fruit of justice (or righteousness) is sown in peace for those who make peace.

The wisdom from above is, of course, the proper content of a true teacher's discourse. By characterizing it in this passage, James is also sketching a picture of his own rhetorical presuppositions and tactics. Here James suggests that the new teaching is disruptive and serving the purposes of jealousy and strife, and that his own teaching will prove to be "peaceful, mild," generous, consistent, and honest. Certainly, he has gone out of his way, up to this point, to avoid offending his audience. He has repeatedly addressed them as ἀδελφοί. Only in 3:1 does he first claim authority as a teacher. Even though he has challenged their treatment of poor visitors, he has presented it as a hypothetical situation. His sharpest words for the rich have been reserved for those outside the community of faith, though he has not altogether neglected those within.

James has criticized no one directly. The closest approach to such a thing is the vocative ὦ ἄνθρωπε κενέ ("you empty person") in 2:20. But it would not have seemed directly confrontational, since it is part of a section already set up in diatribe style in 2:18: "But *someone* will say. . . ." It is the hypothetical "someone" who is addressed as an "empty person," not the audience as such. There is no personal affront here, even if there may be an element that touches them in substance. This restraint will no longer be possible, however, in what follows; for James, having demonstrated his ability to be meek and peaceable, will now raise some quite direct questions with his addressees, concerned no longer with hypothetical, but with actual behavior. And he will even break, at first, with his repetitive salutation of the audience as "sisters and brothers."

Coming to Grips

The language of the letter now becomes quite sharp:

4:1Whence the wars and whence the fights among you? Are they not from this: from your pleasures on the march among your members? 2You desire and you do not have. You kill. And you are jealous and you cannot get. You fight and war. You do not have because you do not ask. 3You ask and do not receive because you ask badly, so that you may spend on your pleasures. 4You adulterous women! Do you not know that the world's friendship is inimical to God's? So whoever wants to be the world's friend is really God's enemy. 5Or do you suppose that the Scripture speaks in empty words? Envy is what the spirit that has taken up residence among us hankers after, 6but [God] gives a greater grace. That is why it says:

"God resists the proud,
but gives grace to the lowly" [Prov 3:34].

7So subordinate yourselves to God. And resist the slanderer (*or* devil) and he will run away from you. 8Come close to God, and he will come close to you. Clean your hands, you sinners, and dedicate your hearts (*or* make your hearts chaste), you two-souled people. 9Be wretched and grieve and weep. Let your laughter be turned into mourning, and your joy into dejection. [10]Bring yourselves low before the Lord, and he will lift you up.

[11]Do not speak against each other, brothers and sisters. The person who speaks against a brother or judges his brother is speaking against the law and judging the law. But if you judge the law, you are not a doer of the law but [its] judge. [12]The lawgiver and judge is one, the one who can save and destroy. And you, who are you that judge [your] neighbor?[24]

The power of this passage lies partly in the way in which it breaks with what has gone before. After the indirection and politeness of the earlier part of the letter, this direct denunciation seems quite sharp indeed.

After repeatedly addressing his audience as "brothers and sisters," James now addresses them as "adulterous women," "sinners," and "two-souled." The first label will have sounded like a double insult, given the cultural context of the letter, for James, by his repeated use of ἀνήρ has communicated a view of his audience as, in the first instance, male. The last links up with the criticism of the "two-souled man" in 1:8, precisely the sort of person who can expect to receive nothing from the Lord. The shock of these insults is the greater because they represent such an abrupt shift. But James does not allow the harsh language to go on very long. By v. 11, he has returned to addressing them as "brothers and sisters," thus reassuring them that he is not setting himself over against them.

His determination to remain in association with his addressees even as he denounces them is nowhere more vivid than in the awkward and surprising sentence: "Envy is what the spirit that has taken up residence among *us* hankers after" (4:5). Even though James is speaking in reproof, he does not disassociate himself from the community, even in its sins—and this despite the fact that he has consistently spoken, in the preceding seven and one-half verses, in the second person plural, not the first—*your* sins, not *ours*. The pronoun gains even more significance from the opening sentence of this argument, emphasizing "wars" and "fights" among the congregation. James might at first seem himself to be launching a new attack, a further extension of such battles, but he soon chooses, instead, to identify himself as part of the sinful community.

James links the conflicts in the community to other problems of particular concern to him: unanswered prayer and the desire to make influential friends in the larger community (which was leading to favoritism toward the rich). James contrasts this, implicitly, to what he said earlier of Abraham: that he was God's friend. Becoming friends with the world means that one cannot be God's friend. It is the devil (literally, "the slanderer") or some equivalent evil spirit that is animating the community's life. A great act of repentance is demanded so that the community can return to its trust in God and be exalted again. The character of this repentance is summed up, as one would expect of James, in terms of behavior toward others. If you mistreat your brother or sister in the faith, you are behaving contemptuously toward the law itself, that is, the royal law of loving one's neighbor as oneself (cf. 2:8).

Given that this passage is the most overtly passionate of the whole letter, one must suspect that it is designed to drive home rhetorically a point of great importance to the whole document, perhaps even of central importance. There is conflict within the congregation. James ascribes it to the desire of some for personal gain at the expense of others and speaks of it as an alien or diabolic spirit inhabiting the group (in tacit contrast, perhaps, to the Spirit of God that ought to be their animating force). He goes so far as to list murder among the resulting sins (4:4), which recalls and reinforces his earlier, uncomfortable choice of murder as the illustration of his argument about the unity of the Law (2:11). One result of all this is that the congregation's prayers are not answered. They can correct the problem only by contrition and conversion. And, despite the harsh language that James has used, he calls for a return to a nonjudgmental stance toward the neighbor. He saves himself from being condemned on his own criteria mainly by including himself as part of the group he is denouncing in 4:5. Still, his parting shot is a drastic warning: Change your ways at once or risk being found in a position of claiming superiority to the royal law itself.

The Culprits

The next segment of the letter seems so unrelated to what precedes that one is at first completely perplexed about how to understand the transition. It consists of two exhortations connected with each other by anaphora (repetition) of the phrase "Come on, now":

> 4:13Come on, now, you who say, "Today or tomorrow, we'll go to this city and do a year there, and we'll trade and make money"—14you who do not know what sort of life you will have tomorrow morning. For you are a mist, appearing for a little while and then disappearing. 15[This is] instead of your saying, "If the Lord is willing, we will both live and do this or that." 16But as it is you boast in your pretensions.

All such boasting is evil. [17]So for the person who knows how to do good and does not do it, it is sin for that person.

[5:1]Come on, now, you rich, weep, wailing over your coming miseries. [2]Your wealth has rotted and your clothes have gone moth-eaten. [3]Your gold and silver are rusted and their rust will serve as testimony against you and eat your flesh like fire. You have been gathering treasure in the last days. [4]Look! the pay of the workers who mowed your fields, held back by you, is shouting aloud, and the outcries of those who harvested have entered into the ears of the Lord Sabaoth. [5]You have enjoyed yourselves on the earth and lived in luxury; you have fattened up your hearts on slaughtering day. [6]You have condemned, you have murdered the righteous one. He does not resist you.

The use of anaphora here suggests to the addressees that they should hear these denunciations as parallel. Yet the sins denounced in the two cases seem scarcely comparable. One is a failure of devout speech; the other is destructive of the lives of workers and is treated in apocalyptic terms.

As to the first issue, when we remember how much James has already emphasized the importance of the tongue, we may be prepared to think that he would weigh errors of language more heavily than we; and that must surely be part of our difficulty. Yet there is something else involved, too. James has repeatedly emphasized the idea of God as giver of all good gifts and such related themes as friendship with God (friendship routinely included exchanges of gifts in antiquity), absolute confidence in God, singleness of devotion, and God's choice of the poor. All these can be read as facets of a single exhortation—to rely on God rather than on one's own power to ensure one's welfare. For James, this seems to be the most basic foundation of Christian life. Therefore, wrong language in expressing one's plans (for it is the language, not the plans, to which James objects) is not merely incidental; it represents a still-unconverted mind at work, desiring to ensure itself against harm. It embodies the very opposite of the patience and endurance praised at the beginning and end of the letter.

It is not difficult to imagine that members of James's audience might have been guilty of expressing their plans in wrong terms—or even of holding the mistaken spirituality that James saw embodied in such language. But what about the accusations and threats leveled at the rich in 5:1–6? Are these, too, members of James's audience? Or is this an example of the rhetorical figure of apostrophe, in which the speaker turns away from the actual audience to address persons not present? Most commentators have chosen the latter explanation on the grounds that such behavior is unthinkable within the Christian community.[25] James, to be sure, has written earlier of rich outsiders, saying that they are oppressors of the community and blasphemers of the name invoked over Christians (2:6–7). On the other hand, we have seen that the Christian synagogue is well furnished and that James can speak of "the rich [brother]" (1:9) and claim that the congregation is playing favorites among themselves, not merely among their visitors (2:4).

Can we suppose that some rich, landowning members of the Christian community or communities to which James writes were in fact withholding wages from day laborers to support their own luxurious lives—perhaps with the consequence of one or more deaths? Yes, we can. The Synoptic Gospels agree that Jesus had rich as well as poor followers. Certainly, the majority of the rich (like the majority of all people) remained non-Christian; and we need not doubt James's claim that some of them were hostile to the Christian synagogue. Yet the Christian community included some relatively prosperous people; and these people would not have been immune to the temptations that attend their social equals in every era, above all the temptation to maximize the incomes from their estates by means that deserve condemnation. Since it was hard to prosecute the rich effectively in the ancient Mediterranean world, there was little means of redress available.[26]

One may *guess* that, in addition, the rich offenders in James's audience justified their pursuit of personal advancement by saying that they had to protect the church as a whole in a dangerous situation. In any case, they might claim they were being disadvantaged by their connection with the church, and that the church needed to gain more rich converts in order to spread the burden more equitably. To do this, it would need to give the rich the sorts of special privileges that were the norm in ancient voluntary associations.[27]

If 5:1–6 is really addressed to members of the Christian community, however, one can only be staggered by the intensity of the denunciation. The description of the rotting of their goods (5:2–3) is couched in perfect tense, announcing it as an accomplished fact. Rust, which does not normally affect gold, here has a supernaturally threatening power. The metaphor of fattening hearts on slaughtering day is vivid and distressing. The passage ends with a fairly long asyndeton (5:5–6), composed of short, clipped clauses and conveying a sense of great urgency. And at the end, James allusively identifies the Christian rich with the very murderers of

Christ. (This is hardly an unthinkable comparison; a similar charge is leveled at Christian apostates in Heb 6:6). They are the ones who condemn and kill the righteous person. He does not resist. In one sense, the "righteous person" here is presumably the laborer who is being ground down by deprivation. The behavior of the landowners is at least life-threatening, and perhaps there have been actual deaths as a result. But the laborer is being presented here in the image of Jesus.[28] Why would James, who has been so careful to identify himself with his audience in the earlier part of the letter, now level such a devastating charge at a portion of them?

The easiest answer is that this is the point of the letter as a whole. If so, the point turns out not to have been quite so close to the end of the letter as my theory had led me to expect. Yet it could scarcely have occurred much earlier than this. James needs the whole of the preceding pages, rhetorically, to prepare this one onslaught. He has given the whole audience ample opportunity to identify him as one of themselves, even in their sins. He has emphasized the all-sufficient goodness of God, the importance of endurance, the relationship between justice and the answering of prayer, the sinfulness of favoritism, the centrality of the royal law of love for neighbor, and the failure of the congregation as a whole. He has argued for a certain kind of patient listening and undercut most of the potential arguments rich offenders could use to defend themselves. Only now can the direct confrontation have its desired effect.

Yet the passage falls short of absolute clarity. Are the evil rich people Christian or non-Christian?[29] Precisely! James, like Jesus telling a parable, leaves it to them to decide. And he does not specify what they must do. But he lets them know in what terms their decision needs to be made.

Full Circle

At this point, we reach the materials we studied at the beginning of this chapter—materials constituting the conclusion of the letter. They return to earlier themes and also to the more diffuse manner of the beginning of the letter. They are calm, dignified, and somewhat sententious in the way valued in wisdom traditions. James returns immediately to addressing his audience as "brothers and sisters." He encourages patient endurance. It is a virtue that, when practiced by the poor, would deprive the rich of any excuse for their mistreatment of workers and shame them for it. But it is also an appropriate virtue for the rich, who must accept the disadvantages attendant on their membership in the Christian community. He again presents the theme of judgment day, now in a positive rather than negative light. He reasserts that God is well disposed and responds to the prayers of the just—who are, after all, quite ordinary people, just like the addressees of the letter.

James interrupts all this to assert the importance of plain, direct, and honest speech. Christians are to use no oaths. Everything they say is to be true. This is of a piece with his reiterated plea for care in speech and in listening. There are no cases where truth is to be deemed less than essential or where Christian speech is less than truthful—which means, incidentally, whatever restitution the repentant rich undertake to make, they must be sure to perform. Finally, he concludes with his reminder that the great thing among Christians is not that some should prove that they are right and others wrong, but that one should turn back those who have wandered away from the truth. Once the communities have resolved their internal conflict, there is to be no ongoing animosity. The return of the straying "will cover a multitude of sins."

James's Relationship with His Addressees

James assumes that he has authority in relation to his addressees, authority that he ascribes to his relationship to Jesus as Jesus' slave. His repeated appeals to the "royal law" and to Scripture have a similar effect of suggesting that he is not speaking on his own. His authority emerges from his relationship to a tradition, a person, and a message. This is also suggested in his use of wisdom language, which identifies him as a successor to the tradition embodied in Solomon.

James expects to be listened to, but he also takes pains to approach his addressees in a way that encourages them to listen. His frequent use of ἀδελφοί ("sisters and brothers") identifies him with his audience, as does his use of the first person plural at critical moments. He describes the good hearer, giving the addressees a model to live up to. He elaborates on the heavy burden born by teachers, thereby encouraging his audience to remain in the role of hearers.

James carefully prepares his confrontation with the rich wrongdoers. He introduces the issue of justice (and even the topic of murder) at first in indirect ways; then gradually he concretizes it and sharpens the focus. His reproof of the community as a whole for their excessive interest in social standing precedes his attacks on the two specific groups that he holds particularly at fault. In this way, he allows even the sinful members of these groups to remain a part of the larger group and so to avoid the loss of honor that would result from their being singled out.

Since there is a good chance that the offenders included some of the community leadership, confronting them carries with it the risk of alienating them and endangering the welfare of the community as a whole. Accordingly, James concludes the letter with a strong emphasis on peace and serenity. All this suggests that he assumes the community will survive and his relationship with it will continue.

Rhetorical Flow of the Letter of James

One might describe both the opening and closing of the letter as being in "soft focus"—relatively indirect and ambiguous. James is not in a hurry to specify the precise concern of the letter; and once he has confronted the wrongdoers, he moves rather quickly to diffuse the spotlight he has placed on them. His use of traditional wisdom material, with its dignified, calm, sententious, and miscellaneous style, makes this rhetorical move easier.

Since wisdom traditions are often proverbial in character, they tend to consist of short units whose meaning becomes clear only in application. It is easy enough to play "dueling proverbs": "A bird in the hand is worth two in the bush" can be countered by "Nothing ventured, nothing gained." As with liturgical language, then, the alert listener is waiting not just for familiar language, but for the particular choice and combination of sayings. Even so, the beginning of the letter can rightly be said to circle round its objective. When that objective does come into sharper focus in the middle of the letter, beginning with the example of the two visitors, James continues to work by juxtaposing topics rather than by logically developing the argument. There are no really extended arguments here except insofar as the letter as a whole may be said to constitute one.

In the course of all this, James makes artful use of the second person plural. It begins as a way of describing the addressees, then moves to denunciation, and finally embodies an emphasis on mutuality. By comparison, James's use of "we" is more static, but even here there is a dialectic: he sometimes uses the first person of himself (and other teachers) as opposed to his addressees; at other times he uses "we" to include himself in one community with his addressees.

James's inclusion of himself in the community has the effect of modifying his authority without resigning it. Like Elijah, he is just one faithful person among many. This approach to the question of authority squares with the traditions from Jesus, particularly Jesus' use of story, which James also uses in his example of the two visitors. It also leaves room for the offenders to repent of their wrongdoing without losing their place in the community. And perhaps it may help the ordinary folk of the congregation to retain their dignity in the face of maltreatment by the leaders.

James's Greek is good, but his rhetoric does not seem very Hellenic. He makes use of occasional verbal figures (e.g., the rhyming of ταχύς and βραδύς in 1:19) and wordplay;[30] and his rapid-fire denunciation of the rich in chapter 4 is impressive. On the whole, however, his rhetorical method belongs to the more indirect tradition of Hebrew Wisdom literature, circling around the topic until the argument has acquired substance from the process.

And?

It is easier for later readers to enter into conversation with James than with Jude. James's letter is longer and, at least as I am reading it, more explicit. And James's concern for justice is easier to connect with modern issues than is Jude's polemic against intercourse with angels. To be sure, James belongs to an unfamiliar tradition. Hebrew Wisdom books, such as Proverbs, are not favorite reading for most of us, even though they have come to hold increasing interest for scholars. But James strikes a reader today as an heir not only of the Wisdom writers but of the prophets, founding his passion on a love of justice and peace.

Particularly pertinent to us here and now is his way of engaging in confrontation and polemic within the Christian community while still insisting on the bonds of unity. He stands as a kind of opposite pole to not one but two failures on the part of later Christianity. One is the church's historical tendency to cater to the powerful and, by extension, to serve as a kind of chaplaincy to the status quo. The other is the propensity of modern Western Christianity, particularly since the Reformation, for angry fragmentation.

With some notable exceptions, the Christian churches have seldom been willing to speak truth to power. The resulting hypocrisy that officially proclaims God's goodwill toward the poor and oppressed but does not speak to the powerful, even the powerful within the church, about their failures and offenses, threatens to invalidate the church as a bearer of the gospel. Such behavior justifies the intense NT hostility toward hypocrisy, for it has the effect of suggesting that the good news is without practical consequences in the everyday world of here and now. However difficult it is to confront this-worldly power, the Christian community is under a necessity to do exactly that.

What is more, the accepted, this-worldly distribution of power has a constant tendency to invade the church's own perceptions of reality. For James, there is a significant continuity between the shocking behavior of the Christian landowners he attacks and his earlier example of discordant treatment accorded to different kinds of visitors within the Christian assembly. Even the language of Christian merchants who speak of their work not as vocation undertaken in cooperation with God, but as something purely secular and under their own control, is critical evidence that these communities, though Christian, are not fully converted. They do not, deep down, *trust* that the God of grace is in charge of the world or believe that the royal law of loving God and neighbor is a possible way of living in this world.

This is not to say that James's response is a perfect example for later Christians. As I suggested above, he does not seem to aim at disciplining the offenders, serious as their offenses were. Much less does he seem to hope for any drastic remodeling of the social world. He does not seem to have a vision for a world in which there are no longer any great landowners with life-and-death power over the weak, though he does hope that the Christian teacher can recall the powerful to their faith and show them their sin. Since he has already insisted that the addressees must hear with the whole life, not just with the intellect, he certainly expects some practical reformation and restitution. But he leaves the social institutions otherwise unchanged. Whether he could have done more is a question worth asking. Whether we can do more is another question worth asking.

In any case, James does offer one rhetorical model for the difficult task of addressing these issues. When he finally comes to speaking directly on the matter of the crimes of the rich, he is forthright—so much so that subsequent readers have had difficulty accepting that he is actually talking about members of his audience. But he spends most of the letter setting a context and renewing community bonds, both before and after issuing his challenge. When Christian churches, at a later time, came to be more or less coextensive with the secular society, such careful rhetorical provisions may not have been necessary. But they are certainly needed again in our own time when Christian churches are again voluntary organizations. The person who would speak against abuses by the powerful within the church will need not only to denounce, but also to take pains in reasserting and reconfirming the common faith and identity of the community—and the possibility of μετάνοια (change of mind) and the renewal of community bonds.

In this way, James also becomes a useful conversation partner with regard to fragmentation within the Christian community. The step from

disagreement to schism has long been relatively short for Western Christians; and after a half century or so of ecumenical goodwill, the schismatic
drive seems once again to be reasserting itself. Whenever a group finds
itself angered by the behavior or teaching of its cobelievers, the first step,
typically, is to form a partisan group and attempt to drive the offenders out
of the denomination. If that fails, the second step is to separate from the
existing community oneself. James identifies the roots of this illness in a
common human tendency to speak too quickly and too much out of anger.
Hence, the letter's preoccupation with the tongue and the harm it can do.
Far from being merely a topos of paraenesis, arbitrarily selected, it forms, in
this letter, an urgent commentary on a fundamental ecclesiastical temptation and explains why James builds his denunciation of the rich so carefully.

Concern to preserve unity may also lie behind the particular way in
which James presents his own role. He writes with the assurance of an
authoritative teacher, and yet he does not merely demand compliance.
James was functioning within a cultural context that took patriarchal
authority for granted, and he seems to possess a good deal of that sort of
authority. Yet he is surprisingly restrained about trading on it—far more so
than Jude. Instead, he encourages his addressees to rely on their own gifts,
even as he discourages them from adopting the role of teacher. He repeatedly identifies himself, explicitly and implicitly, as their equal, even though
he is also writing authoritatively as a teacher.

Over all, the most striking thing I find in James's approach to his
addressees is the way it embodies the gospel itself. Though he does not
avoid confrontation, his goal is not submission by the offenders but conversion—μετάνοια, change of mind and heart—and restoration of the
community. That is why he can leave his letter as open as he does, gesturing
toward a proposed solution rather than prescribing it in detail. He might
have been able to press some of the offenders into cooperation through
social shaming—though that might simply have driven them out of the
church; yet social shaming would not accomplish what he most wants to
achieve. In their life together, he wants the whole community to realize the
mutuality of the royal law, which is also the law of freedom.

Notes

1. For a useful summary with rich bibliography, see Luke Timothy Johnson, *The Letter
    of James: A New Translation with Introduction and Commentary* (Anchor Bible; New
    York: Doubleday, 1995), 11–16.
2. The paraenetic character and formlessness of the letter were made axiomatic by

Martin Dibelius, *James: A Commentary on the Epistle of James,* rev. Heinrich Greeven, trans. Michael A. Williams (Hermeneia; Philadelphia: Fortress, 1976), 2–5. Dibelius regarded the material as mainly traditional but does allow for occasional authorial intervention; e.g., 235.

3. Johnson, *James,* points out, correctly I think, that these alternatives may not be absolutely opposed to one another; 16–26.

4. "Indeed the task of moral philosophers was to integrate the competing expectations of life into a comprehensive and systematic whole. Paraenesis provided the content for shaping and integrating the moral life." Leo G. Perdue, "The Social Characteristics of Paraenesis and Paraenetic Literature," *Semeia* 50 (1990): 19.

5. 1:8, 12, 20, 23; 2:2; 3:2.

6. For a persuasive account of James's manifold closeness to Matthew, see Massey H. Shepherd Jr., "The Epistle of James and the Gospel of Matthew," *JBL* 75 (1956): 40–51.

7. Complaining about each other is also a sin of the tongue and therefore preparatory to the sentence about oaths in 5:12.

8. Contrast the mode of addressing the audience as "children" in 1 John.

9. Both audience and dating are uncertain. On the whole, however, it seems to me simpler to posit an early date and a Jewish-Christian audience. The alternative is to dismiss the many "primitive" elements of the letter as deliberately "archaizing." Cf. Johnson, *James,* 118–21.

10. Or perhaps "have a mature work." One might normally expect a definite article with ἔργον to justify the translation given in the text; but James tends to omit articles.

11. Δίψυχος means "indecisive," but I have created an etymological equivalent in English that, I hope, will convey the same sense while maintaining the connotations of "soul" relating to life and character.

12. There is a long tradition of disagreement as to whether the rich person here is a "brother." Robert W. Wall is not unusual in assuming that the congregation is composed entirely of poor and oppressed persons; *Community of the Wise: The Letter of James* (Valley Forge: Trinity Press International, 1997), 56. Neither the noun ἀδελφός nor the verb καυχάσθω is repeated in 1:10; but given the parallelism with v. 9, the translation I offer is the easiest and most literal interpretation. Cf. Joseph B. Mayor, *The Epistle of St. James: The Greek Text with Introduction, Notes and Comments* (London: Macmillan, 1897), "Notes," 42–44. The idea that early Christian congregations had no rich members, while both venerable and widespread, is a mistaken generalization: Countryman, *The Rich Christian.*

13. So LSJ, s.v.; Dibelius asserts otherwise; *James,* 100–101. It is, at the least, verbally close to the technical term παράλλαξις ("parallax").

14. Τροπή (1:17) could mean "solstice." Since in ancient reckoning the sun was a planet, this may be yet another way of distinguishing God as being like a fixed star, not a planet.

15. The verb ἀποκυέω, though AV translated it "begat," refers to the mother's act of giving birth.

16. Even in 1:21, however, the immediate context suggests that James has in mind a metaphorical sense of "filth," one that might allude to the works of human anger (1:20). This also makes better sense of the phrase "with gentleness," which seems odd if it refers to physical purity. The *manner* in which one seeks to avoid the contagions of physical impurity has little to do with one's success.

17. Countryman, *Dirt, Greed, and Sex,* 66–143.

18. Hershel Shanks, *Judaism in Stone: The Archaeology of Ancient Synagogues* (New York: Harper & Row, 1979), 80–82.

19. Free status (as distinct from slavery or even the status of the emancipated) meant, ideally, freedom of speech and a high degree of self-determination, albeit within the always powerful context of the ancient community. Anyone who had to cultivate the goodwill of others in order to have basic needs met was less than free. Cf. Roberto Calasso's brief but vivid discussion of the meaning of exile in *The Marriage of Cadmus and Harmony*, trans. Tim Parks (New York: Alfred A. Knopf, 1993), 365–66. In the full, classical sense of "freedom," probably no subject of the Roman Empire was free. The earliest Christians' effort to achieve some kind of internal equality was therefore a revolutionary encounter with class presuppositions deeply embedded in their contemporary society.

20. Countryman, *The Rich Christian*, 22–32.

21. I see no indication that James is responding to a Pauline text or to Paul himself. Paul's arguments were presumably bruited about by Christian travelers far beyond the narrow confines of Paul's own foundations. Whether one ascribes an early date to the Letter of James or a late one, it is easiest to read this passage as responding to a filtered version of Paul, created by people justifying their own failures of generosity.

22. *Didache* 11–12. Note, too, that *Didache* 13 prescribes that when an itinerant teacher does settle down, the gifts otherwise given to the poor are now given to the teacher. One may guess that the teacher was then responsible for the community's ministry to the poor, but this is not made explicit.

23. First Cor 16:22; Gal 1:8–9.

24. I owe the punctuation of 4:7 to Mayor, *James*, "Notes," 130–31. The inclusion of murder or killing here is even more outrageous than the previous reference to it in 2:11, since it actually accuses the congregation of committing such an act. This is part of a gradual escalation of the charge leading toward the beginning of chapter 5.

25. E.g., Johnson, *James*, 306.

26. The withholding of wages was an obvious ploy for callous employers and is specifically forbidden in the Torah, where Lev 19:13 requires that wages be paid daily. In the highly marginal existence of day laborers, failure to do so could have life-threatening consequences.

27. Countryman, *The Rich Christian*, 149–82.

28. The majority of commentators reject the idea of a reference to Jesus here, but there seems to be no reason why the passage may not refer to both victims at once. Indeed, that is the source of its power. Richard Kugelman offers a brief but good analysis in *James and Jude* (New Testament Message, 19; Wilmington, Del.: Michael Glazier, 1980), 57.

29. I have probably found it easier than most scholars to see them as Christian because of my own early work on the subject of rich Christians in the church of the early Roman Empire.

30. Johnson, *James*, 8.

8. Interpreting Paul's Letter to Romans

It is a major step from Jude and James to Romans, not only because Romans is much longer than these other letters, but because it is a central work of the NT in a way that not even James has been. Not surprisingly, it is the subject of a vast amount of modern scholarship as well as a principal authority for much Christian theology. One criterion for deciding whether the present process is useful will be its ability to unveil new possibilities of reading what may seem to be an exhausted text, trapped in its history of theological and scholarly use. Another will be to see whether it helps us read as a whole a letter that has been valued, in subsequent Christian history, primarily for its first eight chapters.

Romans does not carry with it the kinds of uncertainties about authorship and date that characterize Jude and James. We know the ethnically mixed Christian communities in which Paul moved far better than any other strand of first-century Christianity. To be sure, the church at Rome was too large and complex (and too little documented) for us to understand it fully, but we can set it against the background of what we do know of such metropolitan Christianity and try to discern its particular characteristics as we examines the clues the letter itself gives to us.

Given the length of Romans, treating it at the same level of detail as Jude or James, much less taking account of other interpretations of it, would overwhelm the present work. The following study, therefore, will necessarily treat the work selectively and make some use of summary presentations. And the reader may justly complain at times that the modern scholarly discussion is being slighted. I will, however, make every effort to ease the reader's process of carrying this interpretation of Romans back into a reading of the full text of the letter and at least to suggest some points of contact with other scholars' concerns.

Reading Back to Front

Benediction (16:25–27)

It is difficult to be sure exactly where and how Romans really does end. Given the disagreement of textual authorities, we cannot be certain whether the benediction that is usually numbered 16:25–27 is an original part of the work or, if so, whether it is correctly located. I credit its history of disappearance and/or dislocation to the desire of early editors or scribes to universalize Romans by omitting or downgrading the personal greetings that occupy most of chapter 16; but there can be no certainty about this.[1] We begin with the benediction, then, in a provisional manner. We shall have to decide, after surveying the whole of Romans, whether we still think it is part of the larger rhetorical whole. This is not as great a difficulty as we might imagine, however, since we have already seen, in the case of Jude and James, that the precise conclusion of a letter, in the sense the present method emphasizes it, may be hard to define. Even in a letter as short as Jude, it is not simply the last one or two sentences. The admonition to begin at the end can only serve as a kind of directional pointer.

The benediction runs thus:

> To the One who is able to strengthen you according to my gospel and the preaching of the Lord Jesus—according to the revelation of the mystery kept quiet for endless periods but now revealed through prophetic writings, made known according to the eternal God's command in order to produce the obedience of trust among all the Gentiles—to the only wise God, through Jesus Christ, to whom be the glory forever. Amen. (16:25–27)

This translation carries over some of the roughness of syntax in the benediction, which actually, on the least forced reading of the Greek, winds up ascribing glory to Jesus rather than, as it began, to God.

What are the basic elements underlined in this liturgical language? Most obvious, among them, given the Pauline context, is the emphasis on divine authorization of the mission to Gentiles. The emphasis on this as expressing God's purpose from the beginning has the apologetic force of insisting that Paul's gospel, however revolutionary it seems, does not really depart from the tradition of Israel. It is indeed very old ("the revelation of the mystery kept quiet for endless periods"); but it has only now become intelligible to readers of the ancient texts that contain it ("now revealed through prophetic writings"). Paul's gospel, then, is a true understanding of what had previously been hidden in the prophetic oracles.[2] The addressees can join in this benediction only insofar as they are willing to accept this interpretation of recent events in the history of the Christian community. As we have seen in Jude, the affirmations here serve to rule out alternative perspectives.

The reference to "the only wise God" may be a way of contextualizing this claim in terms of Jewish Wisdom theology, which described God's Wisdom as the agent of creation and as being accessible throughout the world, while still reserving a particular role for Israel as her supreme dwelling place. The Wisdom literature preserved in the Scriptures of Israel even included materials explicitly ascribed to non-Israelites (Prov 30–31; Job).

Greetings (16:1–23)

Before the benediction, we find a long series of greetings to and from individuals of Paul's acquaintance.[3] They begin with a commendation of Phoebe, deacon of the church at Cenchreae (16:1–2) and quite possibly the bearer of the letter, and then continue through a long list of names, most of them known to us only from this passage. While it is surprising that Paul would be so well acquainted in a place he has never visited, Rome was a magnet for the Mediterranean world of the time. In any case, the length of the list is less important for us than its recurrent themes. Paul identifies these people in relational terms: they are co-workers, kinsfolk, fellow-prisoners, beloved. Similar language is used in the shorter list of those who send their greetings along with Paul in the letter (16:21–23).

Paul concludes the list of those who receive greetings with a short exhortation and blessing. They are to beware of people who continue to make trouble "contrary to the teaching you have learned"—a vague phrase that could refer to long-held beliefs or to the contents of the letter itself or both. Such people are slaves not to "our Lord Christ" but to their own belly—again a vague phrase, but an interesting choice of words, since part of the body of the letter is concerned about issues of food purity.

Paul then quickly reassures the addressees that their obedience is well-known and he has every confidence that they will behave well in the matter

(16:17–20). This brief shift to hortatory mode is likely to be significant. Even with Paul's expression of confidence in the addressees, it defines the letter as being concerned with a risk of division, which is occasioned by divergent teaching and by personal ambition on the part of some in the community—and perhaps concern over certain foods. Paul expresses confidence in his addressees, but he also contrives to say once again, "This is a critical set of issues. Be careful how you proceed."

If this brief exhortation has the effect of refocusing the letter on a point of major concern, the greetings that surround it serve to underline Paul's connection with the church at Rome. He did not found it. He has never visited it. Why would they care to listen to him at all? The greetings respond to this inevitable question in two ways: first, by emphasizing how deeply interconnected he is already with their community, including the Jewish-Christian part of it; and second, by showing that he is well-regarded and supported by the Corinthian church, which he did found and which joins him in greeting the Romans in the person of individual co-workers and kinsfolk and of prominent local citizens like Erastus, the city treasurer.

Even Paul's commendation of Phoebe is an element in establishing his relationship with the Roman church. If it accepts her and assists her, it will imply some sort of recognition of him and establish a bond with him. All this suggests that Paul is more interested in the prospect of future relationships with the Roman church than in the specific questions about food purity to which the exhortation at most alludes.

A Personal Note (15:14–33)

Preceding the commendation of Phoebe and the extended greetings is a "personal" note. Paul lays aside the tone of exhortation and instruction that characterizes the preceding chapters to compliment the Romans and, in effect, to apologize for writing them things they already know. It is a gracious way to avert irritation on the part of addressees who feel (perhaps rightly) that they have not only been lectured rather severely, but have been pressed to move in a direction that they did not particularly want to go (15:14–15a). Paul also speaks about his own work, noting that God has accomplished great things through it, even though Paul has scrupulously avoided working where others had already established the gospel (15:15b–21). This strategy of giving God credit for the accomplishments allows Paul to claim some measure of achievement without the sacrifice of honor that might come from having to boast of one's own achievements. (In any case, he will shortly name people, in the list of greetings, who can testify to his accomplishments.)

Paul goes on to say that he is running out of room for work in the eastern Mediterranean and would like to visit Rome and be sent forward by them on his way to new work in Spain. Interpreters have long debated how important this intention was to the writing of Romans.[4] While it may not have been the only reason, we can easily imagine that it played a part. A controversial figure like Paul, if he hoped to be well received in Rome, would need to make himself known to the congregation in an acceptable light. Even if the Spanish project was a principal occasion for the writing, it will not go far toward explaining the actual contents of the letter, which probably have more to do with issues Paul was aware of within the Roman church at the time. As a controversial figure, he cannot commend himself without saying something about the way his presence would affect the local scene. His assurance that he does not build on others' foundations will reassure the addressees that they do not have to deal with him on a long-term basis. But they still want to know what kind of influence he will bring to bear at Rome.

As Paul continues to tell of his personal plans, he mentions a forthcoming trip to Jerusalem, which raises the theme of Jew and Gentile, to be found again in the letter's concluding benediction. The occasion of his visit will be to deliver a gift from Gentile churches he has founded, to the overwhelmingly Jewish church at Jerusalem. As with Paul's commendation of Phoebe in Romans, the gift, if accepted, will have the effect of cementing relations between the two. Paul emphasizes, in 15:25–28, the mutuality between Jewish and Gentile Christians that he considers normal and proper. Perhaps he also feels some anxiety about how he will be received; in any case, he asks for the Romans' prayers that "my service for Jerusalem will prove to be acceptable to the saints" (15:31). He expects only then to come to Rome "in the fullness of Christ's blessing" (15:29) and to enjoy some rest alongside the Roman Christians (15:32). This suggests that he sees the visit to Jerusalem as a critical step in resolving tensions in the ecumenical church.

The section concludes with a brief blessing: "The God of peace be with you all. Amen" (15:33). Its language echoes Paul's hope for peace between Gentile and Jewish churches.

An Issue at Rome (chapters 14–15)

As I have suggested, even if Paul's projected trip to Spain provided the occasion for the writing of Romans, the contents of the letter are determined by other factors. Even in the letter's concluding matter, we see Paul returning repeatedly to the issue of relationship between Jews and Gentiles within the Christian community. This was, of course, an issue of major concern for him, given his own life and work. And it was his role in relation to the presence of Gentiles in the Christian community that made him a controversial figure. Perhaps he addresses the subject simply because his own identification with it made it unavoidable for him. On the other hand, if he is hoping for a relationship with the church at Rome, he is likely to have asked himself whether that church cared about the subject and, if so, why.

Was the association of Gentiles and Jews in the church an issue at Rome? If so, what form did the issue take? Paul goes out of his way to designate certain of those he greets in chapter 16 as "kinsfolk." At the very least this suggests that they were Jews, regardless of whether they were also more closely related to Paul. Paul also emphasizes the right of Gentiles to be a part of the Christian church. Any reader of Romans is likely to notice that this is indeed an issue earlier in the letter as well. But nowhere does it become quite so explicit as in the last part of the body of the letter, where Paul takes up the question of eating foods classified as unclean—presumably an issue arising from observance of Torah.

For Christians at Rome at this particular time, this could easily have been the key practical issue about including Gentiles and Jews in one church. This is not to say that the church was split into two neatly defined ethnic groups: Jewish Christians who kept *kashruth* and Gentile Christians who did not. It is more likely that the lines of dispute cut through both groups. There may well have been Gentiles who advocated the keeping of kashruth and Jews who were quite ready to set it aside at least as far as concerned the Christian community. Paul himself speaks elsewhere of being "all things to all people" (1 Cor 9:22), and it may have been difficult for him, as a Jew who lived most of his life among Gentiles, to keep kashruth in any serious way. But it was not a matter Paul could simply ignore. His earlier experience as a Pharisee (Phil 3:5) would have left him strongly aware of the issues involved; these could not be matters of easy indifference for him. Paul seems to speak of incipient partisan stances on the subject among his addressees; and he calls them "Strong" and "Weak," not "Gentile" and "Jew."

Given the substantial amount of attention devoted to all this, I suggest that the Letter to Romans is shaped more by issues about food purity in the Roman congregation than by Paul's intended visit on his way to Spain. This is not to set these two "occasions" in opposition to one another. If Paul wants to be welcomed and supported at Rome, he must acknowledge that he is an object of suspicion for many members of the congregation, specifically the party of the "Weak." If his presence is not to divide the church further (and thereby bring reproach on him, despite his claim not to build on others' foundations), he must demonstrate not only that he is not a threat but that he can actually be of help to them in preserving their unity. Indeed, it is precisely in his role as "apostle of the Gentiles" that he must do this.

Paul will scarcely have been able to write anything at all in this situation without accepting this burden and making use of it. This challenge is thus the major external force shaping the Letter to Romans. The great rhetorical interest of the letter is to see how Paul will create a solution consistent with his own principles but also acceptable to people who belong to the other side in the dispute—people deeply suspicious of him and what he stands for.

Reading in Forward Motion

Proem (1:1–17)

Salutation (1:1–7)

The salutation in Romans is by far the longest in any unquestioned Pauline letter[5]—and this despite the fact that Paul writes entirely in his own name, without associating other members of his missionary group with him in the salutation. Two things are conspicuous in the construction of this long passage: one is the recurrence of the verbal adjective "called" (κλητός). Paul uses it first for himself ("called as apostle," 1:1), then in the plural as part of a description of the addressees ("among whom are you yourselves, called of Jesus Christ," v. 6), and finally in the dative a passage that names the addressees ("to all who are at Rome, beloved of God, called as saints," v. 7). The repetition of the term serves to underline a common experience for both the writer and the addressees, the experience of having been called from one way of life into another, the experience of conversion and therefore of change. At the same time, the difference between being called as an apostle (which Paul further underlines by describing himself as "set apart for the good news of God," v. 1) and simply "called as saints" suggests a claim to authority on Paul's part—a claim to be listened to as a teacher of the Christian community.

Paul also introduces himself here as having received ἀποστολὴν εἰς ὑπακοὴν πίστεως ἐν πᾶσιν τοῖς ἔθνεσιν ("an apostleship to bring about obedience of trust among all the nations/Gentiles," 1:5). The use of "among" and the ambiguity of the word translated either "nations" or "Gentiles" avoids confining Paul's mission or audience to Gentiles; in fact, Paul lumps his addressees as a whole in this group: "among whom are you yourselves, called of Jesus Christ." Since we see indications elsewhere in the letter that the addressees include both Jewish and Gentile Christians, he is, in effect, broadening his scope in order to raise a critical question for both: What constitutes obedience appropriate to trust/faith among Gentiles—that is, in the context of a largely Gentile society? This cannot be a question for Gentile believers only; it affects the whole Christian community.

We may also note briefly here that Paul appeals to the prophets and the Scriptures as showing that what he preaches is not really something new, but has been God's purpose all along. It is the same theme that we have already noted in the benediction with which we began our reading (16:26). This and other similarities (for example, the phrase "obedience of trust/faith") may tend to confirm that the benediction is original, though one cannot absolutely rule out the hand of an astute scribe.

In sum, Paul opens this letter with a strong assertion both of his own authority and of what he shares with his addressees. He presses his claim to have a special duty toward Gentile Christians, but does it in a way that implicitly includes the Jewish Christians at Rome, who could certainly describe themselves as living "among the nations/Gentiles," even if they wished to maintain a clear distinction from them.[6]

Thanksgiving (1:8–17)

The thanksgiving that follows (in accordance with Paul's usual practice) continues this ambiguity about the ethnic makeup of the addressees. Paul thanks God περὶ πάντων ὑμῶν ("for you all," 1:8). He expects "to gain some fruit" ἐν ὑμῖν καθὼς καὶ ἐν τοῖς λοιποῖς ἔθνεσιν ("among you just as among the other nations/Gentiles," v. 13). Paul is indebted Ἕλλησίν τε καὶ βαρβάροις ("to both Greeks and barbarians," the latter being a Greek term that included Jews among others, v. 14). Yet he insists that there is a certain priority in the gospel for Jews (v. 16). The two statements are tied to one another by chiasmus (reversal of order): "Greeks and barbarians" in 1:14, and "the Jew first and also the Greek" in 1:16. Paul even says that the very diversity of the Roman church is his reason for wanting to evangelize there (vv. 14–15).

Since Paul is addressing the church at Rome as a relative stranger, despite knowing some individuals there, he must of course take pains to ingratiate himself with his audience and prospective hosts. This thanksgiving is also performing the role of *captatio benevolentiae* (encouraging the goodwill of the addressees). Compliments abound. The faith of the Roman Christians is known everywhere (1:8). Paul has been eager to visit them (vv. 11, 13). He expects *mutual* benefit from such a visit (v. 12). To be sure, he also maintains his dignity and independence. He says, "I am indebted to both Greeks and barbarians, to both wise folk and foolish—thus my particular eagerness to share the good news with you who are at Rome as well" (vv. 15–16). And he goes on to insist that he is "not ashamed of the good news, for it is the power of God to bring about salvation" (v. 17).

Perhaps Paul simply could not sustain the mode of ingratiation for long. But there is more at work here than temperament. Paul must also assert and establish a kind of authority in a community that has no prior reason to take him seriously. He can be complimentary, but he cannot give away his claim to be a voice worth listening to. Hence, he must sustain his claim to having an apostleship dedicated to the proclamation of the gospel—a message still capable of bringing about change in its hearers here and now. The "salvation" of which Paul writes in 1:17 is hardly to be understood solely in the narrow, later Christian sense of a guarantee of eternal salvation. The term σωτηρία is associated, in antiquity, with healing of the individual and of the body politic.[7] When Paul speaks of "salvation," he expects it to have an immediate import for the life of the Christian community—one consistent with, but not confined to, the life of the age to come.

Address to Jewish Christians (1:18–8:39)

I have pointed out the ambiguity of Paul's initial address to the Roman church. While his claim to apostleship is based, as he acknowledges, specifically on his commission to preach among Gentiles, he manages to word his opening remarks in such a way as to suggest that his authority stands to benefit Jewish Christians as well. There is nothing in the opening remarks or in the remainder of what we now denominate "chapter 1" of the letter to suggest any narrowing of this multiethnic audience. And yet, Paul makes a striking departure at 2:1, where he begins to address a hypothetical individual—one whom he will later (at 2:17) identify as Jewish.

This person is not, however, an outsider to the congregation; he stands, rather, for one possible way of interpreting the relationship between Jews and Gentiles within the Christian community. It is an interpretation that Paul will argue against.

This sort of address to a hypothetical individual was familiar in Paul's time as a device used in ancient diatribe. It served to concretize or personify a position that the speaker wished to argue against. By concretizing it in this way as opposed to, say, holding an open debate with a representative of an opposing philosophical camp, the speaker or writer remained in control of the presentation of the material and is able to simplify it and organize it in a way that would lead to the desired end of the presentation. In addition, it had the virtue of allowing members of the audience to work out their own stance in relationship to the topic without being put directly on the spot. They can decide for themselves how far they wish to identify with the interlocutor. There is never any question which way they are being nudged, but they are not being confronted in a way that might result in loss of honor. Instead, they are spectators at a debate between the author and a fictive person.

The fictive interlocutor allows Paul to focus on a particular way of asserting Jewish priority within the Roman congregation. He nowhere dismisses the rest of the addressees. They must be assumed as "listeners-in." But they are not the focus of the exchange. Paul does gradually relax the tight focus on the hypothetical Jewish Christian, and eventually (chap. 9) he makes the Jewish people his topic, treated in the third person, rather than his interlocutor. Finally, in 11:13–16 he specifically names the Gentile members of the congregation as his audience. Accordingly, we ought to see him, at least through 8:39, as addressing, explicitly or implicitly, a particular Jewish Christian perspective about issues of concern for the congregation. We have already seen reason to think that these include issues of food purity, but of course purity was a practice and presupposition that extended to many areas of life besides food, and purity served as a basic dividing line between Jews and Gentiles in Mediterranean antiquity.[8]

Paul's address to the Jewish Christian interlocutor, however, does not begin only with the apostrophe of 2:1. He leads into it with a denunciation of Gentile culture of a type common in Greek-speaking Judaism at the time. In fact, the confrontation with the fictive individual of chapter 2 becomes intelligible only if we see the person as having enjoyed this denunciation—entirely too much so, from Paul's perspective. The rhetorical maneuver is like one used by Amos, who begins by denouncing the sins of Damascus, Tyre, Edom, the Ammonites, and Moab, before turning on the Israelite hearer with a parallel denunciation (Amos 1:3–2:16); satisfaction with the condemnation of others becomes an opportunity to surprise the hearer. Paul sets a rhetorical trap, into which his hypothetical interlocutor must, like any good hypothetical victim, fall.

This trap becomes useful, however, only if people in the actual audience can first identify with the attack on Gentile culture and then be brought to entertain the possibility that their familiar perspectives might perhaps embody a selfish exemption for themselves—something human beings typically find difficult to grasp. This means, in turn, that the trap cannot be completely artificial or it will not work. It must express some of the realities of the current situation—real perspectives and their emotional implications. In this respect, we have ample evidence to show that what Paul writes was relatively conventional discourse in Hellenistic Judaism and therefore easy enough for many in his audience to identify with.[9]

A Classic Hellenistic-Jewish Denunciation of Gentile Culture (1:18–32)

Paul begins with a quite general third-person evocation of the wrath of God against human impiety (1:18). Gradually this reveals itself as an attack on Gentile culture, which Paul characterizes as idolatrous. He denounces this idolatry as a demonstration of willful stupidity, since the truth about God was there for anyone to see in the reality of the creation itself (vv. 18–23). God, angered by this betrayal, has punished the Gentiles with a culture that is unclean: "God handed them over in the desires of their hearts to impurity so that they would dishonor their bodies among themselves" (v. 24). Paul's primary evidence for this claim is the openness of Greek culture to sexual relations between people of the same gender, both male and female (vv. 26–27).

There is nothing particularly unusual in Paul's choice of this theme. By his time it had a venerable history among Greek-speaking Jews, and his contemporary Philo of Alexandria made heavy use of it. To contrast Jewish antagonism toward same-gender sexual relationships with Gentile tolerance of them became a kind of shorthand summary for all the differences between the two cultures. In many respects, Greek-speaking Judaism was not all that distinct from its Hellenistic milieu. The preservation of the Jewish nation as a distinct ethnic group, therefore, depended partly on formulating and maintaining this difference. In the era of the Maccabean Revolt (from 168/7 B.C.E.), that difference had been defined as centering on four elements: worship of the one God, circumcision, the Torah-based purity system that connected temple cultus with daily life, and the keeping of Sabbath.

ie, in Paul's era, opp. to homosexuality a principal identity marker.

The prohibition of anal intercourse between men in Leviticus (18:22) was only one small part of the purity code, but it could stand for the whole. In fact, it was particularly convenient for this purpose, not only because it embodied a dramatic difference between Judaism and the dominant Greco-Roman culture, but also because it was an element of the Jewish purity system that found affirmation in some schools of Greek thought as well. The point at which most Gentiles became aware of the Jewish purity code was probably not in the area of sexuality but in the area of food. In fact, Jewish concern for food purity elicited negative comment from Greco-Roman writers since the code tended to prevent Jews from eating with their Gentile acquaintances and business partners. On the other hand, late Stoic thinkers, unlike their predecessors, taught that sexuality existed only for the sake of producing children and was otherwise to be treated as a dangerous passion; hence, their teaching converged with at least one aspect of the Jewish purity code: its prohibition of male-male intercourse. Thus, this element of the purity code proved particularly useful to Greek-speaking Jewish writers. (It seems to have been of less concern to their Aramaic-speaking counterparts). It served not only to distinguish Judaism from Hellenism, but to do so in such a way that one could claim superiority for Jewish culture by the standards of the dominant culture itself.[10]

It is not surprising that a Hellenistic Jewish writer like Paul would make use of this, then, but the particular way he handles it in this passage is distinctive. His choice of vocabulary is precise and notably specific. Despite having a large stock of words denoting "sin," Paul does not use them when referring to same-gender sexual intercourse here.[11] It is later Christian heterosexism that reads them into the passage. Instead, dominating the passage are the vocabularies of impurity, of social disgrace, and (in Paul's own rather individual version) of the Stoic concern for "nature." Paul speaks of "uncleanness" (1:24), "dishonor" (vv. 24, 26, 27), and "unnatural" usages (vv. 26, 27). He does not, however, treat these as acts chosen by the Gentiles. He stresses repeatedly that this unclean and disgraceful behavior was actually inflicted on the Gentiles by God as the recompense for their root cultural sin of idolatry (vv. 24–25, 26, 27, 28).

The closest Paul comes to calling same-gender sexual intercourse "sinful" here is to describe these acts as τὰ μὴ καθήκοντα ("things that are not fitting," 1:28). Like the language of "natural and unnatural," this terminology emerges from contemporary Stoic usage. We find the term only here in Paul's writings.[12] In a Stoic writer, it might carry a heavy weight of disapproval. How heavily weighted it was for Paul is impossible to say, but if we look at the parallel case of his use of the language of "natural" and "unnatural," we shall see that he was not committed to (and may not even have known) the fine points of Stoic usage. Paul could evoke the criterion of "nature" not only to attack same-gender sexual intercourse, but to define hairstyles (1 Cor 11:14-15). Elsewhere in Romans (11:17–24), he could even describe *God* as acting unnaturally—very problematic language from a Stoic perspective—by including Gentiles in the Christian community.

In short, Paul's denunciation of Gentile culture evoked the tradition of Greek-speaking Jewish polemic, but could be heard as falling somewhat short of the tradition's full negative potential. The language is certainly pejorative; and yet it stops short of actually saying that this aspect of Gentile culture is intrinsically sinful or deserving of God's wrath. Paul's argument is rather that God has "handed over" the Gentiles to their disgusting culture as punishment for another sin, idolatry. This evokes a certain parallelism with two familiar texts in Genesis: the fall of humanity, which God punishes with such innovations as heavy labor and pain in childbirth (Gen 3), and the Tower of Babel, which God punishes with the multiplication of human languages (Gen 11:1–9). Neither punishment is intrinsically sinful.

Later Christian misreading of this passage owes much to a long history of Christian hostility to sexuality in general and homosexuality in particular.[13] This has been, officially, a fixed element in Christianity for a long time. (Unofficially, the church's practical concern has been not to suppress same-gender sexual relationships but to keep them hidden.)[14] As a result, later readers of Romans simply assumed that this must be what Paul intended to say, on the rather circular argument that he could not possibly have thought otherwise.

In the process, later readers also distorted the connection between the attack on same-gender sexual intercourse in 1:24–28, and the more general list of condemned vices in vv. 29–32. Most readers (and translators) have assumed that same-gender sexual intercourse is, in effect, the first item of the list that follows. In fact, the list is set up quite differently. In v. 28, Paul writes of God having "handed [the Gentiles] over to a disapproved mind, to do things that are not fitting"; he then continues by describing the Gentiles as "having [already] been filled up with every injustice" and the rest of the vices in the list (vv. 29–31). I have introduced the adverb "already" into my translation here to indicate the precise relationship implied by Paul's use of a perfect participle in the passage.[15] It describes a state of being that has come into existence *prior to* the time of the main verb ("handed over"). The participle could be translated more freely (but still well within the norms of translation into English) as either "people who were already filled up" or "since they were already filled up." What it does not do is to function simply as a way of adding a list of further, associated transgressions.

The syntax of the passage, then, presents a three-stage process, with the second stage mentioned only in the participial phrase at the end: first, the Gentiles abandoned the worship of the true God for idols (1:18–23); second, they also committed all sorts of other appalling sins—a favorite broadside of ancient anti-Gentile polemic (vv. 29–31); third, God punished them with a culture that was disgustingly unclean from a Jewish perspective (vv. 24–28). Who, then, could find fault with God's decision? The second stage, after all, demonstrates that the Gentiles were so evil that any punishment could have been justified. God would even have been justified in killing them all, for, as Paul writes, "those who do such things [i.e., the things mentioned in 1:29–31] deserve death—and not only the people who actually do them but also those who concur with the people who do them" (1:32).

One may well ask how Paul's Gentile-Christian hearers might react to this material. After all, the focus of this section of the letter on the Jewish-Christian hearer has not yet been revealed at this point, and this passage will appear to be Paul's first word to the whole church at Rome. Reactions may have been varied, with some being irritated by this attack on Gentile mores and others affirming this judgment on their Greco-Roman world. What we cannot assume is that the Gentile Christians inevitably accepted all aspects of the Jewish standards of purity, for chapters 13–14 indicate that some Roman Christians did not in fact adhere to the laws of food purity.

To some degree, Gentile response would have depended on their understanding of Paul's mission. As we have already noted, Paul is not an altogether unknown quantity for this audience. They at least know that he has a reputation for setting purity considerations aside in the case of Gentile converts. Two options, then, are open. One is that Paul treats same-gender sexual relationships as an exception to his general rule that purity does not condition the Gentile convert's approach to God; the other is that Paul makes no such exception. In the first case, his attack on same-gender sexual relationships has the straightforward sense of condemnation and rejection familiar from contemporary Jewish polemic. If his audience knows that this is his position, then those Gentiles who might object would already have been marginalized, and so their response does not count. On the other hand, in the absence of any evidence for the first alternative, it is also possible that Paul maintains his basic "bracketing" of purity even in relation to same-gender sexual intercourse; that is to say, he does not forbid the keeping of purity, but also does not require it. This would mean that he is using the familiar language of ethnic polemic to make some other point. If Paul's reputation among Gentile Christians at Rome corresponds to this latter possibility, those members of his audience may well have caught the particular "spin" Paul was putting on the familiar polemic. They would have heard a familiar ethnic attack, delivered in somewhat restrained terms. While it would still have surprised them, coming from Paul, they would have had reason to suspend judgment while they waited to see how he would use it.

And how would the Jewish-Christian hearer react? The material was familiar to them as well. It would have the effect of reaffirming Paul's Jewishness and his commitment to the superiority of Jewish culture. Accordingly, it could help Paul gain a hearing—at least tentatively. To both groups, however, it may well have seemed a departure from Paul's norm, which was to insist that Gentiles did not have to become Jews in order to be Christians.

In any case, the shift from straightforward anti-Gentile polemic into the vice list of 1:29–31 would have been less comfortable. It is true that Hellenistic Jewish apologists routinely accused Gentiles of all sorts of vices, just as Greeks had their corresponding account of the faults of Jews and other "barbarians." But there is nothing specifically Gentile about any of the elements in this list. What is more, it is an extraordinarily miscellaneous list, setting gossip alongside murder and coupling loosely related offenses by means of wordplays.[16] It would be difficult to find anyone who was not conscious of having committed at least one sin in this list. The purpose of this organization of material becomes evident only in what follows.

Rebuke to the Person Who Feels Superior (2:1–29)

Paul assumes that the foregoing portion of the letter will result in some of his addressees feeling superior. Superior to whom? To Gentiles, of course, who have just been denounced. It is a mistake to read the previous passage as a denunciation of homosexual persons as such. Quite apart from the problem that first-century Mediterranean culture apparently defined no such category,[17] the center of Paul's interest is not homosexual desire, but Gentiles, especially what he would consider the root-sin of the Gentiles—idolatrous worship offered to images of human beings and animals. The Gentile community has been punished and, as it were, branded for its sin of idolatry by God's having surrendered them to dishonorable and unclean desires. Same-gender sexual acts are treated here not as sinful, but as consequences of a prior sin.

In chapter 1 of Romans, the object of attack, then, is Gentile culture. And the person who is invited to feel superior is the Jewish-Christian listener. Paul assumes that some of them, at least, will have taken his bait, and he closes the trap by cross-examining the person who has felt superior. But he does this indirectly, addressing a hypothetical person in the second-person singular: "So, then, you are without excuse, fellow, whoever you are that are sitting in judgment" (2:1a). The reason why Paul has placed his list of serious sins deserving mortal punishment last in the preceding passage (and not second, as chronological order would have dictated) now becomes evident, for this is what he returns to now. The accusation that the critic is condemning the very things that he himself commits would have no meaning if Paul were primarily concerned with same-gender sexual intercourse. Instead, he wants the listener who has relaxed into a sense of ethnically defined superiority to Gentiles to recognize that Jews are not, as a group, any more sinless than Gentiles.

The distinction between Jew and Greek is that Jews know the Law. But what pleases God is not knowledge of the Law, but repentance and right behavior. The priority of Jews may as easily be a priority in judgment as in reward:

> Tribulation and anxiety for every human soul that commits wrong, Jew first and also Greek. But glory and honor and peace for everyone who does the good, Jew first and also Greek. For there is no favoritism with God. (2:9–11)

The parallelism of the two statements underlines their comprehensiveness and conclusiveness and also renders them memorable.

Gentiles, on the other hand, may do law (νόμος) in a kind of generic form without knowing it:

> For whenever Gentiles that don't have the Law do by nature the things the Law prescribes, these people, even though not having law, are law for themselves. (2:14)

One notices that Paul frequently omits the definite article with "Law" in this passage. While this is not a definitive distinction in Greek, as it might be in English, it does suggest a universalizing of the idea of the Torah, not in order to invalidate its association with the Law of Moses, but to suggest that Gentiles may have a sense of God's will for them, too, even without the advantage of the written Torah with its ethnic distinctions. This is not unrelated to the notion found in Jewish Wisdom literature that wisdom, while available generally in the world, is concretized and embodied particularly in the Law of Moses.[18]

While Gentiles, then, who do not know the Law may still have a sense of law and follow it, Jews may know the Law par excellence and still not do it. After a passage extolling Jewish superiority in the style of contemporary Jewish apologetic (2:17–20), Paul even gives examples of possible Jewish offenses:

> You who tell people not to steal, do you steal? You who say not to commit adultery, do you commit adultery? You who regard idols with revulsion, do you rob temples? You who boast of law (ἐν νόμῳ) dishonor God through your transgression of the Law (τοῦ νόμου). (vv. 21b–23)

Note that these offenses are not presented as being exclusively Jewish. To the contrary, they are precisely the kinds of offenses that might be found in Gentile and Jewish communities alike. They are property offenses, likely to be regarded in much the same light by both Gentiles and Jews; they are not purity offenses that the two cultures would define differently. Paul gives the charge of temple-robbing an ironic twist, however, by suggesting that the revulsion Jews should feel toward idols (a purity reaction) is not strong enough to protect Gentile sanctuaries from Jewish robbers.[19] The implication is that the desire to avoid contact with Gentile "abominations" is selective and inconsistent. But precisely because Jews are the people who have the Law, the Jewish offender makes God's name to be blasphemed among the Gentiles (2:24).

The easy sense of ethnic superiority, then, that the Jewish listener might gain by contrasting the purity of Jewish culture with the impurity of Gentile culture, does not really mean much, according to Paul. But, if so, the standard Jewish ethnic apologetic of the era does not hold up. What, then, is the good of being Jewish? (2:25–29). Not much, says Paul, for everything really depends on behavior, not on circumcision—not, that is, on simple membership in the circle of the pure Jewish ethnos (ethnic group). This, finally, is the closing of the rhetorical trap that Paul began laying in 1:18. After encouraging one portion of his addressees to feel superior to others, he catches them up short by rejecting any sense of superiority that might accrue to them purely from their ethnic and cultural identity, even though that was sacralized in the Torah.[20]

It is worth saying, at this point, that this critique of the Jewish interlocutor is only incidentally a critique of Judaism; fundamentally, it is a critique of ethnocentrism—or, better yet, of the general human tendency to categorize one's own group as intrinsically superior to others, whether as an act of aggression against weaker groups or, as in the case of Hellenistic Judaism, an act of defense against stronger ones. Paul's insistence on the priority and superiority of Judaism is integral to his argument because it grounds his treatment of idolatry as the fundamental Gentile sin. Jews really are right in rejecting idols and multiplicity of gods. But equally important is his placing of Jews and Gentiles on the same level with regard to sin and the possibility of recognizing and fulfilling God's will. Judaism is better than Gentile religion; Jews are not better than Gentiles. These principles intersect and conflict at the borders between the Gentile and Jewish communities—borders defined substantially in terms of purity. The tendency of Jewish apologetic was to present Jews as superior to Gentiles in the same way that Judaism was superior to Gentile religion. Paul is severing that link.

What Is the Value of Being Jewish? (3:1–20)

At this point, some in Paul's audience will assume that he has completely reversed fields. After attacking Gentile culture as unclean and shameful, he has now rejected the notion that Jewish identity is in any way superior. He has, in effect, put both parts of his audience at a disadvantage. At least, neither can complain of partiality on his part. He has reproved both in a confrontative way. Now he will have to move in a different direction if he wants to build some positive result on this foundation.

Paul begins this shift by asking quite openly the question that is certainly in the minds of some of his hearers: "So what is the advantage of the Jew? Or what is the good of circumcision?" (3:1) To this he replies, "Much in every way." As he explicates that claim, he moves away from addressing the hypothetical listener and shifts into the third person plural to make a confident assertion about Jewish identity: "In the first place, they have been entrusted with God's oracles" (3:2). Use of the third plural here extends the scope of the statement to include all Jews, not limiting it to the hypothetical interlocutor or even to Jewish Christians.

The Law embodies God's hidden, oracular wisdom.[21] As such, its value is not dependent on the excellence of Jewish stewardship. However false human beings may prove, God's purposes are not defeated; God is not implicated in their failures. Paul objects to those who might see in this teaching a doctrine of "anything goes." This is not a way of dismissing the importance of human action, but rather a recognition of God's generosity and power (3:8).

The point of the rhetorical plan thus far has been to "bring the accusation that both Jews and Greeks, all alike, are under sin" (3:9). Paul has begun in a situation where at least some of his Jewish auditors assume that Jews are more virtuous than Greeks and that the Greek openness to same-gender sexual relations is evidence of this—exactly what contemporary Jewish apologetic typically asserted. Paul reworks this classic Hellenistic Jewish apologetic by treating Greek culture not as sinful in itself, but as divine punishment for the Gentiles' root sin of idolatry. Still, his presentation evoked familiar ethnocentric presuppositions to elicit the semiconscious assumption of his Jewish addressees that Gentiles are sinners and Jews are not. Having brought this assumption to consciousness, he then makes it untenable.

Accordingly, the purpose of the Law is to convict those who have it of sin. The Law (ὁ νόμος) speaks to those who are "in the Law" (ἐν τῷ νόμῳ), that is, culturally and religiously determined by it. And it does so "in order that every mouth might be shut and the whole world be subject to God's judgment" (3:19). In the present rhetorical context, it is more specifically the mouth of the Jewish interlocutor of chapter 2 that is being shut. This interlocutor had no doubt about Gentile sinfulness; but the Law, according to Paul, presses him, however unwillingly, to join the scorned Gentiles in an acknowledgment of guilt.

Even though the Law *is* the advantage of the Jewish people (3:1–2), it does not resolve the problem of sin or the way sin complicates the relationship of humanity and God. "On the basis of works of Law, no flesh will be found innocent in the presence of [God], for Law is how we come to recognize sin" (3:20). The Law exists as a gracious expression of God's will—the oracles of God—and yet, its effect is to demonstrate that the Jewish auditor is as much a sinner as the Gentiles. Far from being the basis for a presumption of ethnic superiority, the Law can only serve as a way of prompting its hearers to humility and repentance.

Paul's earlier claim that Gentiles may do the works of the Law (τὰ τοῦ νόμου) without "having law," just by who they are ("by nature," φύσει, 2:14), and that all will be judged by their works (2:10, 12–15), effectively establishes parity between Gentile and Jew. It is what you do that counts, not the superiority of your ethnic identity nor any particular practice that serves to distinguish Jew from Gentile. The present passage concludes that, even for Jews, works of the Law will turn out to be inadequate to guarantee one's relationship with God, if only because Jews cannot claim to be any more sinless than Gentiles.

Trust, Not Law—the Same for Jew and Gentile (3:21–30)

All this gives Paul the opportunity to turn the focus away from the claims of human beings and back to the centrality of God. He has already said that he views the gospel as "God's power for salvation" (1:16). He has insisted that Jewish failure to keep the Law does not diminish God's faithfulness (3:3–4). Now he speaks about God's δικαιοσύνη, a word classically translated, when Paul applies it to God, as "righteousness," and when Paul applies it to sinful humanity, as "justification." We shall experiment here with the awkward but pertinent "righting" or "putting right" so as to include in the word not only God's own integrity but also God's desire to cooperate with humanity in "putting things right" again in the world. In 1:17, the term has already appeared almost as a synonym of the phrase "God's power for salvation" in 1:16.

This divine "righting" is perfectly in accord with the Law and the Prophets (3:21); it is therefore deeply embedded in Jewish faith. At the same time, it is manifest in a new form in relation to Jesus. Exactly how Jesus plays this decisive role is difficult to determine here, but Paul is at least clear about the *consequence* of what God has done in Jesus: the distinction between Jew and Gentile is no longer significant in relation to God.

As a result, there can be no further "boasting" (3:27). The boasting thus excluded, of course, is specifically, in this part of the letter, that of the Jewish Christian who feels superior to Gentiles. "For we reckon that a person is righted by faith/trust apart from works of Law" (3:28). The point is that God is God of *Gentiles* as well as of Jews (3:29–30). Accordingly, those elements of legal observance that distinguish the two—precisely issues of purity, including but not limited to circumcision—are no longer of ultimate significance. This is what Paul means, at least at this point, by insisting that "works of Law" (a phrase that here has the narrower sense of distinctive Jewish practices) are no longer decisive.

This Teaching Does Not Nullify, but Fulfills the Law (3:31–4:25)

When Paul insists that he is not nullifying the Law with this teaching but reaffirming it (3:31), many of his listeners will, of course, be skeptical. That is all right, because he is using this claim to introduce a proof. He has posed the challenge he hopes to meet; the argument will follow. Paul begins it in a way calculated specifically to draw in his Jewish-Christian auditors. He starts out in the first person plural: "So what shall we say . . . ?" This is, in itself, an invitation to the audience to join in an inquiry. But Paul goes on to make it specifically an invitation to the Jewish portion of the audience: "What shall we say that Abraham, *our ancestor in terms of the flesh,* found?" (4:1). In brief, Paul proposes to show the Jewish-Christian auditors that the inclusion of the Gentiles is implicit in the Law itself, embodied in the foundational promise to Abraham.[22] Paul's argument works in accordance with ancient norms of textual interpretation, even though it may be difficult for the modern reader to follow. In a nutshell, Paul argues from a psalm text[23] that Scripture blesses the person to whom righting is *reckoned*—as opposed, by implication, to the person who *earns* it (4:1–9). Abraham was uncircumcised and therefore unclean—outside the standards of Jewish ethnicity—when he received the blessing; and this makes him father of *all* who believe, not just of Jews (4:10–12).

The Law is not contravened if God's promise accomplishes something that the Law could not. Quite the contrary, Paul argues, this is all deeply in accord with the principles of Jewish faith. At the end of 4:17, he reminds the hearers that God can raise the dead and make something out of nothing. In that case, the surprises found in Paul's gospel should not seem incredible or unthinkable to them. To the contrary, Abraham's faith is the model for our own in expecting the unimaginable (4:18–25). In this way, Paul draws from the Law itself, in the broader sense of "the Scriptures of Israel," his sanctions for a move that might well appear to many of his hearers to nullify the Law in another sense, the sense of "the distinctive observances that separated Jew from Gentile."

In making such an argument, Paul is certainly departing from broadly acknowledged Jewish norms of self-understanding. This does not make his argument non-Jewish, however, much less anti-Jewish. As Daniel Boyarin has demonstrated, Paul is dealing with a tension implicit in Judaism itself, particularly in its most Hellenized (and therefore Platonized) form. While Judaism necessarily focuses on the relationship between God and Israel, there is always the question "What about the Gentiles?" The Platonizing element in Paul's Judaism, with its stress on the one as opposed to the many and therefore on the unity of the Holy, would have made this tension particularly difficult.[24]

Trust Brings Peace with God for All Humanity (5:1–21)

As I have noted, Paul shifts toward including Gentile-Christians in his "we" at 4:16. By the beginning of chapter 5, the "we" includes the whole Christian community without distinction, though this is implied rather than stated. Salvation is dependent only on the grace and love of God as evidenced in the gift of Jesus. Jesus died for us while we were still weak and sinful, while we were still enemies (5:6–10). In contrast to the hypothetical Jewish-Christian interlocutor of chapter 2, Paul has now firmly included Jews in the category of sinners and enemies of God alongside Gentiles. Therefore, God can deal with both in the same way.

God's love is unfailing and unconditional and therefore evokes trust, which in turn has the power to turn ordinary human expectations on their heads. "Once we've been put right on the basis of trust, . . . we even boast in the midst of our troubles," for we see them simply as producing the good result of hope through the love of God suffused in our hearts (5:1–5). Paul is appealing here to the Christian experience of conversion,[25] with its transformation or even reversal of previously held certainties.

By "conversion," I do not mean change of religion. For Paul and his Jewish-Christian hearers, there has been no change of religion. There has, however, been a critical discovery: the God whom they knew already is not quite as they supposed; and therefore the world and their own lives are now different. To the person who has experienced conversion in this sense, the world is new, even though it is still continuous with what one knew before.[26] Paul implies that for a Jewish Christian to give up claims of superiority based on distinctively Jewish practice is simply an extension of the initial conversion by which this person became a Christian in the first place, reposing trust in God's grace through Christ rather than in one's own perfection. That initial conversion entailed no rejection of the Law; but it did place something else in the center—the grace of a God who is willing to sacrifice his son to benefit his enemies (5:6–11).

What God has done in Jesus has to do with all humanity, not just Jews. It is symmetrical with the transgression of Adam and represents the same kind of major turning point in the history of humanity. Adam's sin brought death into the world, even for those who did not themselves transgress in the same way. Paul may be thinking of apparently sinless figures such as Enoch and Elijah, who are indeed spared death, but only by a direct divine intervention without which they, too, would presumably have died. Or he may be distinguishing between Adam, who violated a particular commandment, and others who sinned without having such a commandment to violate.[27]

The Law did not make a radical change in the situation inaugurated by Adam. It served only to introduce an element of conscious awareness of that situation. Before the Law, sin was "not reckoned" (οὐκ ἐλλογεῖται, 5:13). In one sense, this made little difference; death followed on sin anyway. But in another sense, the Law allows humanity to come to grips with its Adamic reality by becoming aware of sin and by choosing or rejecting it. Paul's argument is not entirely clear here, but there may be a parallel with his insistence on the importance of "reckoning" (ἐλογίσθη) in the earlier argument about Abraham (4:4). The important thing is not simply what happened, but how it is counted. The Law provides a clear basis for reckoning sin, and God chooses to make use of it in that way. Yet God retains the power to "reckon" apart from the Law, as when Abraham's faith was reckoned as righteousness. Law entered in to multiply "the transgression" (τὸ παράπτωμα, 5:20). In the light of the previous comment about "reckoning" sin, one might well take this to mean simply that the Law allowed humanity to become conscious of sin as sin. In this case, "Law" would not mean simply the Law of Moses, but law in the broader sense that Paul used earlier (2:12–16), a sense in which it is accessible to Gentiles as well as Jews. The value of the Law in this regard was to prepare the way for the magnifying of God's grace in Jesus. The Law makes the multiplicity and the magnitude of sin visible, so to speak.[28]

For Jesus' work is not *only* symmetrical with the sin of Adam. The symmetry is indeed there: through Adam "the many were constituted sinners" and through Jesus "the many will be constituted righteous" (5:19). But "the gift is not like the transgression" because its results exceed (ἐπερίσσευσεν) those of the transgression and bring life in place of death (5:15–17). The Law, then, belongs essentially to the Adamic era of human history as a way of concretizing it and making its sinfulness fully apparent.

Paul Answers Three Possible Objections (6:1–7:25)

Thus far, Paul, even though he has never mentioned the issues of food purity that trouble the Roman church, has been constructing a context for dealing with them. He has relativized the spiritual importance of those practices (primarily purity practices) by which Jews distinguished themselves from Gentiles while, at the same time, insisting on identity between the God of Israel and the God of Jesus. By itself, however, this will not be sufficient, since some of the addressees will still be harboring objections to his line of reasoning, objections that they feel invalidate it. To counter these, Paul makes a lengthy excursus in the middle of his argument. He will return to the main thread of his own thought only in 8:1.

There are three objections that Paul takes up and attempts to refute. Each is heralded by repetition of the phrase "What then . . . ?" (Τί οὖν . . . ;) (6:1, 15; 7:7). In each case, Paul responds with an expression not unlike the English "God forbid!" (Μὴ γένοιτο, 6:2, 15; 7:7). And each time he appeals to what he believes will be shared assumptions by asking, "Are you ignorant of . . . ?" (6:3; 7:1) or "Don't you know . . . ?" (6:16), or by asserting shared knowledge with "We know . . . ." (7:14).

In each case, the objection is one that would be raised by someone who wants to retain the full Torah, including its distinctive purity practices, as authoritative for all Christians. The objectors fear that Paul's gospel will demolish all ethical norms and leave the faithful without reliable guidelines to moral behavior. After all, the Jewish apologetics they have known have repeatedly contrasted moral Judaism with immoral Gentile culture. This may well constitute a problem not only for some of Paul's Jewish-Christian hearers, but also for some Gentile Christians, whose conversion to Christianity seemed to them to imply a far-reaching (if not absolute) accommodation to Jewish ethnic practice; "ethnic" and "ethical" are effectively indistinguishable for them, as they are for many human communities.

The first objection is roughly this: Aren't you making sin actually a *good,* since it gives rise to grace? Wouldn't this imply that Christians should continue to sin, since this would increase the amount of grace? (6:1). "Not at all," replies Paul, appealing to the shared experience of baptism. Grace has come to us (note the free use of the first person plural in the passage) through Jesus' death and resurrection. We participate in this death through baptism, and we are therefore implicated already in the life of the age to come. Sin cannot be a good for anyone or for any purpose in the age to come, which is the realm not of law but of grace (6:2–14).

The second objection runs thus: If we're no longer subject to Law, can we do anything we like? (6:15). Paul replies: No! We all understand that a slave cannot have dual loyalties. You have passed from one allegiance to another. The Law was only relevant while you were slaves of sin. (After all, it served as sin's bookkeeper; 5:13.) The idea that his Jewish as well as his Gentile hearers had been slaves of sin is, of course, of a piece with his whole argument to this point (6:15–23).

Death is emancipation from this slavery. Paul proves this point with an argument by analogy from the Torah. Just as the widow is no longer bound to her deceased husband, but is free, so too the Law is nullified by death in general, proving that it belongs to the world ruled by sin (and therefore characterized by death), not to the one ruled by grace. At this point, Paul returns to emphasizing the Jewish segment of his audience. In introducing this argument, he says specifically, "I am speaking to people who know the Law." But he is appealing, yet again, to the idea that the Torah, in this case, supports its own relativization in favor of grace (7:1).

The third objection asks, "Is the Law sin?" (7:7). Paul replies: No, but sin is able to use the Law to the destruction of the person who is "fleshly" (σάρκινος, a term Paul sometimes uses to denote what is opposed to God in the human being; 7:14) because the Law concretizes and particularizes ways of being sinful (cf. 5:13). The inner person can will the good, but not do it. We are divided within ourselves, as each of us knows. Paul shifts here to the first person singular: "I know that the good does not dwell in me, that is, in my flesh" (7:18). This statement of self-knowledge invites a similarly honest and modest self-appraisal on the part of his hearers—a gentler invitation to such reappraisal than the rhetorical trap of chapters 1–2.

Paul does not, however, want this negative appraisal of humanity to be the only word on the subject. It would amount to returning the whole discussion to the question of what humans deserve, after moving it emphatically to the subject of God's generosity. The concluding sentence of the section reiterates the divided nature of the human being. But just before it is an exclamation of hope: "Who will deliver me from this body of death? Thanks be to God through Jesus Christ!" (7:24b–25a).

I am treating this whole rather long section, often seen as virtually the heart of Romans, as merely a long aside. That is not to say that it is unimportant, only that it does not further the main thread of Paul's argument. His aside here is essential in order to establish that his bracketing of "the Law" in the sense of "what makes Jews different from Gentiles" does not have the effect of abolishing all distinction of right and wrong. To the contrary, Paul affirms the importance of "law" in the broader sense of faithful living, even as he asserts its limits as a means of transforming humanity. His objective is not to reject standards of ethical behavior but to undercut a sense of ethnic superiority.

Death/Flesh/Sin versus Life/Spirit/God (8:1–39)

Paul returns to the main track of his argument in chapter 8, where he also concludes it with a handsome peroration. He signals the return with a particle (ἄρα) that suggests a major summing up will follow: "So then! There is no condemnation at all now for those who are in Christ Jesus" (8:1). Having disposed of the various objections raised in chapters 6–7, he feels free to use a sweeping formulation of his basic premise that those elements of Torah that were purely distinctive of Jewish practice are no longer critical.[29] Paul remains quite clear that the Jewish people are central to the drama of salvation and that the Scriptures of Israel are the authentic oracles of God. None of this is in question. The focal point is rather those practices that served to distinguish the Jewish ethnos from Gentiles and therefore created divisions within mixed Christian communities. Paul's argument is less abstract than Christians have often assumed; it centers on a specific topic of immediate concern. Since the Christian's standing with God is based on something quite different from ethnic uniformity, namely, grace, distinctive ethnic practices have no absolute significance.

In a surprising turn, however, Paul reverts here, for the first time since chapter 3, to the use of the second singular pronoun: "For the law of the Spirit of life in Christ Jesus has liberated you (σε) from the law of sin and death" (8:2). At least, this is the probable reading. Some ancient authorities read "liberated me," and some read "liberated us." Both of these readings, however, can readily be understood as accommodations to what has preceded. Paul has just exclaimed, "Who will deliver me?" And in chapters 6 and 7 he has repeatedly emphasized the first person plural as embodying the shared faith of the Christian community. The shift to the second person singular, however, both continues and contrasts with the use of the first singular "me" in 7:24. There Paul used himself as example. Now he is inviting his addressees to join him in this exemplary mode. Yet his previous use of the second person singular was for the hypothetical objector of chapters 2–3—and, of course, all those hearers who may have identified with that objector. Now he invites those hearers to return to something he regards as central to their original calling/conversion: their move from a confidence centered on ethnic identity to one centered on Jesus and the Spirit.

Most Jewish Christians, before or apart from the influx of Gentiles into the community, would not have experienced any tension between Jewish identity, based in Torah, and Jesus. They would have continued to live in general accord with practices that defined their ethnicity as much as their religion. Locally slaughtered meats, for example, would have been kosher in any case, since that was simply the prevailing cultural standard. Still, their conversion (again, their experience of μετάνοια, not "conversion" in the sense of a change of religion) represented a major shift in focus that made the ensuing developments within the Christian community at least thinkable if not inevitable. The very mix of followers that Jesus is said to have drawn after him suggests that he had already minimized the importance of Levitical purity, even within the Jewish community.[30] And both

John and the Synoptic Gospels suggest that he welcomed Samaritan followers.

This was not to say, even for Paul, that the Law was somehow wrong, only that it could not achieve the desired end because of the way the weakness of human "flesh" was able to sabotage it. God could achieve the goal of reconciling humanity only through Jesus and the Spirit—that is, through the transformation worked in the faithful through their conversion. Paul can say confidently to his addressees: "But *you* are not in flesh, but in Spirit, if indeed the Spirit of God is dwelling among you" (8:9). This formulation has both the positive effect of assuring the addressees that they can trust their experience and the negative one of suggesting that those who disagree with Paul and insist on full Jewish practice do not have the Spirit. To belong to God, to have the Spirit, is a guarantee that the faithful belong to the life of the age to come. Now, nothing can stand in the way of God's good purpose toward you (plural; 8:11). We need fear neither earthly troubles (8:18–24; cf. 2:9; 5:3) nor supernatural powers (8:38–39). Despite appearances, "all things are working together for good to those who love God" (8:28).

There is no further occasion to be concerned about the Torah, though Paul politely avoids putting the matter quite so baldly. Instead, he says that we are no longer indebted to the flesh, nor have we received a "spirit of slavery" (8:12–15). Both flesh and slavery have previously been associated with our experience of the Law. In place of the Law, at the center of the Christian's experience of God, Paul puts the experience of "sonship," the experience of finding oneself part of God's family. This happens not through the Law but through our sharing in Christ's sufferings and therefore in his glory (8:16–17).

Paul steps up the emotion of his peroration by reasserting once again that this faith is a shared possession: "We know that all things work together . . ." (8:28). The remaining verses of the chapter build up, through elements of sound and word order, to a powerful statement of Christian hope. Note for example, the "climax" (ladder-construction) of verses 29–30:

> For those whom [God] foreknew, he also foreordained as sharers in the image of his Son . . . ; and those whom he foreordained, these he also called; and those whom he called, these he also righted; and those whom he righted, these he also glorified.

Each clause picks up and builds on the one before.

In verse 31, Paul again asks, "What then shall we say?" But now it is not the introduction of an objection but an invitation to the addressees to join him in a confession of shared faith: "If God be for us, who is against us?" This inaugurates a series of rhetorical questions emphasizing the shared belief that no one can negate God's goodwill for God's chosen people. The series concludes with a polysyndeton (a surplus of conjunctions) that serves to underline the impossibility:

> Who will separate us from the love of Christ—tribulation or distress
> or persecution or famine or nakedness or danger or sword? (8:35)

The implied answer, of course, is "none of the above," and the use of polysyndeton gives the whole list a sense of completeness, as if we have now rejected every possibility of contradiction. Paul then cites Scripture—"the oracles of God"—to give further authority to this thought. Yes, we have suffered and will suffer again, but we are bound to God in love and are therefore "more than conquerors" (8:36–37).

A final long polysyndeton brings the section to a conclusion (8:38–39):

> For I am persuaded that neither death nor life nor angels nor princi-
> palities nor things present nor things to come nor powers nor height
> nor depth nor any other created thing will be able to separate us from
> the love of God that is in Christ Jesus our Lord.

The careful composition and the expansiveness of this passage tell the hearers that they have reached the end of a major section in the letter. It is scarcely surprising that later readers have sometimes responded to this peroration as if it concluded everything of importance in the letter. In reality, it has a more limited purpose. In this whole first part of his argument, Paul has had a single focus—to exclude the possibility of maintaining that distinctively ethnic practice makes Jewish Christians intrinsically superior to Gentiles. The one exception to this equation of the two cultures is idolatry, which Paul identifies as the Gentiles' root sin. Here, Paul clearly sees a significant difference—but nowhere else.

Address to Gentile Christians (9:1–15:13)

Paul begins a new major division of the letter at this point, but at first the hearers are given only a few clues as to what is different. The rhetorical power of the preceding peroration is the first of these clues. But Paul blurs the transition a little by continuing his use of the first person singular. The last main verb of the preceding peroration was "I am persuaded." The first sentences of the new division of the letter are "I am telling the truth. I am not lying." The content that follows, however, signals a new departure.

For the first time in the letter, Paul begins to speak of the Jewish people consistently and at length in the third person. This does not mean that he is distancing himself from other Jews. To the contrary, his first reference to them is as "my brothers, my kinfolk according to the flesh"; only after establishing this relationship does he add a proper noun, "the Israelites" (9:3–4). Nor is Paul merely dismissive of those Jews who have not become believers in Jesus. He still describes them as the people who have "the adoption and the glory and the covenants and the legislation and the worship and the promises," and also "the ancestors" (9:4–5). From them, he reminds his hearers, "is the Christ as far as the flesh is concerned" (9:5). While "flesh" here must be inferior to "spirit," it is still essential to the divine work.

At first, this might appear to be only a shift in subject matter. Having finished his discussion of Law and grace, Paul now turns to a different theological topic, the (for him and his addressees) perplexing reality that the majority of Jews have not perceived in Jesus the fulfillment of God's will. When we recall, however, how much of the preceding eight chapters was addressed specifically and sometimes quite explicitly to the Jewish portion of the Roman Christian community, we will suspect that something more is going on here. From the second person—whether singular, as in the case of the hypothetical objector, or plural, as more often—the Jews have now come to be characterized in the third person; they have become a topic to be discussed, much as the Gentiles were in 1:18–32, even though Paul affirms that he is a member of the group at issue.

I have labeled this division of the letter "Address to Gentile Christians." In fact, however, it is not until 11:13 that Paul will make this explicit by saying, "I'm talking to you Gentiles!" This direct address is surprising because at first reading it seems that nothing has prepared us for it. What is there to suggest that Paul would be speaking specifically to Gentile Christians already as early as chapter 9? At the beginning, there is no clue except his subtle shift of the Jewish nation into the third person.

What Paul is up to here becomes fully evident only in 11:17, where Paul returns again to the use of the second person singular to pinpoint a hypothetical objector; but in this case the objector exemplifies Gentile, not Jewish, pride. The use of the second singular again in this way suggests that Paul's discussion of the fact that most Jews have not become believers in

Jesus (chaps. 9–10) is parallel to the attack on the filthiness of Gentile culture earlier (1:18–32). It is a disguised act of provocation, a trap, a device to lure Gentile prejudices into the open where they can be identified and rejected.

This is not to deny that Paul is indeed interested in the question of ongoing Judaism in its own right. Indeed, it is intimately linked to the central issue of Romans. Paul, after all, represents the influx of Gentiles into the Christian community, and the presence of these converts, who are still Gentiles and not committed to the distinctive practices that set the Jewish ethnos apart, is part of what makes the Christian community an object of suspicion for many Jews. Paul cannot really dismiss the issue, even if he wishes to.

The Failure of the Gospel to Win All Jews (9:1–33)

Paul's criticism of those Jews who have rejected the gospel is not couched in terms as contemptuous as his attack on Gentile culture in chapter 1. It is phrased rather in terms of Paul's personal distress—particularly apparent when he exclaims that he would be willing to be outcast from Christ if it would benefit his coreligionists (9:3)—and of his perplexity about what God is doing at this moment in history.

In search of a theological explanation, Paul offers, as often, multiple avenues of thought. One is to say that the descendants of Jacob, like those of Abraham and Isaac, are perhaps not all to be considered the true Israel. This idea derives from earlier prophetic images of a faithful remnant, to whom God will still make good the promises to the ancestors despite the failure of the majority (9:6–9).[31] Another possible direction is an appeal to God's sovereignty and the idea of predestination, rooted in the Exodus account of the hardening of Pharaoh's heart (9:10–23).

The idea of predestination is, of course, found widely in NT writings, but its real importance there is apt to be lost on the modern Western reader. Because of our Augustinian theological tradition of "metaphysicalizing" predestination, turning it into one of several successive steps in God's dealings with humanity, we are apt to think of it primarily in terms of dogmatic theology. In many cases, we go on to assign it to the theological archives as a notion that has outlived its usefulness, thanks to the way in which some followers of John Calvin pushed it to extremes. In the NT, I am persuaded, the importance of predestination has less to do with a dogmatic theology that had not yet come into existence than with a critical issue of Christian spirituality, grounded in the experience of conversion. Conversion often comes as a surprise, not as something carefully prepared for and thought through. It is not the convert who is "in charge," but rather the grace that evokes the conversion.

The early Christians saw themselves as people who had been claimed by God—"called as saints," to use Paul's own language (1:7). If the members of the Christian community, however, owed their acceptance of the gospel to the experience of grace intervening and redirecting them, how were they to explain the many people who heard the same message and did not respond to it in the same way? In many different ways, NT writers ascribe both acceptance and refusal of the gospel to God's work as distinct from that of the human being. "Predestination," with all its later theological history, is a clumsy word for this; but we lack an alternative. Paul's second-person-singular objector returns here (9:19) to make the inevitable objection that this is not just. Paul responds by appealing to God's unlimited sovereignty. As the Creator of all, God is free to make one pot for destruction and another for glory (9:22–23). This actually places the refusal of many Jewish hearers of the gospel to accept it in a context that invalidates any effort to place blame on them. It was not their choice; it was God's choice.

Paul does not mind putting alongside this, however, another argument that says it *was* their choice and that they chose badly. (The need to sort out the precise mutual limits of predestination and free will is the particular demon of Western Christianity, not of the NT authors.) What was their error? "Israel, though pursuing a law of righting, did not attain the law. Why? Because they proceeded on a basis not of trust/faith, but of works," that is, ethnic distinctiveness (9:31). Accordingly, says Paul, they found the Torah a stumbling block rather than an opportunity of conversion.

By offering these variant explanations of what he saw as a distressing turn of events, Paul is also furthering an almost subliminal rhetorical process of shifting his focal audience. The vessels God intended for glory, he says, are "we whom God has called, not just from among the Jews but from among the Gentiles" (9:24). Just as Paul has begun to use the third person to refer to Israel at the beginning of this chapter, he now uses "we" to shape a specifically Christian community inclusive of Gentiles as well as Jews.

Paul confirms this move by appealing to Hos 2:1, a passage he interprets as meaning that those who were not God's people in the past (i.e., Gentiles) are now to be understood as God's people.[32] By way of contrast, Paul then cites Isaiah as authority for the doctrine of the remnant that he had earlier invoked as one possible way of explaining the refusal of the gospel by many Jews. Paul even adds a second quotation from Isaiah that includes a threatening comparison between Israel and Sodom and Gomorrah (9:29). No doubt, Paul is fully conscious of the irony of this comparison, since by his time, the example of Sodom was part of the Jewish polemic against Gentile tolerance of same-gender sexual relationships.[33] Paul makes no reference to the Sodom story in his own treatment of same-gender sexuality in chapter 1; but here, with Isaiah, he turns it against the Jewish nation instead.

Beyond the Law (10:1–11:12)

The next segment of Paul's argument consists mainly of Scripture quotations to show that grace is equally available to Gentiles and that Israel's failure to respond to the gospel was predicted all along. There is little that is new here, but it is important for Paul to build a solid array of scriptural support for his claims. It is one thing for modern Christians, almost entirely Gentile, to accept the reality of ongoing Judaism as simply a given. It was another thing for Paul and his contemporaries. They were laying claim to represent the true tradition of Judaism despite the reality that the majority of their coreligionists did not agree with them.

Paul can interpret the situation in several ways, as we have already seen, since his cultural environment did not insist that there ought to be a single, exclusive explanation for such events. In this passage, he adds the claim that Christ is the telos of the Law—its culmination and fulfillment, and also its conclusion (10:4). Paul can speak of Jesus in this way because he sees Jesus as a principal topic of the Scriptures of Israel. He was spoken of already in Deuteronomy, according to Paul, as "the word" that is "near you" (10:8). Jesus, then, is not only the opposite, in some sense, of Law, but also its continuation and fulfillment.

The development of a church increasingly Gentile in membership and increasingly at odds with the mainstream of the Jewish nation, Paul presents as the playing out of a process already predicted and outlined in the Scriptures. The practice of distinctively Israelite Law is no longer to be the way to God, though it was a necessary intermediate step. Now the central path to God is the trust that arises from hearing the proclamation about Jesus. And the corollary of this is that access to God is as open to Gentiles qua Gentiles as to the people of Israel.

Paul reemphasizes the importance of his own role as apostle in this process (10:14–15). This, too, he sees as prophesied in the Scriptures. The refusal of the many in Israel, then, is partly a result of ignorance: they did not really understand what God was doing in giving the Law. It was not intended, in itself, to bring about "salvation" (10:1–3). It was intended to

bring both Israel and the Gentiles to a new level of trust in God's willingness to put things right. At the same time, Paul is willing to say that Israel
should have recognized and understood this process (as, indeed, the Gentiles should have known better than to worship idols). After all, the events
unfolding in his own time—the inclusion of Gentiles and the hostile reaction of some Jews—were already foretold in the Scriptures for anyone with
an eye to see them (11:19–21).

The emphasis throughout this passage is on what Paul sees as the failure of Israel. Even with his expression of deep personal concern (10:1), he
is profoundly critical of his coreligionists. He concludes the argument with
a pair of questions, both prefaced by "I say then" and both answered by
"Unthinkable!" (μὴ γένοιτο). The first question is "Has God thrust his people aside?" (11:1). The second is "Have they stumbled so badly as to fall
completely?" (11:11). Paul's negative answer to these questions relies
partly on the fact that the Christian community is in fact full of Jewish
members, Paul among them. They vindicate the doctrine of the remnant,
for which Paul now cites the story of Elijah at Horeb (11:2–7). The remnant, then, will achieve what all Israel hoped for, while the majority will be
hardened. And yet Paul also maintains a broader hope: if God has hardened them, it is only for a time; and the ultimate expectation is for their
return (11:11–12). One cannot emphasize too strongly that Paul is not dismissing the distinctive relationship between God and Israel. To read the
passage in that sense, in fact, is precisely to fall into the trap it lays for Gentile arrogance.

Paul is still addressing a community divided along ethnic and theological lines. How might different portions of the audience hear this passage?
Other Jewish Christians may well have shared Paul's concerns. Some of
them, in fact, may have blamed Paul's apostolate to Gentiles for creating or
exacerbating tensions between Christian Jews and the mainstream Jewish
community. Gentile Christians at Rome, on the other hand, may well have
found themselves responding much as the hypothetical Jewish-Christian
hearer responded to Paul's attack on Gentile culture in chapters 1–2. The
Gentiles can now think of the Jews as those who did not understand or live
up to the role God assigned them and of themselves as the faithful ones,
succeeding to Israel's place.

To be sure, Paul has described the rejection of the gospel on the part of
some Jews as evidence of a kind of hardening of heart—a divine act, not
merely a human one. In this, his attack on Jews is comparable to his attack
on Gentiles in chapter 1; for there, too, the filthiness of Gentile culture is

described not as a choice, but as a punishment divinely visited on them. But that did not keep the hypothetical Jewish-Christian respondent in chapters 2–3 from feeling superior. And here, too, Paul has, in effect, invited the Gentile-Christian audience to feel superior to the Jewish people, particularly to those who remain outside the Christian community.

Paul will now shift to speaking directly to the Gentile Christians. But he has already prepared the whole audience for this change in addressees, since he has been speaking about Israel in the third person since the beginning of chapter 9, a distancing so complete that it comes almost as a surprise when he again asserts his own identity as a Jew in 11:1. (This time, he does not reassert his communion with his Jewish-Christian addressees by using "we.") The stage, then, has been set. Paul has tacitly invited Gentile Christians to assume a role of superiority to their Jewish coreligionists. Ironically, Paul constructs this trap with the help of numerous Scripture citations, which means that he has also tacitly reaffirmed the Gentiles' debt to Israel. He now springs the trap he has constructed—this time in a less leisurely way.

Address to Proud Gentiles (11:13–36)

Paul has suggested that the "fall" of Israel is a divinely chosen way of bringing "salvation" to Gentiles (11:11). Now he turns directly to the Gentile-Christian part of his audience, whose presence was recognized in the salutation, but who have been referred to largely in the third person up to now:

> It's you I'm talking to, you Gentiles. Inasmuch, you see, as I am apostle to Gentiles, I make much of the service I perform in the hope that somehow I may provoke my own flesh to jealousy and save some of them. (11:13–14)

Thus far, Paul may even seem to be holding Gentile Christians up as models, further encouraging a certain self-satisfaction on their part.

But then Paul moves from the second plural to the second singular, marking the Gentile objector, like the Jewish one of chapter 2, as a hypothetical person rather than identifying the whole Gentile audience of the letter as committing this mistake:

> But if some of the branches have been broken out and you (σύ) wild-olive though you are, have been grafted in among them and become

a sharer in the domestic olive's root of fatness, don't lord it over the branches. If you do—it's not you that support the root, but the root you. (11:17–18)

Paul then goes on to remind the Gentile interlocutor that what was grafted in can be taken out again. Gentile Christians must never imagine that they are present in the community by some virtue or entitlement of their own.

In yet another parallel between this passage and the entrapment of the Jewish interlocutor in chapters 1–3, Paul returns to the language of "nature" and speaks of God's "grafting in" of the Gentiles as "contrary to nature" (11:24). This language he last used to describe same-gender sexual intercourse in chapter 1. The inclusion of Gentiles in the Christian community represents a break with the preceding order of things as substantial as God's handing over of the Gentiles to their unclean culture. God's willingness to contravene "nature" can thus lead in more than one direction. The constant, in both cases, is an assumption that there was a clear Gentile identity that God has altered not once, but twice: first in punishing the Gentile foundational sin of idolatry, and now, a second time, in incorporating Gentiles into the Christian community for reasons entirely of God's own grace. Both were "unnatural" acts.

But God's grace cannot become a basis for boasting because it never implies that there is anything superior about the recipient. It demonstrates rather God's propensity for putting things right. Hence, there is no more room for Gentile Christians to feel superior to Jews than for Jewish Christians to feel superior to Gentiles.

Paul now addresses the Gentile-Christian component in the Roman church again in the second person plural, abandoning the hypothetical interlocutor, whose arrogance he has condemned. He moves to set a standard of humility for the whole of the Gentile-Christian group:

> For I don't want you to be ignorant, brothers and sisters, of this mystery, so that you won't be wise in your own sight—the mystery that hardening has settled, in part, on Israel until the full complement of the Gentiles comes in, and so all Israel will be saved. (11:25–26a)

God's dealings with the Jews (their "hardening") have been motivated by a desire to save the Gentiles, not by any intention to dispossess Israel. Indeed, "all Israel will be saved." As Paul reminds both sets of listeners, "The gifts and the calling of God are inalterable" (11:29). And God gives to each group at least partly for the sake of bringing about some good for the other.[34]

Finally, Paul concludes this large section of the letter in a way as emphatic as the previous one. There, at the end of chapter 8, he constructed an elaborate summing up of his teaching about God's unfailing generosity. Here, he creates a conclusion that belongs more to the tradition of psalmody or hymnody. It begins with two exclamations:

> O the depth of the wealth and wisdom and knowledge of God!
> How unsearchable are his judgments and untrackable his paths!
> (11:33)

And, after a quotation from Isaiah emphasizing that God is beyond any human influence, Paul moves to a doxology:

> Because from him and through him and for him are all things. Glory
> be his for ever. Amen. (11:36)

This benediction brings closure to the argument against Gentile superiority.

At the same time, this conclusion, however beautiful, is relatively brief and therefore makes less of an impression than the "peroration" at the end of chapter 8. One might expect something more memorable if the present address to Gentile Christians were fully parallel to the previous section addressing Jewish Christians. The difference, I think, is that while Paul is concluding his two-sided preparatory argument at this point, he is also preparing to move to a discussion of the specific problem of food purity. These verses are as much transition as conclusion. Paul cannot bring the address to Gentile Christians to a sharp close because it is the immediate foundation for much of what he wants to say next and because, in a certain sense, he must now address the Roman church as a whole through the medium of its Gentile members.

This has not been necessary up to this point because Paul was constructing an argument about general principles. Jewish and Gentile members of the Roman church had different investments in it and were addressed separately; yet all were free to listen to the argument. The use of the second-person-singular interlocutor, for example, kept anyone from being directly attacked. From here on, however, Paul is going to propose certain standards of behavior immediately affecting both Jewish and Gentile Christians. He has just reiterated his own role as apostle to Gentiles

(11:13); and, if the benediction is genuine (16:25–27), he will return to that claim near the end of the work. He expects this role to establish some bond between him and the Gentile-Christian portion of the audience and so to gain a respectful hearing from them. Even if they are not themselves his converts, they know of him as a principal champion of their right to be a part of the community.

On the Jewish-Christian element of the Roman community, however, he has little claim beyond some, probably remote, degree of kinship. Indeed, some of them may well be hostile toward him because they see him as one who is indifferent to Jewish distinctiveness and who tends to encourage indiscriminate mingling between Jews and Gentiles. In this situation, Paul will have to be cautious about how he makes his recommendations to the church as a whole. Rather than sacrifice the momentum of his argument by bringing the address to the Gentiles to a full conclusion, he merely slows the pace enough to suggest that a shift is taking place. In the process, he allows the following passage to be heard as a continuation of his address to Gentile Christians, even though it will contain ideas directed at Jewish Christians as well—or more precisely, at those who are attached to the observance of distinctive Jewish purity law.

Admonition Addressed Increasingly to the Whole Community (12:1–15:13)

After the doxology, Paul continues in the second person plural. Even though there is nothing to suggest any change of audience, there is actually no further focus on the Gentile identity of the "you" addressed. The good advice that follows in chapter 12 and the beginning of chapter 13 applies to all members of the community alike. In fact, much of this advice is of such amiable and self-evident good sense that it is almost impossible to take exception to it. It therefore serves to establish a prejudgment, on the part of the whole audience, of agreement with what Paul will subsequently propose.

A new element, however, enters into Paul's description of the audience in this section of the letter. The distinction that will emerge in chapter 14 is no longer between Jew and Greek, but between Weak and Strong—two groups that are apparently defined principally by their attitude toward the eating of unkosher food. The Weak are those whose consciences are troubled by such food; the Strong are those who believe that the purity or impurity of food is of no concern to Christians. It would be a mistake to identify these as purely ethnic distinctions. We have reason to think that some Greek-speaking Jews of the first century held the concern for food purity lightly if at all. Philo objects to those who feel that the laws on this subject were of allegorical significance only.[35] And Mark claims that Jesus taught that the purity of food was unimportant (7:19). Some Jewish Christians, then, may have been among the Strong.

At the same time, it is not at all difficult to suppose that some Gentile Christians chose to adopt the Jewish food-purity code. There was great attraction to "oriental" religions in the early Roman Empire. And Luke indicates that an important part of the earliest Christian communities was made up of people he calls "God-fearers"—Gentiles who had accepted Judaism in principle and, to some extent, in practice, but without becoming full converts to it. (Such conversion, of course, involved not merely a religious transition, but a legal, political, and ethnic one as well.) In Paul's letter to Galatians, we encounter Christian communities made up almost entirely, it seems, of Gentiles, who are nonetheless fascinated by a "new" version of Christianity that requires of them the practice of distinctively Jewish rites, particularly circumcision of their males. In short, the two perspectives on purity attributed to the Weak and the Strong are not simply disguised ethnic identities. While the majority of the Weak may well have been Jewish and a majority of the Strong Gentile, these two perspectives on purity actually mark a somewhat different and, as it were, more principled division.

Paul does not, however, move directly to try to resolve these issues. Instead, he begins by establishing himself as a giver of good advice that anyone could safely follow. Even if there is no explicit expansion of the "you" here, the Jewish members of the audience will feel as much at home with the material as the Gentiles.

Relatively Noncontroversial Admonitions (12:1–13:14)

Paul commends the importance of a life focused on God, not the world. He directs his addressees to "offer your bodies as a living sacrifice, holy, pleasing to God, which is your rational worship" (12:1). This might well strike a chord with those to whom purity was important. After all, purity in the Torah is at its highest level in relation to the sanctuary and altar. He also tells them to be "transformed by the renewing of your minds" (12:2), which he expects will help them to discern what is genuinely good. This reminds the addressees that they are Christians by virtue of having already experienced such a change of mind, that they are not strangers to such an experience.

Paul has distanced himself from the addressees at the beginning of this section with a first-person-singular verb: "So I exhort you . . ." He does it again in 12:3: "For I am telling—by virtue of the grace given me—every person who's among you not to credit yourself with more than is right." But he will quickly move to reidentify himself with the audience. He does stand apart as a teacher; yet he is part of the community, too. Using the image of the body and its many members, each with its own praxis, he shifts to first person plural: "We who are many are one body in Christ" (12:5). Accordingly, we have gifts that differ. One of those he names is the gift of "encouragement" or "exhortation" (12:8), using the same word he had used of himself in 12:1: "I exhort . . ." Paul, then, is implying that his role as exhorter here exists for the sake of the community as a whole. He thus suggests that he will abide by that understanding of his gifts, and the community can afford to listen to him since he is not seeking credit for himself.

The admonitions that follow all have to do with maintaining the unity of the community. "Let love be without hypocrisy" (12:9), Paul begins. And the rest follows in the same vein. He wants the community to be consistent in its judgments, hospitable, considerate, humble, hopeful, patient, generous. Bland as the list sounds, it is actually quite topical. If we convert these virtuous adjectives into their antonyms, we have a description of the agents of disintegration who bedeviled first-century urban Christian communities: changeable, suspicious, self-centered, arrogant, grasping, impatient, greedy.[36]

Even to their persecutors, the community is to respond with blessings, not curses (12:14, 17–20). How much more ought they to prefer others to themselves within the Christian community (12:15–17). In sum, "Don't be conquered by evil, but conquer evil with good" (12:21). Paul is preparing his audience for the moment, not far off now, when he will ask all alike to take active—and, for many of them, less than attractive—roles in overcoming the existing suspicions among them.

Paul seems to make a kind of digression with a third-person admonition to respect the government (13:1–7). It begins with a third-person imperative ("Let every soul be subject . . ."), continues with a discourse on the divine ordination of earthly governments (13:1b–4), and results in a "therefore" that applies to the congregation at large. In particular, Paul insists on the necessity of paying taxes and other dues (13:6–7). We can guess that there may have been some particular local history behind these remarks. There were tensions at various times between the Jewish community at Rome and the government. Paul may have wished to keep the Christian community out of the way of urban disturbances. But it is also possible that he is using this short lecture on public obedience as a surrogate for encouraging obedience to authorities within the church community. Hierarchy was, after all, one way of trying to maintain unity.

Finally, Paul sums up all this good advice in terms of two standards of behavior. One is love (13:8–10). Loving behavior, says Paul, cannot possibly run counter to what the Law really demands. Indeed, "the person who loves the other has fulfilled law" (13:8b), since "love does not work harm to the neighbor" (13:10a). Paul can even say that "Love is the fulfilling (πλήρωμα) of law" (13:10b), where the word "pleroma" might mean that love always performs the specifics that the law commands or, more likely in the context of this letter, that what love commands is enough to satisfy the Law, even if it does not fulfill its letter. The latter interpretation allows for the fact that Paul is about to bracket the Torah's purity requirements.

Paul's second standard of behavior is the image of "daytime," as opposed to "nighttime," behavior (13:11–14). He speaks of the "hour" in which "we," the Christian community, find ourselves—the end time, the time to wake up. And he uses that image to describe an appropriate kind of behavior for the community—the kind of behavior one is not afraid to have seen by others. He contrasts it with "revels and drunkenness, sexual intercourse [literally, "beddings," κοίταις] and dissolute behavior"—a fairly obvious set of nighttime behaviors. But he also contrasts it with "strife and jealousy" (13:13). In other words, Paul is still drawing the addressees' attention back to the unity of the Christian community—to the particular vices that threaten it and the virtues that can help maintain it. When he tells the addressees to "clothe yourselves in the Lord Jesus Christ and have no forethought for the flesh to [fulfill] the desires" (13:14), he is not speaking simply of "flesh" in the modern sense of sensual temptations, but of the selfish, grasping quality in the human being that produces social disruption.

The Problem of Food Purity (14:1–15:6)

It seems odd, then, that Paul continues with "Welcome (προσλαμβάνεσθε) the person weak in trust/faith, but not in order to get into arguments with him" (14:1). For the last two chapters, the second-person-plural infinitives would be heard as addressed to the community as a whole. Now Paul takes a part of the community, the Weak person, out of the group he addresses in the second person; he is therefore, by implication, speaking only to the Strong. Yet he has made no explicit shift here. This serves subtly to identify the Strong as the core of the community.

In any case, Paul needs to keep the Strong in view here because he has more leverage with them. After all, they are the people who most readily accept the presence of Gentiles in the Christian community. In the material that follows, we find that Paul regularly addresses himself to them and even gives directives to them. Only incidentally, in asides, does he develop the implications of these directives for the behavior of the Weak.

It may well be that the terminology of Weak and Strong was already familiar at Rome. In any case, Paul makes certain that the addressees now see exactly where he has been headed all this time. The issue at Rome is distinctive Jewish observance, as instanced initially in matters of food purity: "One person trusts that it is all right to eat everything, but the weak person eats vegetables" (to avoid unkosher meats; 14:2). He even offers a hint of each group's characteristic stance toward the other when he tells each of them how *not* to behave: "Let the person who eats not be contemptuous of the one who refrains from eating; and let the person who refrains from eating not sit in judgment on the one who does eat—after all, God has accepted him" (14:3).

The double characterization is neat and effective. It captures each group at its least attractive: the Strong contemptuous of the Weak, who cannot seem to think for themselves or draw the inevitable conclusions from the gospel; the Weak scandalized by the behavior of the Strong and sitting in judgment on their moral laxity. Paul does go on to give a special warning to the Weak. But he reverts to the second person singular, as he has before when he wanted to paint a negative picture of a hypothetical stance without pointing at anyone in particular: "You! who are you who sit in judgment on another's servant? His own lord decides whether he stands or falls. And he will stand, because the Lord is able to hold him up" (14:4).

Paul's earlier discussion of the diversity of gifts becomes relevant again now. The members of the body, he argued previously, do not all have the same praxis, the same work to perform, the same behavior (12:4). Now Paul turns to the issue of holidays to say not only that Gentile Christians do not have to adopt the Jewish calendar (for example, Sabbath observance), but that there is room within the Christian community for differing observances:

One person distinguishes one day from another; another treats every day the same. Let each be fully satisfied in his own mind. The person who observes the day observes it with reference to the Lord. The person who eats, eats with reference to the Lord, for he gives God thanks. The person who refrains from eating refrains with reference to the Lord and gives God thanks. For not one of us lives [merely] with reference to himself or dies [merely] with reference to himself.

> For if we live, we live with reference to the Lord; and if we die, we die
> with reference to the Lord. So whether we live or die, we belong to
> the Lord. For this is why Christ died and returned to life—to be lord
> of both the dead and the living. (14:5–9)

For Christians, relationship to Jesus gives life its meaning. (Notice Paul's
return to the first person plural: we're all in this together.) But what distinguishes the Christian is not a specific list of things one must do—at least,
not the list embodied in the Torah—but rather the way everything one
does has reference to the Lord. This principle can embrace the differing
praxes of those who eat anything and those who eat only what is kosher, of
those who observe the Torah calendar and those who do not. More than
that, it embraces the whole universe, the world of the dead as well as of the
living. In other words, it is of a piece with the Christians' fundamental
trust in God.

Paul has inserted a proviso, however: "Let each be fully satisfied in his
own mind." It does not follow that the Christian can do anything at all.
Paul is not proposing that the faithful person can simply follow the desire
of the moment. He will enlarge on this point a bit later. For the moment,
he is pressing another point—his condemnation of the way the two groups
treat one another.

Paul reverts again to the second person singular—the hypothetical person who is so much easier to confront. He has already rapped the knuckles
of the Weak. This time, he includes the Strong as well:

> You! why are you judging your brother? Or you! why are you regard-
> ing your brother with contempt? For we shall all stand in God's
> court, for it is written:
>
>> As I live, says the Lord, to me will every knee bow,
>> and every tongue will confess me as God. (Isa 45:23)
>
> So, then, each one of us will be giving God an account of himself.
> (14:10–12)

Paul's impartiality here, of course, cannot mask the fact that he himself
belongs on the side of the Strong. Otherwise, he could not have performed
his ministry among Gentiles. Paul is concerned, however, to maintain the
unity of the community. He is not willing to press for a victory on the part
of the Strong that would drive the Weak out. Instead, he must try to

rebuild the mutuality implicit in "we" while resolving the particular issue that threatens it. He has just introduced the first person plural again ("each one of us"). Now he imposes a common directive on all—himself included: "Let's not judge each other any more." In this case, "judging" is not simply the behavior of the weak, but a catchall term for the dismissive behavior of both sides.

The alternative to judging one another is presented with a second person plural imperative: "But make this judgment instead: that you won't put a stumbling block or a scandal in front of a brother" (14:13). Paul then hastens to say that he is not yielding at all on the point of principle. In fact, he puts the basic principle of the Strong in the most emphatic terms possible, introducing his formulation of it with the phrase "I know and am persuaded (οἶδα καὶ πέπεισμαι) in the Lord Jesus" (14:14).

This is not a common phrase for Paul. Even its component parts are not common. In three other places, two of them in Romans, Paul uses οἶδα to introduce statements with theological import. In the first passage in Romans, he declares, "For I know that good does not dwell in me, that is, in my flesh" (7:18). In the second, he says, "And I know that, when I come to you, I will be coming with the fullness of Christ's blessing" (15:29). In both cases, the knowledge seems to express a kind of internal certainty, one based in Paul's own experience of life and the Spirit.[37] It is perhaps surprising that Paul does not use this expression more often, given how frequently he uses this same verb in the first or second person plural. He is quite willing to speak of what "we know" or to ask his addressees, "Don't you know . . . ?" But the locution "I know" is rare with him.

The parallel verb "I am persuaded" also appears twice elsewhere in Romans, but nowhere else in the undoubted Pauline letters.[38] It is found at Rom 8:38, in the elegantly constructed peroration of the first major section of the letter. There Paul uses it to underline a major statement of trust in God: "I am persuaded that neither death nor life nor angels [nor other powers] will be able to separate us from the love of God that is in Christ Jesus our Lord." The final instance of πέπεισμαι in Romans (15:14) serves to underline Paul's good opinion of his Roman addressees: "And I am persuaded, my brothers and sisters, even I myself, regarding you that you yourselves are full of goodness, filled up with all knowledge, quite able, in fact, to instruct each other." Here it combines with other modes of emphasis that I have (somewhat clumsily) translated with such phrases as "even I myself" and "you yourselves." In both these cases, πέπεισμαι indicates a strong conviction.

The combined expression, "I know and am persuaded," then, gives a strong emphasis to what follows it—an emphasis further enhanced when Paul specifies that this conviction has its origins in Jesus. Probably, given what we have seen of his use of οἶδα, Paul refers to his personal experience of Jesus: "I know and am persuaded in the Lord Jesus that nothing is unclean in and of itself, except that for the person who regards something as unclean, for that person it is unclean" (14:14). His calling as apostle to Gentiles would have forced him to grapple with these issues from the beginning.

It would not be a mistake to call this the central affirmation of Romans. I do not say that it is the central affirmation of Paul's faith; chapters 7–8 may give us a closer view of that. But it is the principle that Paul sees as necessary to any resolution of the conflict over food purity in the church at Rome. It is therefore also vital to his own future relationship with that church. If this principle is lost, then Paul's mission would have no meaning there.

This principle has two sides to it. On the one hand, it affirms the idea, central to Paul's ministry, that there is no intrinsic obligation for Christians to observe such Torah commandments as were purely distinctive to Jewish culture. Even something as fundamental as circumcision is not vital when Gentile males are seeking access to God. On the other hand, the principle also affirms that those who have a conscientious commitment to the importance of specifically ethnic-Jewish purity have not only the right but the duty to maintain it.

Paul had already hinted at such an idea a few sentences earlier, when he said that, whether a person observes the food purity laws or not, one needs to "be fully satisfied in his own mind" (14:5). The Christian community can allow, according to Paul, a certain diversity in practice. But each of us must live and die, eat or refrain from eating, with reference to the Lord; and this requires a certain integration of theological understanding, spiritual experience, and practice. Paul does not believe that it requires uniformity throughout the community, but it does demand integrity in the individual.

In an address framed in the second person singular, Paul now goes on to explain the import of this principle for the behavior of the Strong. The second person singular may once again be a way to avoid pointing the finger at particular people, for Paul does not label the person he addresses as one of the Strong. It is also, however, at this point, a way of emphasizing individual responsibility. Paul is offering not a single rule for the whole community, but corresponding norms of behavior for both Weak and Strong. And he begins with the party for which his word carries most weight.

What, then, is the Strong person to do? The simple answer is that the Strong individual must exercise restraint:

> For if, on account of food, your brother is brought to grief, you're no longer walking in accordance with love. Don't destroy the person for whom Christ died by what you eat. (14:15)

This does not, apparently, mean for Paul that the Strong simply yield to the Weak and adopt the Torah's prescriptions about food. Instead, he hopes to create a situation where the Strong continue to maintain their position but do so in a way that is less confrontative and more likely to win respect:

> So don't let the good that you have be blasphemed. For God's reign is not a matter of food and drink, but of righting and peace and joy in the Holy Spirit. For the person who serves Christ in this matter [or way] is pleasing to God and approved by human beings. (14:16–18)

If the community is to maintain its unity in the face of divergent practice, it will have to lower the volume of its internal polemics.

Accordingly, Paul presents as his conclusion (marked by the "summing-up" particles ἄρα οὖν) a proposal for reorientation of the discussion:

> So then—let's pursue the things that have to do with peace and the things that have to do with mutual upbuilding. Don't destroy God's work for the sake of food. To be sure, all things are clean; but it's bad for the person who eats [something he disapproves of] as an act of stumbling. It would be good [by comparison] not to eat meat or drink wine or whatever your brother trips over. As for yourself, hold the faith that you have [in this matter] privately in God's presence. (14:19–22a)

The phrase I have translated "privately" could mean "internally," but it would be more in accord with the argument to conclude that Paul means rather to make a distinction between what is eaten at home and what is eaten at the church's common meal. The Strong are not restricted as to what they eat at home. What Paul wants them to avoid is behavior that would tempt the Weak to violate their own consciences or that would force the issue into open debate again.

Paul repeats the conclusion, this time in terms of what is at stake for the Weak:

> Happy is the person who doesn't judge himself when he makes a decision; but the person who does make distinctions is condemned if he eats, because the action doesn't proceed from trust/faith. And every action that doesn't proceed from trust/faith is a sin. (14:22b–23)

The radical idea that the presence or absence of trust is the determining issue enables Paul to suggest a resolution of the matter. The point is not whether unkosher food is forbidden or permitted in general. The question is how one decides whether unkosher food is forbidden to this or that individual. Paul brings the decision back to the center of his own understanding of the gospel—that, through the gospel, God becomes accessible through trust. What violates trust, then, is sinful because it violates the person's relationship with God.

Paul has implicitly associated himself with the Strong by using the first person plural in 14:19 ("let's pursue the things that have to do with peace"). He makes this association explicit in 15:1:

> We who are Strong ought to bear the weaknesses of those who are not and not please ourselves. Let each of us please his neighbor for good, with the goal of upbuilding. For in fact Christ didn't please himself but, as it is written, "the reproaches of those reproaching you fell on me" [Ps 68:10, LXX]. For all the things written in the past were written for our instruction, so that through patience and encouragement from the Scriptures we might have hope. (15:1–4)

Jesus thus becomes the model of behavior for the Strong. The Strong do not have to have everything their own way, even though they are right. A certain meekness and patience may even be the best way for them to make their point. Paul is not suggesting, after all, that they should simply surrender. They are urged to please their Weak neighbors with the purpose of accomplishing some good through mutual upbuilding. In other words, they expect to convert them over time.

Paul brings this specific discussion of purity issues to an end with a blessing whose language is drawn from his closing plea to the strong:

May the God of patience and encouragement give you the gift of agreeing with one another in accordance with Christ Jesus, so that together you may with one voice glorify God, the Father of our Lord Jesus Christ. (15:5–6)

We might expect something more imposing to round out this critical segment of the letter. But there are two reasons why Paul does not spin a grand rhetorical turn here. First, the passage itself needs to be handled glancingly, as it were, almost as an aside, precisely because it deals with the principal issue of the letter. In order for Paul's suggestion to be acceptable at all, it must not seem heavy-handed. After all, he does not have authority at Rome to impose anything; and he must be careful not to appear to be claiming it. Second, Paul is now ready to conclude not only the admonitory segment of the letter (including the more wide-ranging set of good advice that preceded the discussion of purity), but also the body of the letter as a whole.

Conclusion to Admonitions and to Body of Letter (15:7–13)

Paul begins this closing summation with an echo of 14:1. There he had written, "Welcome (προσλαμβάνεσθε) the person weak in trust/faith, but not in order to get into arguments with him." Now, he writes, "Therefore welcome (προσλαμβάνεσθε) one another, just as Christ has welcomed you into (*or* for) the glory of God" (15:7). The central topic in this summing up, however, is not simply food purity, but the overarching issue of the relationship of Jews and Gentiles in the Christian community. And all alike are included the second person plural here: "Welcome one another" applies equally to all. Paul then appeals to a string of scriptural quotations to show that this mutual welcoming is exactly what God has had in mind all along. And if this is God's purpose, it is the task of the community to figure out how to maintain unity and let it happen.

Paul describes the work of Christ in terms that relate it to both Jews and Gentiles:

For I'm saying that Christ became a servant of the circumcision for the sake of God's truth, in order to confirm the promises made to the ancestors and so that the Gentiles would glorify God for his mercy— just as it is written:

For this reason I will confess you among the Gentiles and sing to your name.[39]

And again, it says:

> Rejoice, you Gentiles, with his people.[40]

And again:

> Praise the Lord, you Gentiles,
> and let all the peoples praise him.[41]

And again, Isaiah says:

> And there will be the root of Jesse,
> even the one who has arisen to rule the Gentiles.
> In him will the Gentiles hope.[42] (15:8–12)

According to Paul's argument, the bringing together of Jew and Gentile in the Christian community is not incidental to the gospel but the very heart of it. Hence, the importance of working out appropriate solutions to the kind of problem that was threatening the unity of the Christians at Rome.

Finally, Paul concludes with another blessing, this one emphasizing the centrality of hope, the forward-looking virtue that can hold the community together:

> And may the God of hope fill you with all joy and peace in trusting,
> so that you overflow with hope in the power of Holy Spirit. (15:13)

It is the future life of a united community that will make sense of these efforts toward unity, not the past definitions that held different groups of human beings apart. In the benediction of 15:5–6, Paul prayed for the gift of agreement in praise. This benediction trumps the previous one, as it were, with its language of filling and overflowing.

Paul's Relationship with the Addressees

In chapter 16, Paul presents himself as well connected to the Roman church in terms of individuals, but he has no prior formal relationship to the community as such. Taking his projection of a mission to Spain at face value, we can guess that he does indeed wish to cultivate such a relationship. He cannot, of course, become the Romans' "apostle." And he puts any potential anxieties about his intentions to rest by insisting that he does not build on foundations laid by others (15:20–21). But he may be hoping for a supportive relationship of the kind he enjoyed with the church at Philippi. Rome would perhaps be the closest major concentration of Christians to his projected mission field and therefore the church most easily able to send assistance.

In order to build a relationship with the Roman Christian community, however, Paul has to do more than just reassure them that he will not try to "take charge." He has to make them a gift of value. In particular, since he is known to be the "apostle of the Gentiles," he must show that he can offer them something that will benefit a community divided about the interactions of Jews and Gentiles within it. Circumcision does not appear to be a grave issue at Rome, but food purity is. And given the importance, for the earliest Christians, of eating together, this could quickly become a serious problem.[43]

Paul remains true to his own position that purity is no longer a condition of access to God. Having been educated as a Pharisee, Paul would not be inclined to blur this issue. Either the full sweep of distinctively Jewish purity must remain in place or, at least in principle, it must be set aside. This would not mean that people were forbidden to observe purity, only that it was no longer required. In an entirely Jewish-Christian community, observance of kashruth might well continue as usual; it was simply normal to Jewish ethnicity. But in a Gentile or mixed Christian community, this simple fact of continuity no longer prevailed. For Paul to depart from his principle in the matter would not only have been a lapse in his own integrity; it would also have opened him to the criticism that he was pandering to potential opponents in Rome because he wanted the congregation's support. This, in turn, would mark him as untrustworthy.

Instead, Paul presents a possible resolution of the conflicts at Rome that asks a good deal of both sides. The Strong, who share Paul's principles on the subject, must back off from demanding that others agree with them and adopt their practice; they are not to place the Weak in a position that would cause them temptation. The Weak, on the other hand, are told not to sit in judgment on the Strong; they are to treat their own observance of food purity as a personal obligation, not a universal one. When the church eats together, one guesses, the foods are to be such as will not violate the conscience of any. This could mean a variety of things: the serving of only kosher food, the serving of a variety of foods clearly distinguished, the serving of only such foods (e.g., vegetables) as are not subject to concern about their purity. Paul does not specify details, nor does he need to.

If Paul's proposal is acceptable, it creates a way for the Roman community to resolve its problem and also inaugurates a bond between him and the community. They are now in his debt for offering this solution and for pressing those who share his perspective to cooperate in it. In return, he can hope for a positive reception when he himself visits Rome and perhaps for further help on his way to Spain. He also hopes for a positive reception of those associated with him, such as Phoebe (16:1); and a welcome extended to her will imply a welcome to him as well.

Rhetorical Flow of the Letter

The Letter to Romans has a large and coherent structure. To be sure, Paul has not marked this structure out with complete clarity; but to do so would betray its purpose. The larger part of it, after all, is constructed in the form of two extended, parallel entrapments. In these, Paul hopes to neutralize potential opposition by showing those who assume an easy superiority to people of the opposite ethnicity that they have no real claim. He must do this in a way that does not alienate his audience as a whole. With the Jewish-Christian audience, therefore, he makes exclusive use of a hypothetical interlocutor addressed in the second person singular. With the Gentile-Christian audience, he can be somewhat more direct, since he has a closer relationship with them, at least in principle.

Later readers of Romans have found this difficult to follow because we have been so far away from the social situation in which the letter was shaped. The issue of food purity was settled for Christians by the de facto separation of Jewish from Gentile churches. This was a result of demographic and historical changes as much as a real decision of principle; and yet, Paul's reduction of purity laws to the level of personal conscience rather than community boundaries must have played a role.[44] As a result, the issue that was central to the writing of Romans could not be central to later reading of it.

As a result, the more specifically theological portions of the letter, which, in its original logical and rhetorical structure, were essentially preparatory, became the center of interest. Chapters 6–8, rather than leading toward some further goal, came to be read as the real focus of the work. These chapters certainly deserve study and reflection in their own right; but their reading will be enhanced by recognizing the letter's larger structure and the vital significance of later chapters. In addition, the two "entrapments" (1:18–32; chaps. 9–11) came to be read as theological set pieces on the evils of homosexuality and Judaism, respectively, instead of playing their rhetorical function of entrapment for two distinct groups of Christians who prided themselves on their ethnicity and looked down on those who differed.

Fortunately, the letter is not without clues to its structure. Many of them are implicit in elements of its rhetorical flow. Paul uses such rhetorical figures as climax, parallelism, anaphora, and polysyndeton to produce a sense that a major division of the letter is coming to a close—most notably at the end of chapter 8. He uses liturgical forms to establish other pauses or closures—for example at 15:5–6, 13.

Paul is also a master of the nuanced use of pronouns. As I have suggested, he is addressing a community with at least two major components, whether they are defined ethnically as Jews and Gentiles or ethically as Strong and Weak. He must address the concerns of each side, but always with the other side listening in. What is more, he must do this while both maintaining the integrity of his own connection with the Gentiles and the Strong and also conciliating those on the other side that might be inclined against whatever he will say. Variation of pronouns is a principal means to accomplish the necessary shifts in audience focus.

The situation he addresses is difficult. His use of the hypothetical objector, addressed in second person singular, allows him to speak to issues and positions without attacking actual persons or, worse yet, defined parties. His often ambiguous use of the second person plural allows him to single out one side of the community or engage the attention of the whole group. The repeated reappearance of "we" implies a kind of collegiality with his addressees—at the time of writing, still largely a hope rather than a reality.

In such a difficult situation, the rhetoric reflects the high risk it undertakes. It is bold; but it would have done Paul no good to be diffident. He is restrained at the critical moment when the decision must be made by others. He suggests kinds of behavior on the part of the Strong and the Weak that would resolve the tensions, but leaves it entirely to the local leadership how to organize the essential practical details of church meals. It would be impossible for anyone to claim that Paul has dictated a settlement. And he has taken care to be as demanding of his own partisans as of anyone else and as critical of Gentile Christians as of Jewish Christians.

And?

This analysis of Romans as focusing on an issue that is long dead within Gentile Christianity may seem to diminish it in the minds of some. I think that would be a misperception. It serves rather to reconnect the whole letter to on-the-ground realities that theology too easily avoids when it has the chance. Paul is not writing a treatise of dogmatic theology or a theological last will and testament in Romans. He is writing a piece of "occasional theology," the kind of theological reasoning elicited by real-world challenges.

If Paul's challenges are not precisely the same as ours, that means not that Romans is of no use to us, but that it affords us a different kind of gift. It provides an experience of disentangling complex practical issues of Christian life that may prompt us to imagine new ways of thinking through those of our own time and place. And it reminds us that even apparently intractable differences of usage can direct us back, in ways productive of new understanding, to the central affirmations of the Christian gospel—above all the principle that access to God is through the trust that God has made possible for us, not through human merit, however measured.

This does not, of course, mean—for Paul or for us—that human behavior is unimportant. It means that it is important for different reasons—not in order to fulfill preexisting prescriptions but in order to express peace and love, to shape a life in hope, to upbuild the human community in peace, to issue, finally, in joy and praise. Paul, in this respect, is more like James than like Jude. He is working hard to maintain the existence of the community even while speaking difficult truths to it.

The Power of Style

One significant aspect of Romans is the rhetorical style Paul adopts in it. We have already seen a significant contrast between Jude and James. Jude's peremptory and insulting style almost succeeds in masking the more affirmative aspects of his message—so much so that the modern reader may be surprised to find anything positive in Jude at all. James, on the other hand, writes in a much more cautious mode. He has authority, it seems clear, but he reaffirms his fundamental identity and even equality with his addressees. Perhaps it is precisely this that makes it difficult for us to hear the attack on the rich (5:1–6) as actually addressed to members of the congregation. Paul's situation in Romans is significantly different from those of Jude and James—and even from his situation in his other letters: he has no direct authority of any kind at Rome.

One might argue that, in the Corinthian correspondence, his direct authority as founding apostle of that community did Paul little good in any case. Still, he could speak to that audience in tones he cannot use with the

Romans. That does not mean that he writes as one without any authority whatever. He claims a divine vocation as apostle to Gentiles. He assumes that he is known to the Roman audience by reputation (and, in some cases, by personal interaction). And I have suggested that his activity on behalf of Gentile Christians gave him a certain connection with those members of the community, even when they had had no direct dealings with him. Accordingly, he can write as a person who deserves the addressees' attention.

He does not, however, presume that he has earned their obedience. The obedience that he praises them for (16:19) is owed to Jesus, not to Paul. Paul hints that it will, of course, lead them to agree with him; but he cannot lay claim to it in his own right. Instead, Paul must present his entire argument in terms of the Christian experience he shares with his audience. If he feels that he is entitled to a hearing, he must still make good use of that hearing in order to persuade his audience that he shares with them a common faith and that, on that basis, he can help them come to a settlement of their internal differences.

In the clatter of claims and opinions that marks the conflicts of contemporary Western Christianity, Paul's approach in Romans might suggest a productive change of rhetoric. Instead of deductive arguments from authority, whether personal or derived from theological systems (including those that masquerade as "the plain sense of Scripture"), we would benefit if more speakers returned to the basic experience of μετάνοια (conversion), of the change of perspective that marks our discovery that, in Jesus, the world and God and ourselves all turn out to be different from what we thought. And yet, there can be no simple return to this, if only because Christianity in the modern West is, to a significant extent, still a culturally (if not politically) established religion. To be a Christian today does not necessarily mean to have experienced μετάνοια—though such an experience is still possible within Christianity, just as Paul found it to be within Judaism. To be a Christian, for many of us, is simply to be reaffirmed in the assumptions and prejudgments of our culture. Or to put it in a slightly different way, to be a Western Christian today is most often not about the discovery of truth, but about the reaffirmation of the cultural construction of reality that we have inherited.

The Pauline rhetoric of Romans, then, cannot work in precisely the same way in our context. It may be, however, that it is increasingly relevant again, at least in urban areas, where one often encounters churches made up primarily of people who grew up without Christian faith or who abandoned the faith of their early years—and then have returned to Christianity only as the result of a new encounter with the gospel and new understanding of what it actually means. For that matter, even those who have been Christian all their lives, may come to an experience of μετάνοια in which their faith comes alive for them in new and compelling ways. There is nothing new, of course, about such an idea. As Christianity became a cultural fixture in antiquity, the faithful quickly began to find a need for a kind of conversion that could move a person from conventional, socially prescribed acceptance of the faith to the discovery of its life-changing and world-changing possibilities. The most visible of such conversions were also the most dramatic—vowed virgins, martyrs, hermits, cenobitic monastics, ascetics—but they served as sacramental pointers to a possibility of conversion within even the most ordinary life.

One challenge, then, for the interpreter today (and, indeed, for any leader of the church) is to learn or devise a rhetorical mode that honors the reality of such conversion, not only by speaking of it but by encouraging it and by making use of it as a means of moving toward resolution of internal differences. The brittleness of modern Western Christianity, particularly in its Protestant manifestations—its propensity to shatter into ever smaller and angrier fragments—is in part an inadvertent legacy of Jude. If genuine unity—not uniformity of belief and practice, but community of conversion and faith—is to become more of a possibility again, it will require a rhetoric more like that of James and the Paul of Romans.

The Capacity of Scripture to Surprise

Another aspect of Romans that is significant for the modern interpreter is Paul's use of the Scriptures of Israel not simply to confirm the faith of Judaism in existing forms but to ground new possibilities. When Paul, in Romans 15:9–12, cites passages from the Scriptures of Israel as demonstrating that the Gentile mission and the inclusion of Gentiles in the church has been a part of the divine plan all along, he is probably not merely repeating traditional interpretation. It is difficult to imagine Paul the Pharisee having read them in this way—not because Pharisees were ungenerous in their religious ideas, but because Pharisaic thought was focused differently and went to the scriptural texts with quite different questions and presuppositions.

Paul the apostle to Gentiles had to read the texts differently because his spiritual experience and focus had changed. His conversion and apostolic calling meant that he had a different perspective on the world and God and that he brought this perspective to everything he did, including the reading of Scripture. This is not quite the same thing as saying that Paul made Scripture mean what he wanted it to, or more generally, that the reader has complete power over the text. It is to say, rather, that all reading is a conversation. As in conversations with living interlocutors, we are often deaf to what does not fit our presuppositions. Only an experience of discovering truth, of finding the places where our presuppositions do not in fact match up with reality, allows us to hear what we could not hear before.

What Paul was hearing, in this case, was indeed there in the texts—not in the form of the full-fledged Gentile Christian mission, of course, but in the more tentative recognition by ancient Israelite authors that a universal monotheism implied some kind of universal comprehensiveness in relation to humanity. Paul's shift in reading was not a matter of inventing new possibilities for the scriptural texts so much as a matter of rebalancing elements that were there all along, but which came to weigh one way in developing Judaism and another in developing Christianity. The universalism implicit in the concept of God as unique Creator of the world, and the particularism implicit in God's calling of Israel, form a tension in the Scriptures of Israel that continues in both Judaism and Christianity, but is formulated variously in each.[45]

To say that Paul has moved in a universalist direction is not to say either that he has abandoned Israelite tradition or that he is importing alien notions into his reading of Scripture. His conversion simply means that he is reading the tradition with new eyes, seeing things previously passed over as unexpectedly central and questioning the centrality of issues such as purity that he previously thought to be of great importance. In Paul's experience, Scripture is not in conflict with change. Indeed, it can, however surprisingly, turn out to ground it.

The way in which conversion and Scripture interact for Paul would provide a better model for scriptural interpretation today than the one most American Christians have inherited from the Reformed and Evangelical roots of our culture. The perception of Scripture as having a single, legally binding sense that has been verified and recodified for all time in a given strand of theological systematics turns out to be a betrayal of Scripture itself: it is a betrayal of the way in which Scripture and its interpretation worked to foster change in earliest Christianity. I do not mean to suggest that the surprising interpretation is always better than the familiar one. I reject all such mechanical criteria. I mean that interpretation must be *open* to surprise—a surprise that emerges in and through the process of conversion, which even the Christian most deeply rooted in culturally approved forms of the faith must still undergo as the gospel transforms our grasp of world, God, and self.

Ironies of Interpretation

In this respect, it is deeply distressing that Romans 1 and 9 have come to be read as affirmations of Christian cultural prejudices, whether against same-gender sexual partners or against Jews. Passages that began as entrapments for the proud have now become bulwarks of our pride. Read in its simplest, most literal sense, neither chapter supports such a use. Paul is quite cautious in chapter 1 to avoid saying that same-gender sexual intercourse is sinful; nor does he suggest that Gentiles must alter their cultural norms to exclude it. Indeed, to read the passage as a prohibition is to imply that Paul was absent-minded enough to insist on retaining one aspect of Israel's purity code in chapter 1 while definitively rejecting the whole principle of purity in 14:14. While the connection between food laws and sexual laws may not seem obvious to the modern reader, the Scriptures of Israel do not make the clear-cut modern distinction between "ritual purity" (meaning those purity laws modern Christians have abandoned) and "moral purity" (those they have retained). Paul is unlikely to have made such a distinction. For him, as we have seen, the key issue is that distinctively Jewish purity laws served to divide Jew from Greek. It is far less forced to read Romans 1 in the way I have suggested here, since it allows it to function in terms of the rhetoric of the letter and does not ask it, in contravention of its own language, to lay down eternal laws. Similarly, it is a more literal reading of chapter 9 to see it as reaffirming the privileged particularity of God's relationship to the Jewish people than to read it as simply replacing Jews with Gentile Christians or even Israel with the church. It is obscene that what began as an exercise in exposing the self-confidence of the proud has so long been an excuse for Christian arrogance and violence against gay-lesbian people and Jews.

Even if the rhetoric of the letter has habitually been misread, however, Romans, taken as a whole, may still be helpful in the modern conflicts over sexuality. If, as I have argued elsewhere, the Torah's prohibition of anal intercourse between men is essentially a purity law, then it is analogous, from Paul's perspective, to the issue of food purity at Rome.[46] That may well be his reason for beginning his argument with the topic of sexuality. The stance of the Strong, who rejected the purity rules that separated Jew from Gentile, would be that there is no valid prohibition of same-gender sexual relationships as such; it was simply a distinction between Jewish and Gentile cultures. While aesthetically disgusting from a Jewish perspective, it was not sinful. (Same-gender sexual intercourse would still be subject to ethical norms based on other principles. Presumably, Paul would insist on love and trust/faith as essential standards for sexual behavior, as he does elsewhere in Romans.) The stance of the Weak would be that the Levitical prohibition of such acts is still in force.

The analogy between food purity and sexual purity, to be sure, is not absolute. Paul himself insists elsewhere that sex and food are not strictly comparable because sex involves the whole person and therefore the person's relationship with Christ (1 Cor 6:12–20). This cannot rule out same-gender sexual partnerships, however, unless they are shown to compromise a person's relationship with Christ. To argue a priori that all such relationships do so is to introduce a claim that Paul never makes; his example of prostitution as compromising the Christian's relationship with Christ is not at all comparable. Whether same-gender sexual partnerships are capable of being open to the relationship with Christ is a question to be determined by respectful spiritual dialogue here and now, not by reference to a priori theological systems. There is, in fact, abundant testimony that they can be.

An analogy with food purity does help in suggesting how a divided church may eventually come to deal with the modern issue of sexual orientation. The church can acknowledge the existence of both Weak and Strong perspectives on the subject, and the two parties can refrain from judging and dismissing one another and trying to force agreement. This is possible, however, only if the freedom of both parties is clearly preserved. Those who object to same-sex partnerships must, of course, absent themselves from blessings of such unions and, still more, refrain from participating in them themselves. Those who believe that the Spirit of God is at work in the movement to affirm a gay/lesbian presence in the community of faith must be free to celebrate that presence in faithful ways.

Paul's admonition that each person is to proceed according to the trust or faith that each has been given still offers a resolution not unlike the one that apparently maintained the unity of the church at Rome in Paul's time. The question for modern Christians is whether we can reach a level of spiritual generosity that will restrain us when we are tempted to tear the church apart over such issues. Those whose conscience (that is, their consciousness of God's will for us) prohibits same-gender sexual relationships must cease to sit in judgment on those who enter in such partnerships in faith. Conversely, those whose conscience allows them to celebrate such relationships are not free to behave contemptuously toward those who object or to encourage such persons to compromise their conscience. The two groups are not free either to dismiss or to draw apart from each other. They must continue in communion and faithful dialogue with one another.

Both groups need to focus on trust and love as the foundations of Christian ethics. "Love is the fulfilling of law" (13:10). "Whatever does not proceed from trust/faith is sin" (14:23). If our behavior compromises our trust in God and leads us toward trust in ourselves, we have gone wrong. This is possible both for "liberals" and for "conservatives," either group being fully capable of substituting its own certainties for the kind of openness to discernment that is the mark of genuine humility. Again, if our behavior is not animated by love but by a desire to prove our superiority to our neighbor or to dictate to our neighbor, we have gone wrong. Again, it is an opportunity for sin equally available to people of all theological camps. What destroys unity is our tendency to sit in judgment on one another or to dismiss one another with contempt while carefully absolving ourselves from any possibility of error.

In any case, the complex dynamics of the Letter to Romans remind us that our search for discernment of God's will must pass through a process of sometimes difficult conversation with the people who share our journey. Paul is committed to the principles that shaped his ministry; indeed, they are part of the gospel that he describes in 1:16 as "God's power for salvation to everyone who trusts." This power of salvation becomes known most particularly in the gospel's ability to evoke conversion and transformation. This proves troubling in that it creates a new setting for our life with God and with one another. It created, for example, a church composed of both Jews and Gentiles in place of the simpler environment of a Christian community that was purely Jewish or purely Gentile. It creates mixture and uncertainty in today's churches as well.

We cannot know all the details of such a community's life in advance. How could we when we have yet to experience it? Even if we had been given a complete set of regulations in advance, we should have lost half of them, not recognizing their potential usefulness, and misunderstood the rest. For Paul, it is only in hindsight that the true meaning of the Scriptures emerges. It is only after the emergence of God's mission to Gentiles that one begins to see that it was there all along, hidden in the prophets. We remain in continuity with the past of faith, but we find that we have to devise our own solutions, with the aid of the Holy Spirit, to the challenges of the present. In doing so, the wise apostle will speak to both the strengths and the weaknesses of the church. The wise apostle will do everything possible to maintain the precarious unity of the mixed community except compromise the good news itself.

Paul is not answering modern questions in the Letter to Romans. We actually understand the letter better when we give up that expectation. On the other hand, the very complexity of the rhetoric, in its response to an extremely complex situation, may be the single most significant gift the letter offers us. A church, in our own time, that cared more for the maintenance of genuine communion among diverse groups than it cared for vindicating the arrogance of the Strong or the paranoia of the Weak would be a voice of creative power.

Notes

1. The problem is immensely complex, and I do not claim any great weight for my own judgment in the matter, which is partly just a reflection of my habitual preference to try making sense of a whole document first and splitting it up into disparate sources only if that seems absolutely necessary. For the complexity of the issues and the earlier history of discussion, see the detailed account of William Sanday and Arthur C. Headlam, *A Critical and Exegetical Commentary on the Epistle to the Romans,* 5th ed. (ICC; Edinburgh: T. & T. Clark, 1902), lxxv–xcviii. For a clear, later summary, see C. K. Barrett, *A Commentary on the Epistle to the Romans* (New York: Harper & Row, 1957), 10–13.

2. This is the implication behind the string of quotations from the Scriptures of Israel in Rom 15; the idea that 16:25–27 is a Marcionite addition to the letter seems to me correspondingly unlikely, since this is precisely a point Marcion would presumably not have wished to make.

3. Since Paul had not been to Rome before, scholars have long questioned whether he could have known so many people there. The concern seems unnecessary. "A priori arguments against St. Paul's acquaintance with some twenty-four persons in the Roman community are of slight weight. Christianity was preached amongst just that portion of the population of the Empire which would be most nomadic in character. It is admitted again that it would be natural that, in writing to a strange church, St. Paul should lay special stress on all those with whom he was acquainted or of whom he had heard, in order that he might thus commend himself to them"; Sanday and Headlam, *Romans,* xciii–xciv.

4. E.g., Anders Nygren, while acknowledging Paul's interest in Spain, argues that one must not "stretch the significance of the outward occasion of the letter, at the cost of the actual contents of the epistle," by which he means that Paul is really engaged here in a work of fundamental theology; *Commentary on Romans,* trans. Carl C. Rasmussen (Philadelphia: Muhlenberg Press, 1949), 3–9. Brendan Byrne, taking a more political approach, argues that the purpose was really one of attaching the Gentile Christians of Rome to Paul's sphere of influence; *Romans* (SP, 6; Collegeville: Liturgical Press, 1996), 8–19. Several studies of the question are included in Karl P. Donfried, ed., *The Romans Debate,* rev. ed. (Peabody, Mass.: Hendrickson, 1991).

5. It amounts to twelve lines in the 26th edition of the Nestle text as compared with nine in the nearest competitor, Galatians; none of the others is more than six lines long.

6. Since a few mss. omit the designation "in Rome," it is possible to question whether the letter was actually addressed to that community; but there is evidence in the letter to suggest a specific destination rather than a completely general letter, and no other destination fits as well as Rome. Barrett, *Romans*, 9.

7. Hence its popularity as epithet for kings (e.g., Ptolemy I Soter) and local divinities.

8. Countryman, *Dirt, Greed, and Sex*, 11–65. Other readers, too, see the distinctive practices of the Jewish ethnos as a major concern of Romans; cf. Daniel Boyarin, *A Radical Jew: Paul and the Politics of Identity* (Berkeley: University of California Press, 1994), 52–56.

9. Countryman, *Dirt, Greed, and Sex*, 57–64.

10. Ibid.; cf. Martti Nissinen, *Homoeroticism in the Biblical World: A Historical Perspective*, trans. Kirsi Stjerna (Minneapolis: Fortress, 1998), 57–102.

11. Robert A. J. Gagnon, in discussing Romans, ignores all distinctions of meaning between varieties of pejorative language; *The Bible and Homosexual Practice: Texts and Hermeneutics* (Nashville: Abingdon, 2001), 229–303. The same is true in his handling of ancient Near Eastern background, in 44–56. It was perhaps the only way he could make his case.

12. Indeed, it appears only one other time in the NT, at Acts 22:22, in a different usage.

13. The hostility has, however, been less universal than sometimes assumed; cf. Boswell, *Christianity, Social Tolerance, and Homosexuality.* Despite subsequent criticisms of Boswell's work, it opened up recognition that the history of this issue was never as uniform as assumed in the first half of the twentieth century.

14. As one example, Mark D. Jordan, *The Silence of Sodom: Homosexuality in Modern Catholicism* (Chicago: University of Chicago Press, 2000).

15. In Greek, the perfect passive participle refers to a state already in existence by the time indicated in the tense of the verb on which the participle depends. Cf. the occurrences of the same verb in this form in Rom 15:14; Phil 1:11; Col 2:10.

16. "Jealousy, murder" (φθόνου, φόνου); "foolish, faithless" (ἀσυνέτους, ἀσυνθέτους).

17. Ancient authors recognized that some males (the gender that primarily interested them) were attracted more or less exclusively either to females or to other males, but assumed most were attracted to both. For a useful summary, see David F. Greenberg, *The Construction of Homosexuality* (Chicago: University of Chicago Press, 1988), 141–60.

18. E.g., Sir 24.

19. The "revulsion" a Jew (βδελυσσόμενος) might feel regarding idols (2:22–23) belongs to the word group usually translated into English with variants of "abomination"; the Greek noun βδέλυγμα is used in Lev 18:22; 20:13 with reference to male-male sexual penetration.

20. "[I]t is not simply hypocrisy that Paul attacks here but the confidence of the Jew that his ethnic status will make the divine judgment lighter for him"; Boyarin, *A Radical Jew*, 88.

21. The term λόγια, "oracles," in 3:2 seems to be functionally synonymous with "Law."

22. The use of the first-person-plural pronoun here clearly places the Gentile-Christian portion of the community on the sidelines of this discussion while Paul addresses their Jewish coreligionists. Only in 4:16 will he begin to let Gentile-Christians into the "we": Abraham is "the father of us all, just as it is written, 'I will make you father of many nations/Gentiles.'"

23. Ps 32:2, but probably using the psalm in a Greek rather than a Hebrew form.

24. Boyarin, *A Radical Jew*, 49–85.

25. As Alan Segal notes, Paul actually prefers to speak of "transformation" rather than "conversion"; *Paul the Convert*, 72.

26. This corresponds to the pattern of conversion to a sect within Judaism; Segal, *Paul the Convert*, 75–84.

27. Boyarin, *A Radical Jew*, 161.

28. Boyarin's interpretation (*A Radical Jew*, 158–67) of how the Law multiplies sin (the commandment to procreate institutionalizes and fosters lust) seems quite possible. If he is correct, then Paul, at this point, is raising a familiar point of intra-Jewish concern to show his Jewish-Christian audience that the Law is not without its grave problems as well as its advantages.

29. One must assume, to be sure, that Gentiles have to abandon idolatry and polytheism in order to have any relationship with the One God; but that is not an issue in dispute at Rome.

30. Countryman, *Dirt, Greed, and Sex*, 80–96.

31. It also represents a major departure from the prophetic theme, however, in that the "remnant" is no longer ethnically defined; Boyarin, *A Radical Jew*, 201–6.

32. The quotation from Hosea, conveniently for Paul's purposes, conveys this message in a useful mix of speech in the second and third person:

> And it will happen in the place where it was said to them,
>   "You are not my people,"
> that they will there be called "Sons of the living God." (9:26)

The third person shows a certain evenhandedness, matching Paul's third-person references to Israel. But the second person, even though the message in it is negative, hints at relationship and therefore the possibility of a shift to come.

33. Countryman, *Dirt, Greed, and Sex*, 57–64.

34. As Boyarin observes (*A Radical Jew*, 202), this is certainly not an anti-Jewish passage, but it turns out to be successionist in another sense: "We thus see the peculiar logic of supersession at work here. *Because* Israel has not been superseded, therefore most Jews have been superseded."

35. *Migration of Abraham* 89–93.

36. The parallelism of the construction in 12:10–13 and the lack of connectives (asyndeton) help suggest that these are all aspects of a single kind of behavior.

37. The remaining passage is in Phil 1:19, where Paul is expressing a certainty that his imprisonment will turn out for the best; also, the subjunctive appears in 1 Cor 13:2 with "mysteries" as its object. A few other instances of the use of οἶδα express simple factual knowledge (1 Cor 1:16; 14:11; 2 Cor 9:2) or a self-deprecating reference to the self (2 Cor 12:2-3). He can also use οἶδα in the sense of "knowing how to . . ." (Phil 4:12). Paul uses the synonym γινώσκω a few times, but not in ways that would alter this picture.

38. It also appears twice in 2 Timothy (1:5, 12).

39. Ps 17:50 in its LXX form; 2 Sam 22:50.

40. Deut 32:43 in the LXX.

41. Ps 117:1.

42. Isa 11:10 in the LXX.

43. "In Paul's growing discussion of Jewish law, dietary laws prove to be the more difficult case; as public rites easily open to view, they are constantly an issue. It is also possible to vacillate between customs. Thus dietary laws become central to Paul's discussion of Jewish ceremonial law in a way that circumcision had not. This irony, that the less severe laws are the most troublesome ones, has been insufficiently appreciated." Segal, *Paul the Convert*, 224.

44. Boyarin (*A Radical Jew*, 94): Paul's "major concern throughout his ministry: producing a new, single human essence."

45. Boyarin is particularly helpful in dispelling any notion that there is or can be a single resolution to these tensions; *A Radical Jew,* 228–60.
46. Countryman, *Dirt, Greed, and Sex,* 30–32.

Epilogue
The Ethos of Interpretation

This book is calling for a change in the way that biblical scholars do business. The change is not absolute or total, but it is significant. It still demands intensive preparation in the knowledge of ancient languages and of ancient culture and history. It does not exclude the use of analytical methods like those that already have a foothold in biblical studies, though it casts a skeptical eye on those that are not primarily heuristic. It calls attention to the importance of complexity, both ancient and modern, to the interpretative conversation, and therefore to the need for synthetic methods alongside and in cooperation with analytical ones. It stresses that biblical interpretation refers not just to the canonical texts but to the larger realities environing both them and the modern reader and, in particular, to the experience of discovering truth, which calls all our culturally constructed humanity into question.

Such an approach to interpretation makes certain demands both on the interpreter and on the community of readers. It prescribes for each a certain *ethos or* character—one that includes or implies a spirituality and an ethic. I begin here with the community, since that is the more external, describable, and verifiable aspect of this change.

The Ethos of the Readers

There have come to be at least two communities of readers for the Bible today: communities of faith and academic communities. For the past two hundred and more years, biblical scholars have often been seen as standing over against the community of faith or at least outside it as they did their

[handwritten note at top: ✗ Perhaps I don't connect w/ book because not my experience.]

work. That perception has probably been wrong. My own unscientific nose-counting suggests that most biblical scholars first became involved in this study because at some point they were drawn to the Bible as a document of faith. Sometimes the communities of faith have misunderstood their questioning and sought to silence them; one result can be that scholars abandoned the faith of their earlier years or at least the effort to converse with their original community of faith. This initial separation has then built on itself, segregating the community of faith, with its suspicion of the biblical interpreter, from the academic community, where the expression of faith may be prohibited as impolite or irrelevant. Consequently, we now have two communities of readers that often deem each other's primary concerns irrelevant or subversive.

The preceding description of the situation is, of course, oversimplified. It would be more accurate to think of these two communities not as independent, clearly distinct entities, but as "ideal types." In practice, the two interpenetrate. Biblical scholars whose writing, teaching, and giving of papers never raises explicit questions of faith may also be members of congregations, may serve their denominations in various regional or national capacities, may preach and teach the Bible in their community of faith— yet without really allowing the two sides of their communal identification to mesh and interact. My own experience is that, if we are asked what our biblical scholarship has to do with our faith and vice versa, we are likely to say, "A great deal," but then we have difficulty articulating what that means.

This is not really so surprising. The "work world" of most biblical scholars is the academy. It is there that one "succeeds" or "fails" in worldly terms—in terms not only of position and income, but also of reputation and a sense of belonging. In this, we are like other professionals in our world. Given past tensions with the churches, the academy by now has defined itself largely in terms that marginalize the faith of those who belong to it. The claustrophobia of academic definition has lessened a little in other respects as the guild opens up to membership by women, people of color, and others who were previously kept out or kept quiet. But it has still not come to terms with the reality of faith or its relationship with communities of faith.

The reader may question whether there is not more conversation between these two in institutions with specific connection to a faith community: Bible colleges, for example, or seminaries. The answer is, "Less than one might expect." In some cases, the sponsoring church body allows no questioning of its official standards. In those cases, its domesticated

[handwritten note in right margin: see above]

scholars typically avoid any aspect of biblical studies that might lead them into dangerous territory. In other cases, the sponsoring church body has drifted into the expectation that biblical scholarship is least dangerous when it is most abstract and unintelligible, which leaves most of us who belong to "mainline" church contexts to define ourselves in terms of our academic communities and seldom presses us to integrate the various sides of our identities.

This is not to say that mainstream scholars fail entirely to communicate with the churches. But our communication tends to take the form of "popularization," talks and articles on how scholars are currently thinking about the Bible. That is not the same as letting our stake in faith and the community of faith become a participant in the interpretive conversation. It assumes, rather, that the academic community is primary and the community of faith can be fed off its scraps. The language here may seem too harsh, and I must immediately affirm that there is a place for abstruse and difficult biblical scholarship. Some things even in a book like this, where I am endeavoring to speak to a relatively broad audience, will seem impenetrable to the nonspecialist reader. But there is a difference, nonetheless, between popularization and the kind of interpretation I am calling for. The difference lies in whether the life of the community of faith is a part of the conversation from the start or is rather the recipient of occasional memos excerpted from the academic conversation in simplified form.

If academic interpretation is to change in the ways I am calling for, it implies an equally substantial change in the churches and the way they talk with, listen to, read, or interpret the Scriptures. If people of faith are earnest in saying that the Bible is, in any sense at all, the "word of God," we ought to assume that it is dangerous, that it can surprise, that it can initiate change in thought and action, that it can threaten the status quo. We should read it under the rubric that Mark uses for Jesus' parables: βλέπετε τί ἀκούετε, "Watch out what you hear!"[1] Instead, our long habit has been to read it in order to confirm what we already think—and perhaps also to disconfirm what our neighbor thinks. As a friend says, with perhaps a little exaggeration, "No English-speaking Christian has ever picked up a Bible except to bash someone else over the head with it."[2] This means that too many Christians are not really engaging with the Bible at all. They are reading it and using it, but not listening to it—not listening for the reality of another voice in it, not listening for the possibility of μετάνοια/conversion.

We owe this habit in large part to certain strands of the Protestant Reformation. Like every great spiritual movement, it has had its negative as well as its positive consequences. The Reformers' appeal to the Scriptures as limiting factor, as the authorization for pruning back the vast shrubbery of medieval Western Christianity so that the main lines of Christian faith could be more clearly seen, was, from my perspective, a positive inheritance. One negative inheritance is the peculiar notion, strongly represented in American Christianity, that the Bible could be reduced to a kind of systematic theology, that one could rephrase it in systematic format without somehow betraying it, and indeed that one could in this way actually enhance it, clarify it, and make it more useful. As a result, Christians where this sort of Protestantism has dominated assume that the Bible is made up entirely of timeless truths and unalterable laws. Some of them embrace this assumption with enthusiasm, while others regard it with suspicion and feel that the Bible is not to be taken "too literally." But both "conservatives" and "liberals" often miss what I believe is the real point of having Scriptures at all.

The problem here is not so much the idea that the Bible contains timeless truths but the way in which Western Christianity tries to grasp and possess such truths. As I posited earlier, truth is not a possession for human beings; it is a discovery. The notion that any believer can grasp the fullness of God's truth and deliver that knowledge authoritatively to others runs aground on the fact of human finitude, not to mention the human talent for self-regard, pride, suspicion, anger, self-hatred, and other faults. It also violates the quite orthodox teaching that God is ἀχώρητος (incomprehensible, uncontainable). It is, for that matter, bizarre and absurd on the very face of it. A God so easily comprehensible would be completely inadequate to the realities of human existence and undeserving of our worship or obedience.

The communities of Christian faith must abandon the fantastic dream of a final and complete "biblical theology" that will answer all human questions in advance. And along with it, they must abandon the notion of a tame Bible that can reassure each variety of Christians that their particular tradition with its familiar attitudes and habits of being is entirely in the right and uniquely pleasing to God. The Bible does not exist in order to confirm the church in its present configurations, but to assist the community of faith in the ongoing process of discerning God's gifts and God's calling here and now, for the present and the future. Systematic theology is a useful discipline insofar as it encourages comprehensive vision and systemic thinking, but it is not a useful model for most of the church's life. The tradition of spirituality, deeply conscious that no two people or communities or moments of history begin from exactly the same point or have exactly the same vocation, is a better model.

Jesus, in the Gospel of John, says of the church's work of ongoing discernment: "When that one, the Spirit of truth, comes, it will lead you in all truth" (16:13). The truth in question is what Jesus has already uttered (e.g., 16:7, 14), but it is not exhausted by a single uttering of it. The truth that the church has yet to discern is continuous with the teaching of Jesus, but it is and will always be new because it is spoken in a new time and place. Truth is discovery and surprise, not possession, not weapon. Indeed, when we treat it as possession or weapon, by that very act we falsify it.

Only by giving up the fantasy of completely mastering the gospel can the church enter into the interpretive conversation. And the resulting conversation with the Bible is part of our larger conversation with God about gifts, about vocation, about discernment in every aspect of life. This process of discernment is also, from the beginning, a conversation within the community of faith, one in which many voices have to be heard with respect while they accord the same respect to others. The one human voice that cannot be honored in this conversation is the voice that claims already to be possessed of the entire truth. That voice has exempted itself from the conversation by claiming a more than human status for itself. And that claim, of course, is a form of idolatry.

When the community of faith brings its own process of discernment, with all its many voices, into conversation with the Bible, it will find that the Bible, too, is a conversation of many voices. This is perhaps the single most important and challenging insight of modern biblical studies, starting with the eighteenth-century efforts to think through the Synoptic problem and the nineteenth-century recognition of the composite nature of the Pentateuch. The Scriptures are most adequately understood not as framing a single, self-consistent biblical theology, but as containing a diversity of voices, without merely submerging any one of them in the rest. We shall learn to look to the whole vast conversation within the Scriptures as our conversation partner, and not just to the individual pieces of it. Interpretation thus becomes a conversation of conversations. And while this may seem a counsel of chaos and despair, the repeated Christian experience of this process of discernment is that the Spirit can in fact lead us forward through it.

Only that confidence—the faith in God's continuing goodwill toward us and the hope that arises from that faith—can give the churches the courage to enter into this quest. And only by entering into this quest can the churches come to appreciate fully the opportunities for new life that lie in the words of the Bible. This means that Christian communities who know too much about God will have to give up dictating to Scripture what it can and cannot say. It also means that those Christian communities that have given up taking the Scriptures seriously as an element in their discernment of truth will have to prepare to be surprised by unexpected good news and the demands that good news makes on its hearers. This is a challenge, in other words, to conservative and liberal alike.

The creation of a livelier context for biblical interpretation in communities of faith will go a long way toward reforming the academy as well. Biblical scholars who engage in interpretive conversation in the community of faith may well find that it energizes their more specialized, academic work. Indeed, there are significant examples of this already in the contemporary scholarly guild, whose most creative figures are often also engaged in lively conversation outside the academy. The academic guild, in turn, may react defensively, out of concern for its turf; but if it is healthy, it may also come to welcome yet another voice in the conversation. For some reason, the guild, still predominantly white, finds it easier to accept religious commitment on the part of scholars of color. I am not sure that this is healthy. It may be yet another projection of something thought of as a relatively "primitive" quality onto people unlike the Western majority. I should hope we might see a situation in which all participants are able to bring their faith into the interpretive conversation, if we can do so in a genuinely critical way, without presuming either that we know all there is to know about it or that others must agree with us in advance.

The Character of the Interpreter

What, then, does the triangular model of interpretation offered here suggest about the character of the interpreter? To begin with, the interpreter needs an appropriate reverence for both text and community. By "reverence," I do not mean an unquestioning stance. Authentic reverence can never be a form of pretense. If I must pretend that the text or the community is better than it is, if I must assume a hypocritical stance in relation to either, then I am concluding, however unconsciously, that they are not in fact worthy of reverence. True reverence embodies a confidence that the text will be of value even when its warts have all been noted and acknowledged, that the community will still be a worthwhile context for being human even as it confronts its own betrayals and admits its incompleteness. Indeed, especially then. The interpreter will not work effectively if hampered by false notions of the perfection of either the text or the community.[3]

Ideas of infallibility or inerrancy, whether applied to the text or to the community, must therefore be rejected. They tend to close rather than open the process of interpretation. Invariably, they will be invoked to suggest that there is neither room nor need for change, for a fresh look, for reflection and reevaluation. In that case, interpretation becomes idle. Only enforcement of norms remains. The interpreter will become, at most, a cosmetician for the corpse of received opinion, giving it a complexion of authenticity and permanence that it cannot rightly claim and that cannot long disguise its decay.

Any preconception about the text, then, that makes the interpreter want to save it from embarrassment is suspect. Reverence for another human being is expressed not in failing to notice that person's flaws, but in taking the person seriously enough to pay attention and come to know them. Reverence for the text is expressed above all in attentiveness, but also in hope—the hope that the cultivation of this relationship will not have been a waste of human energy, that the conversation with the text will even enhance our human encounter with reality.

The same is true of reverence for the community. It does not mean that the interpreter subscribes to every current belief in the community. The interpreter, ideally, bows neither to the dictatorship of the powerful few nor to the tyranny of the many. For that matter, the interpreters' education ought to warn them against taking the agreed preconceptions of the community too seriously. The notion that any text or tradition is perfectly univocal will not stand up to close examination, and the community that indeed speaks with a single voice is a community that is preparing to die. The interpreter who merely seconds the opinions of the community is not maintaining the independence necessary to the interpretive conversation and is actually betraying the community rather than serving it.

On the other hand, the interpreter who abandons the sense of belonging to the community for which one interprets will lose the ability to perform the interpretive role at all. If one has enough reverence for the text to attend to it and learn it, but does not have an equivalent reverence for the community, one will have no real understanding of what issues and questions are being raised from that apex of the conversational triangle. This is often a problem for modern biblical interpretation, since many academic interpreters have allowed themselves the apparent luxury of abandoning the community that cares about the Bible rather than enduring the stress and strain of remaining in it and entering into conflict with it where that seems necessary.

An interpreter needs to know to what communities she or he belongs and for what communities she or he interprets. "The academic community" is seldom if ever a sufficient answer to these questions, since the academic community is an epiphenomenon of other, larger, and more diverse communities, not a self-sustaining reality in its own right. Scholars do in fact live in a larger world, whether they are particularly conscious of it or not. My point is not to treat one's local community or one's ethnic community or one's religious community as if it were perfect. The point is not to agree with it in all respects. The point is to be engaged with the life of a human community that is broader than the academic.

It is possible, of course, that one's work will prove useful even beyond the boundaries of one's own community. But without having a sense of our particular communities, we cannot address ourselves to the task of interpretation at all. To interpret for and with all is to interpret for and with none. For humanity does not exist, practically speaking, as an abstract entity; it exists in the context of specific times, places, and cultures. We may well find analogies and helpful parallels between the complexities of one community's interpretive discourse and those of another; but we have to begin where we are.

In order to fulfill the task of reverence for text and community, the interpreter needs a high regard for truth and integrity. If we believe that anything human—whether a community, an individual, or a human artifact—must be protected from the truth, we are not according it reverence. This is not to say that truth may not be frightening. Indeed, it quite often is. After all, our apprehension of truth, as I have suggested earlier, is rooted in the discovery that our human cultural armor is not perfect. The world is and will always be larger, more dangerous, and more surprising than our cultural constructs will allow.

The interpreter, then, is on the alert for the loose edges, the light glimpsed through the chinks in our existing expectations. The interpreter who has experienced truth as discovery will not expect to *possess* it, to stand above and apart from the ignorant and muddled obsessions of hoi polloi and dictate what truth demands. Such a stance would be the very opposite of a high regard for truth, since it violates the truth of the interpreter's own incompleteness as a human being.

The interpreter has something to bring to the interpretive conversation, but not everything—not "the" truth, but a glimpse of something significant that we have hitherto slighted or even failed altogether to notice. Recognizing this, we shall learn how to maintain an "engaged detachment" in the interpretive conversation. The engagement is with the process of interpretation, with the richness of the text, and with the need of the community to continue growing and changing in changing circumstances while also retaining continuity with its past and a sense of its inherited gifts and weaknesses. The detachment arises from knowing that we are only a part, however critical a part, of where the conversation will head. Our job is not to dictate the results but to add an important element to the process.

The combination of these seemingly irreconcilable elements—engagement and detachment—emerges from the interpreter's integrity, that is to say, the interpreter's willingness to become transparent to glimpses of truth. Perhaps the root sin of the interpreter is the lie told on account of fear or favor—or out of irritation or annoyance, or for the sake of feeling superior, or for any reason at all. When interpreters tell not what they have heard or read in the text but what they believe the listener wants to hear or something they merely choose to say for their own aggrandizement, they commit a fundamental sin. This sin is fundamental because, in the interpreter's mouth, the impact of such a lie is magnified through the way it undermines the whole interpretive conversation.

If the interpreter is genuinely committed to the task of interpretation, this will make itself known in a certain teacherly care and concern. The great aim is not to impress others nor to triumph politically, but to encourage genuine knowledge, thought, and reflection. As the interpreter's great vocation lies in facilitating the encounter between text and community, so the interpreter's great delight lies in witnessing the moment of discovery when the text begins to be heard anew and the community begins to sense new possibilities in its world.

This is not something that will occur without opposition. There is something in each of us that prefers the devil we know to the angel we are meeting for the first time. There is something in religious communities that engenders faction and values partisanship above life itself. Because the interpreter lives and works at the focal point of discovery and change, the interpreter is sometimes endangered. Accordingly, the virtue of courage (or hope, to give it a more biblical name) is something the interpreter would be well-advised to pray for. Perhaps we have entered the vocation of biblical interpretation, many of us, hoping to find a quiet refuge from the disputes of everyday life. Instead, we may find that we are at the center of a storm. Only hope makes that location worth occupying.

The challenge to biblical scholars is to become genuine interpreters: this means not only sitting with the text in the quiet of the study, and not only engaging with the community of faith in its ongoing process of discernment, but also looking for the things that bring text and community into conversation with each other. Biblical scholars cannot single-handedly dominate this conversation or dictate its results. To do so would destroy it. What we can do is to help maintain the voice of the ancient texts against the higher decibels of the living community and to seek the points at which the complex conversation within the text itself and that within the community may make fruitful contact with each other. They will not always be the obvious points, the ones one could find with a concordance, the ones clearly labeled by vocabulary or subject matter.

In creating the present study, for example, I have found my reflections focusing, in ways that I did not expect at all, on the quality of the interchange between writer and addressees in Jude, James, and Romans. I had decided in advance that I would look at the rhetoric of each letter, but I thought of rhetoric as of instrumental rather than substantive importance. I emerge from the study thinking that the quality and character of Christian rhetoric may indeed be an essential point at which our modern efforts at discernment need to enter into serious conversation with our Scriptures. Not every rhetoric is suitable to every occasion. That is not news, but it is an old discovery of truth that is ready for rediscovery. Modern communities of Christian faith need to rediscover how to differ from one another and engage in discernment with one another in ways that do not violate the gospel we share. The importance of rhetoric means that the interpreter who translates the bare gist of a text but neglects its communicative nuances and imaginative power has done only half the job. To bring the Bible genuinely into play in the modern interpretive conversation demands that we be sensitive to more than just the denotative meaning of the text.

No simple rules can be given for our work. We must proceed by intuition as well as method. My own model is that of the good spiritual advisor, who not only knows the traditional methods and their limitations but also knows how to listen for the unexpected in the life and words of the advisee. We could do worse than to cultivate that capacity, both in listening to Scripture and in listening to the community of faith. We are alert to the moment of καιρός, the appointed time, the revelatory instant. Just as the rotation of the earth constantly brings new portions of it into the light, the juxtaposition of the Bible with the ever-changing realities of the world, the church, and our own lives will bring new things to light. We have only to be alert to the possibilities.

And then we have to think carefully about how to communicate what has surprised us. The issue of rhetoric is as important for us as it was for NT writers. Indeed, in a broad sense, it is the same issue. How do we communicate the possibility of new insight to a community that may be wary of it? How do we utter difficult discoveries of truth while also maintaining a sense of communion that may be strained by them? There will never be a time in the future of Christianity, any more than in its past, when these are not significant questions. And we may as well admit in advance that they will not always find entirely adequate answers. The vocation of biblical interpreter is not going to become easy or, in many cases, secure.

In the long run, we interpreters will not succeed in our challenging task unless we are willing and able to cultivate, with the help of the Spirit, the virtues appropriate to our work. The integrity to stand by our discoveries of truth and to let them continue to shape us, the courage to convey the possibility of truth to the communities for whom we interpret, the continuing human affection that makes us desire to serve others in our capacity as interpreters—these are the forms that the basic theological virtues of faith, hope, and love take in our work and lives. To be an interpreter of the Scriptures is only incidentally a job. It is primarily a calling. If we have indeed been called to it, we should also look for the graces that will make our work possible, and we should move forward with both humility and confidence as we facilitate the great conversation of discernment in our own time.

Notes

1. Mark 4:24. It is a typically Markan insight. The warning is not paralleled in Matthew; Luke 8:18 has "Watch out, then, *how* you hear!"
2. M. R. Ritley.
3. "The reader of the Bible cannot claim the privilege enjoyed by the Bible's divine author of being beyond good and evil. By the same token, giving up control when we read the Bible does not entail giving up our responsibility to discern what comes out of the exercise, and to use it in an ethical way"; Schuyler Brown, *Text and Psyche: Experiencing Scripture Today* (New York: Continuum, 1998), 138.

Bibliography

General

Adam, A. K. M., ed. *Handbook of Postmodern Biblical Interpretation*. St. Louis: Chalice, 2000.

Borg, Marcus. *Jesus, a New Vision: Spirit, Culture, and the Life of Discipleship*. San Francisco: Harper & Row, 1987.

Boring, M. Eugene, Klaus Berger, and Carsten Colpe, eds. *Hellenistic Commentary to the New Testament*. Nashville: Abingdon, 1995.

Boswell, John. *Christianity, Social Tolerance, and Homosexuality: Gay People in Western Europe from the Beginning of the Christian Era*. Chicago: University of Chicago Press, 1980.

Brown, Raymond E. *The Community of the Beloved Disciple*. New York: Paulist, 1979.

Brown, Schuyler. *Text and Psyche: Experiencing Scripture Today*. New York: Continuum, 1998.

Buckley, Jorunn Jacobsen. "A Cult-Mystery in the Gospel of Philip." *JBL* 99 (1980): 569–81.

Bultmann, Rudolf. *The Gospel of John: A Commentary*. Trans. G. R. Beasley-Murray, R. W. N. Hoare, and J. K. Riches. Philadelphia: Westminster, 1971.

Countryman, L. William. *Biblical Authority or Biblical Tyranny? Scripture and the Christian Pilgrimage*. Rev. ed. Harrisburg: Trinity Press International, 1994.

———. *Dirt, Greed, and Sex: Sexual Ethics in the New Testament and Their Implications for Today*. Philadelphia: Fortress, 1988.

———. *Living on the Border of the Holy: Renewing the Priesthood of All*. Harrisburg: Morehouse Publishing, 1999.

———. *The Rich Christian in the Church of the Early Empire: Contradictions and Accommodations*. Texts and Studies in Religion. New York: Edwin Mellen, 1980.

———. "Tertullian and the Regula Fidei." *The Second Century* 2 (1982): 208–27.

Draper, Jonathan. "Confessional Western Text-Centered Biblical Interpretation and an Oral or Residual-Oral Context." *Semeia* 73 (1996): 59–77.

Ferguson, John. *The Religions of the Roman Empire*. Ithaca: Cornell University Press, 1970.

Gagnon, Robert A. J. *The Bible and Homosexual Practice: Texts and Hermeneutics*. Nashville: Abingdon, 2001.

Gamble, Harry Y. *Books and Readers in the Early Church: A History of Early Christian Texts*. New Haven: Yale University Press, 1995.

Gibson, Paul. *Discerning the Word: The Bible and Homosexuality in Anglican Debate*. Toronto: Anglican Book Centre, 2000.

Grant, Robert M. *A Historical Introduction to the New Testament*. New York: Harper & Row, 1963.

———. *Second-Century Christianity: A Collection of Fragments*. London: SPCK, 1957.

Grayston, Kenneth. *The Johannine Epistles*. The New Century Bible Commentary. Grand Rapids: Eerdmans, 1984.

Green, Joel B. "Rethinking History (and Theology)." In *Between Two Horizons: Spanning New Testament Studies and Systematic Theology*. Ed. Joel B. Green and Max Turner. Grand Rapids: Eerdmans, 2000. Pp. 237–42.

Greenberg, David F. *The Construction of Homosexuality*. Chicago: University of Chicago Press, 1988.

Jordan, Mark D. *The Invention of Sodomy in Christian Theology*. Chicago: University of Chicago Press, 1997.

———. *The Silence of Sodom: Homosexuality in Modern Catholicism*. Chicago: University of Chicago Press, 2000.

Kennedy, George A. *New Testament Interpretation through Rhetorical Criticism*. Chapel Hill: University of North Carolina Press, 1984.

Klawans, Jonathan. *Impurity and Sin in Ancient Judaism*. Oxford: Oxford University Press, 2000.

Klein, Julie Thompson. *Interdisciplinarity: History, Theory, and Practice*. Detroit: Wayne State University Press, 1990.

Martin, Dale B. *Slavery as Salvation: The Metaphor of Slavery in Pauline Christianity*. New Haven: Yale University Press, 1990.

McKenzie, Steven L., and Stephen R. Haynes, eds. *To Each Its Own Meaning: An Introduction to Biblical Criticisms and Their Application*. Rev. ed. Louisville: Westminster John Knox, 1999.

Meeks, Wayne A. *The First Urban Christians: The Social World of the Apostle Paul*. New Haven: Yale University Press, 1983.

Moule, C. F. D. *An Idiom-Book of New Testament Greek*. Cambridge: Cambridge University Press, 1971.

Nissinen, Martti. *Homoeroticism in the Biblical World: A Historical Perspective*. Trans. Kirsi Stjerna. Minneapolis: Fortress, 1998.

Patte, Daniel. *Ethics of Biblical Interpretation: A Reevaluation*. Louisville: Westminster John Knox, 1995.

———. *The Gospel According to Matthew: A Structural Commentary on Matthew's Faith*. Philadelphia: Fortress Press, 1987.

Perdue, Leo G. "The Social Character of Paraenesis and Paraenetic Literature." *Semeia* 50 (1990): 5–39.

Raposa, Michael L. *Boredom and the Religious Imagination*. Charlottesville: University Press of Virginia, 1999.

Rousselle, Aline. *Porneia: On Desire and the Body in Antiquity.* Oxford: Blackwell, 1988.

Sanford, John A. *Mystical Christianity: A Psychological Commentary on the Gospel of John.* New York: Crossroad, 1993.

Schine, Cathleen. *Rameau's Niece.* New York: Ticknor & Fields, 1993.

Schneiders, Sandra M. *The Revelatory Text: Interpreting the New Testament as Sacred Scripture.* San Francisco: HarperSanFrancisco, 1991.

Scholem, Gershom G. *Major Trends in Jewish Mysticism.* New York: Schocken Books, 1961.

Segovia, Fernando F., and Mary Ann Tolbert, eds. *Reading from This Place.* 2 vols. Minneapolis: Fortress, 1995.

Shanks, Hershel. *Judaism in Stone: The Archaeology of Ancient Synagogues.* New York: Harper & Row, 1979.

Smith, Wilfred Cantwell. *What Is Scripture? A Comparative Approach.* Minneapolis: Fortress, 1993.

Smyth, Herbert Weir. *Greek Grammar.* Cambridge: Harvard University Press, 1959.

Staley, Jeffrey L. *Reading with a Passion: Rhetoric, Autobiography, and the American West in the Gospel of John.* New York: Continuum, 1995.

Temple, William. *Readings in St. John's Gospel (First and Second Series).* London: Macmillan, 1955.

Theissen, Gerd. *Sociology of Early Palestinian Christianity.* Trans. John Bowden. Philadelphia: Fortress Press, 1978.

Tolbert, Mary Ann. "Christianity, Imperialism, and the Decentering of Privilege." In *Reading from This Place,* ed. Fernando F. Segovia and Mary Ann Tolbert. 2 vols. Minneapolis: Fortress, 1995. 2:347–61.

———. "The Politics and Poetics of Location." In *Reading from This Place,* ed. Fernando F. Segovia and Mary Ann Tolbert. 2 vols. Minneapolis: Fortress, 1995. 1:305–17.

———. "Reading for Liberation." In *Reading from This Place,* ed. Fernando F. Segovia and Mary Ann Tolbert. 2 vols. Minneapolis: Fortress, 1995. 1:263–76.

———. "When Resistance Becomes Oppression: Mark 13:9–27 and the Poetics of Location." In *Reading from This Place,* ed. Fernando F. Segovia and Mary Ann Tolbert. 2 vols. Minneapolis: Fortress, 1995. 2:331–46.

Wilder, Amos N. *Early Christian Rhetoric: The Language of the Gospel.* Cambridge: Harvard University Press, 1971.

———. "Scholars, Theologians, and Ancient Rhetoric." *JBL* 75 (1956): 1–11.

James and Jude

Boobyer, G. H. Jude. *Peake's Commentary on the Bible.* Ed. Matthew Black & H. H. Rowley. London: Thomas Nelson, 1962. Pp. 1041–42.

Charles, J. Daryl. *Literary Strategy in the Epistle of Jude.* Scranton: University of Scranton Press, 1993.

Cranfield, C. E. B. *I and II Peter and Jude.* London: SCM Press, 1960.

Dibelius, Martin. Rev. by Heinrich Greeven. *James: A Commentary on the Epistle of James.* Trans. Michael A. Williams. Hermeneia. Philadelphia: Fortress, 1976.

Johnson, Luke Timothy. *The Letter of James: A New Translation with Introduction and Commentary.* AB, 37A. New York: Doubleday, 1995.

Kelly, J. N. D. *A Commentary on the Epistles of Peter and of Jude.* New York: Harper & Row, 1969.

Kugelman, Richard. *James and Jude.* New Testament Message. Wilmington, Del.: Michael Glazier, 1980.

Mayor, Joseph B. *The Epistle of St. James: The Greek Text with Introduction, Notes and Comments.* London: Macmillan, 1897.

Neyrey, Jerome H. *2 Peter, Jude: A New Translation with Introduction and Commentary.* AB, 37C. New York: Doubleday, 1993.

Plumptre, E. H. *The General Epistles of St Peter and St Jude.* Cambridge: Cambridge University Press, 1910.

Reese, Ruth Anne. *Writing Jude: The Reader, the Text, and the Author in Constructs of Power and Desire.* Leiden: Brill, 2000.

Reicke, Bo. *The Epistles of James, Peter, and Jude.* AB, 37. Garden City, N.Y.: Doubleday, 1964.

Shepherd, Massey H., Jr. "The Epistle of James and the Gospel of Matthew." *JBL* 75 (1956): 40–51.

Vögtle, Anton. "Der Judasbrief/Der Zweite Petrusbrief." *Evangelisch-Katholischer Kommentar zum Neuen Testament,* 22. Solothurn: Benziger Verlag; Neukirchen-Vluyn: Neukirchener Verlag, 1994.

Wall, Robert W. *Community of the Wise: The Letter of James.* Valley Forge, Pa.: Trinity Press International, 1997.

Watson, Duane Frederick. *Invention, Arrangement, and Style: Rhetorical Criticism of Jude and 2 Peter.* Atlanta: Scholars Press, 1988.

Paul and Romans

Anderson, R. Dean, Jr. *Ancient Rhetorical Theory and Paul.* Kampen, The Netherlands: Kok Pharos, 1996.

Barrett, C. K. *A Commentary on the Epistle to the Romans.* New York: Harper & Row, 1957.

Boyarin, Daniel. *A Radical Jew: Paul and the Politics of Identity.* Berkeley: University of California Press, 1994.

Byrne, Brendan. *Romans.* SP, 6. Collegeville: Liturgical Press, 1996.

Donfried, Karl P., ed. *The Romans Debate.* Rev. ed. Peabody, Mass.: Hendrickson, 1991.

Furnish, Victor Paul. *The Moral Teaching of Paul.* Nashville: Abingdon, 1979.

Kern, Philip H. *Rhetoric and Galatians: Assessing an Approach to Paul's Epistle.* Cambridge: Cambridge University Press, 1998.

Kittredge, Cynthia Briggs. *Community and Authority: The Rhetoric of Obedience in the Pauline Tradition.* Harrisburg: Trinity Press International, 1998.

Malina, Bruce, and Jerome H. Neyrey. *Portraits of Paul: An Archaeology of Ancient Personality.* Louisville: Westminster John Knox, 1996.

Nygren, Anders. *Commentary on Romans.* Trans. Carl C. Rasmussen. Philadelphia: Muhlenberg Press, 1949.

Sanday, William, and Arthur C. Headlam. *A Critical and Exegetical Commentary on the Epistle to the Romans.* 5th ed. ICC. Edinburgh: T. & T. Clark, 1902.

Segal, Alan F. *Paul the Convert: The Apostolate and Apostasy of Saul the Pharisee.* New Haven: Yale University Press, 1990.

Index